This Book Belongs To

(So Please Don't Color In My Sh*t)

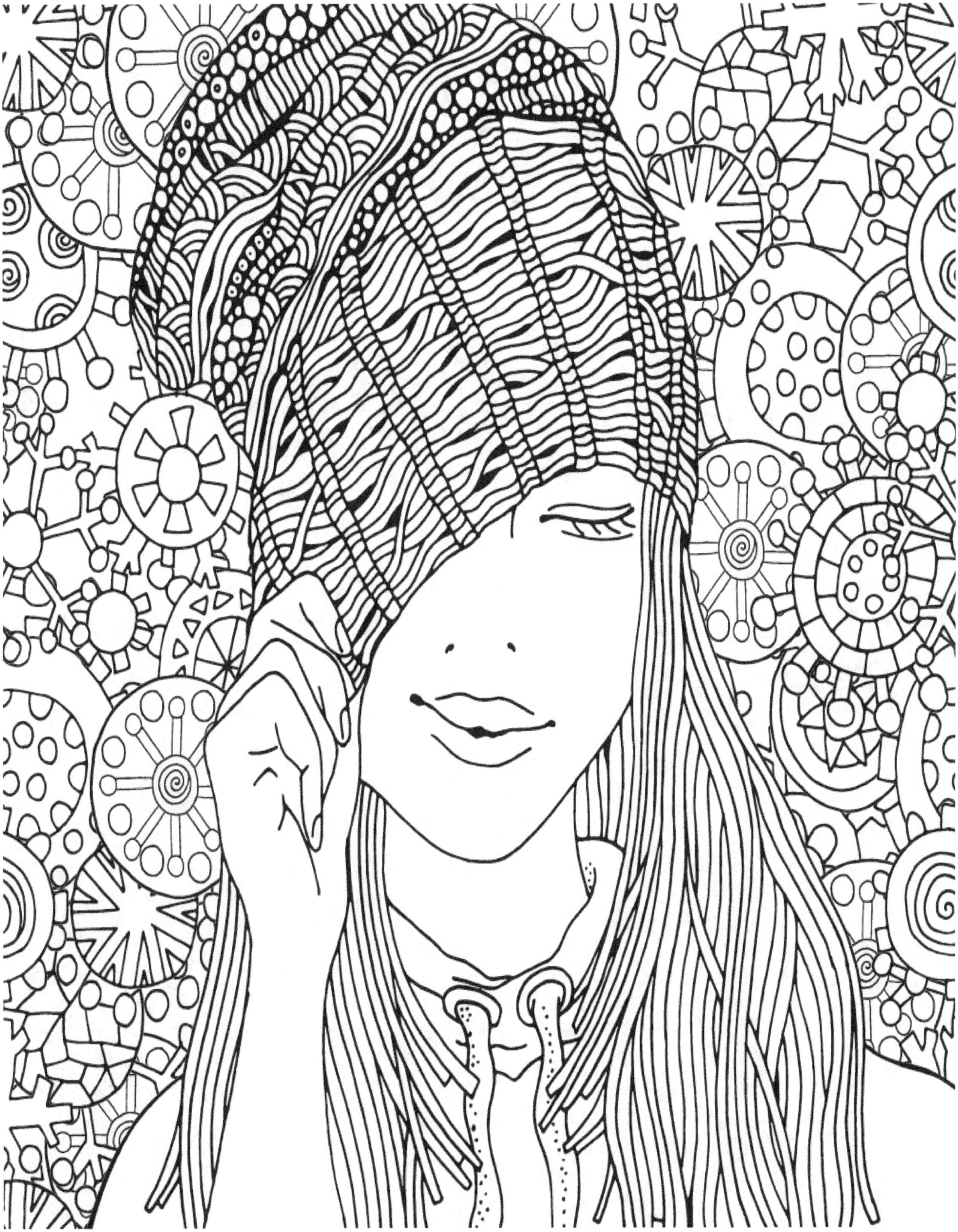

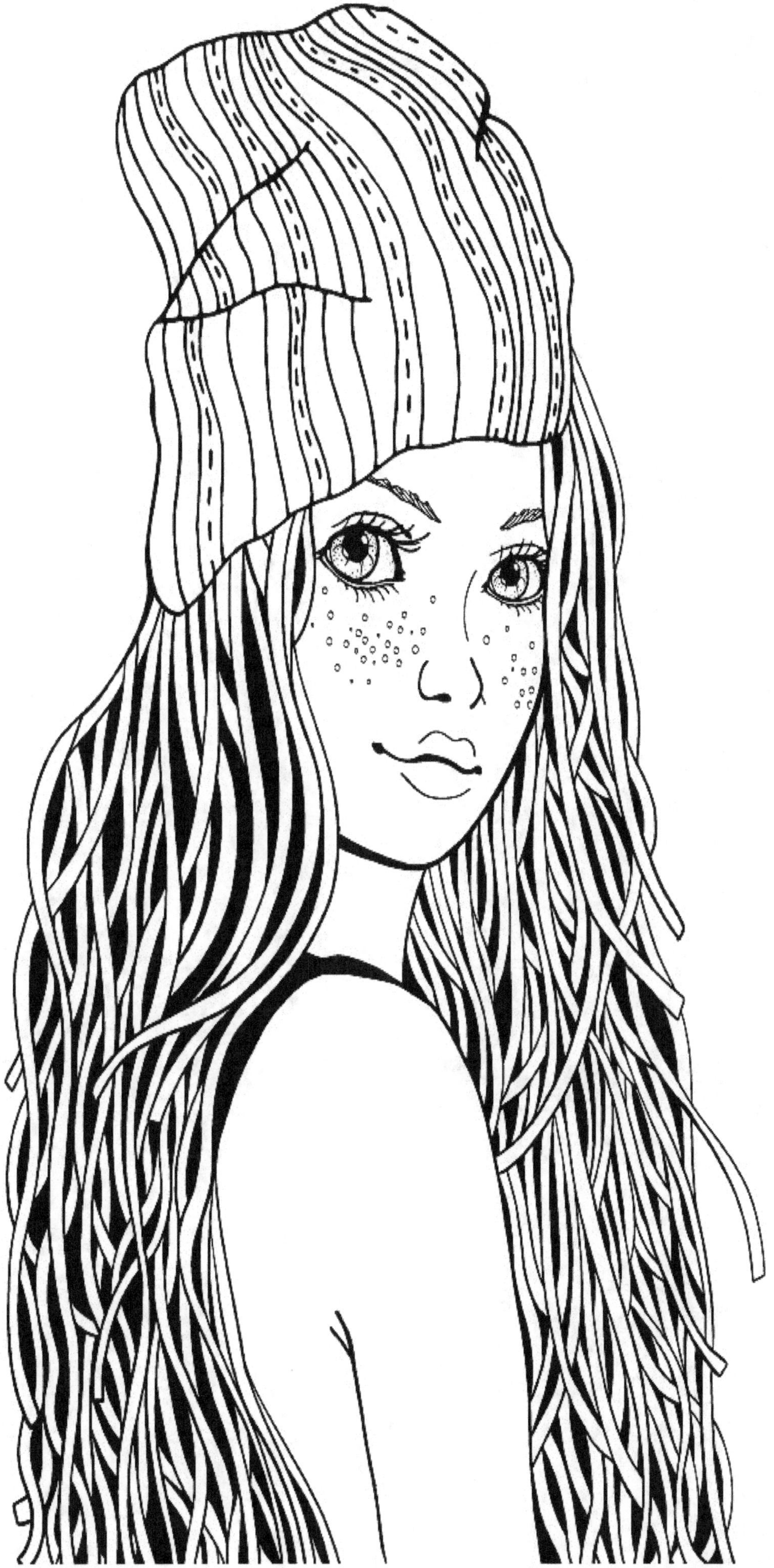

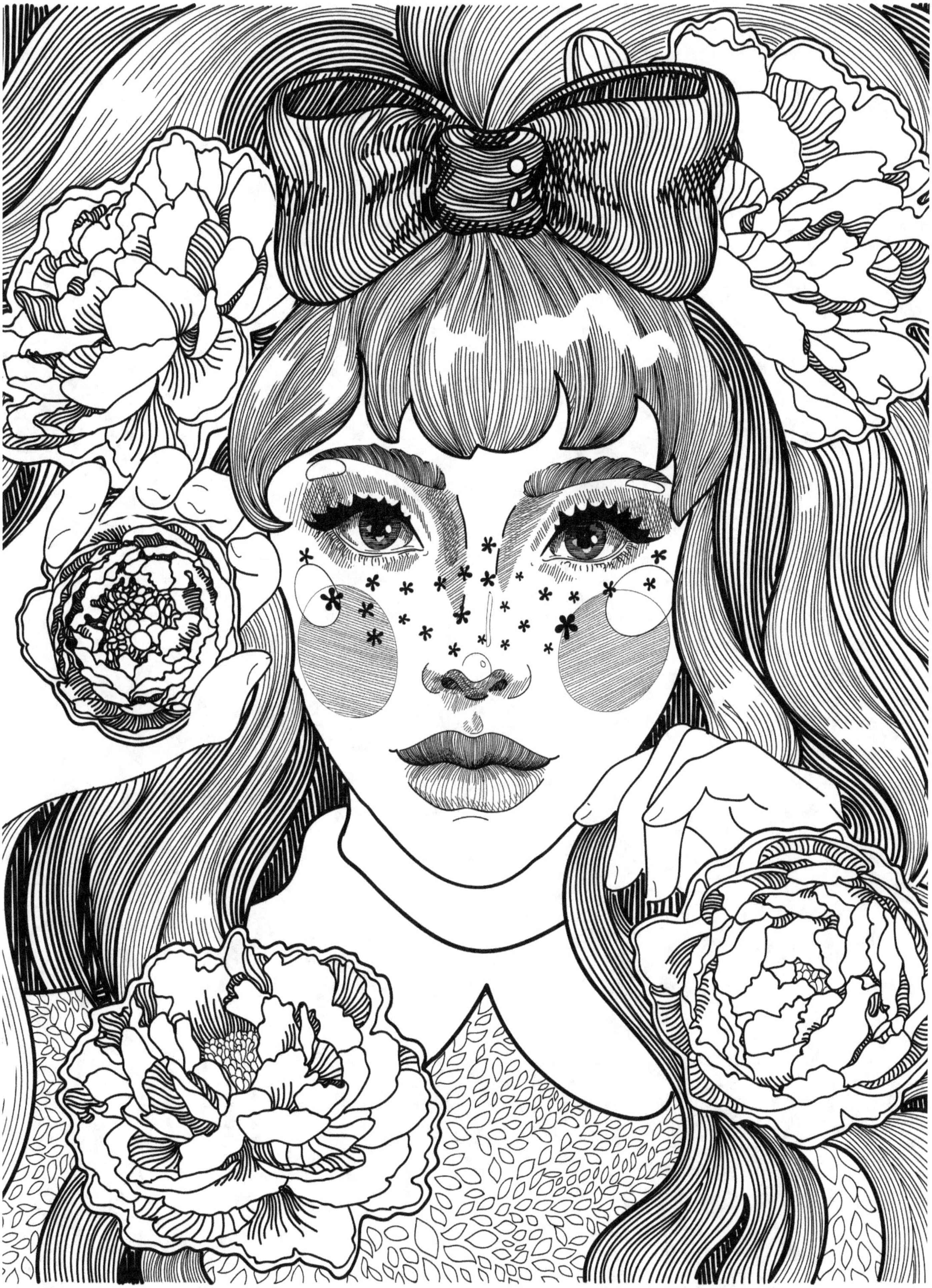

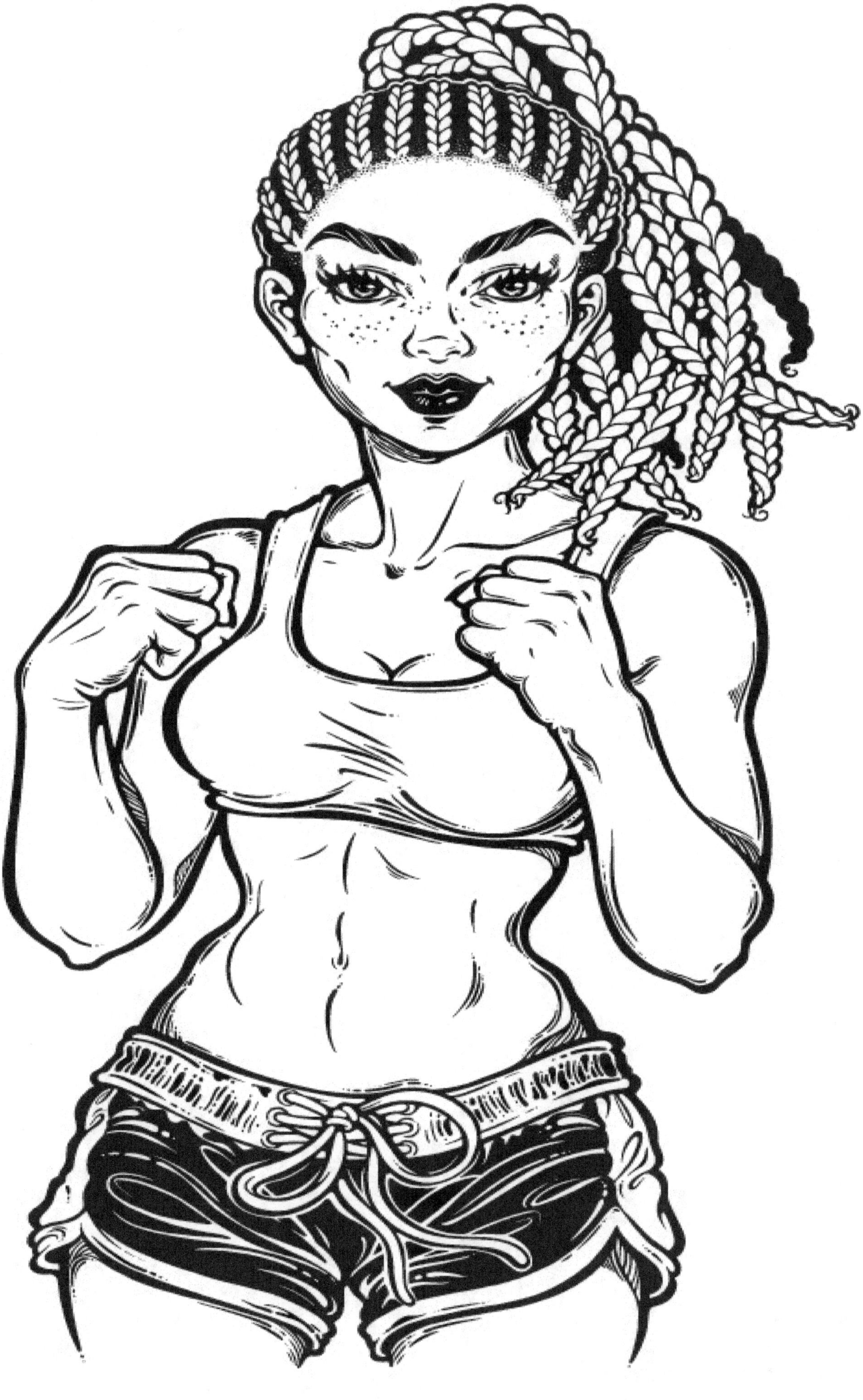

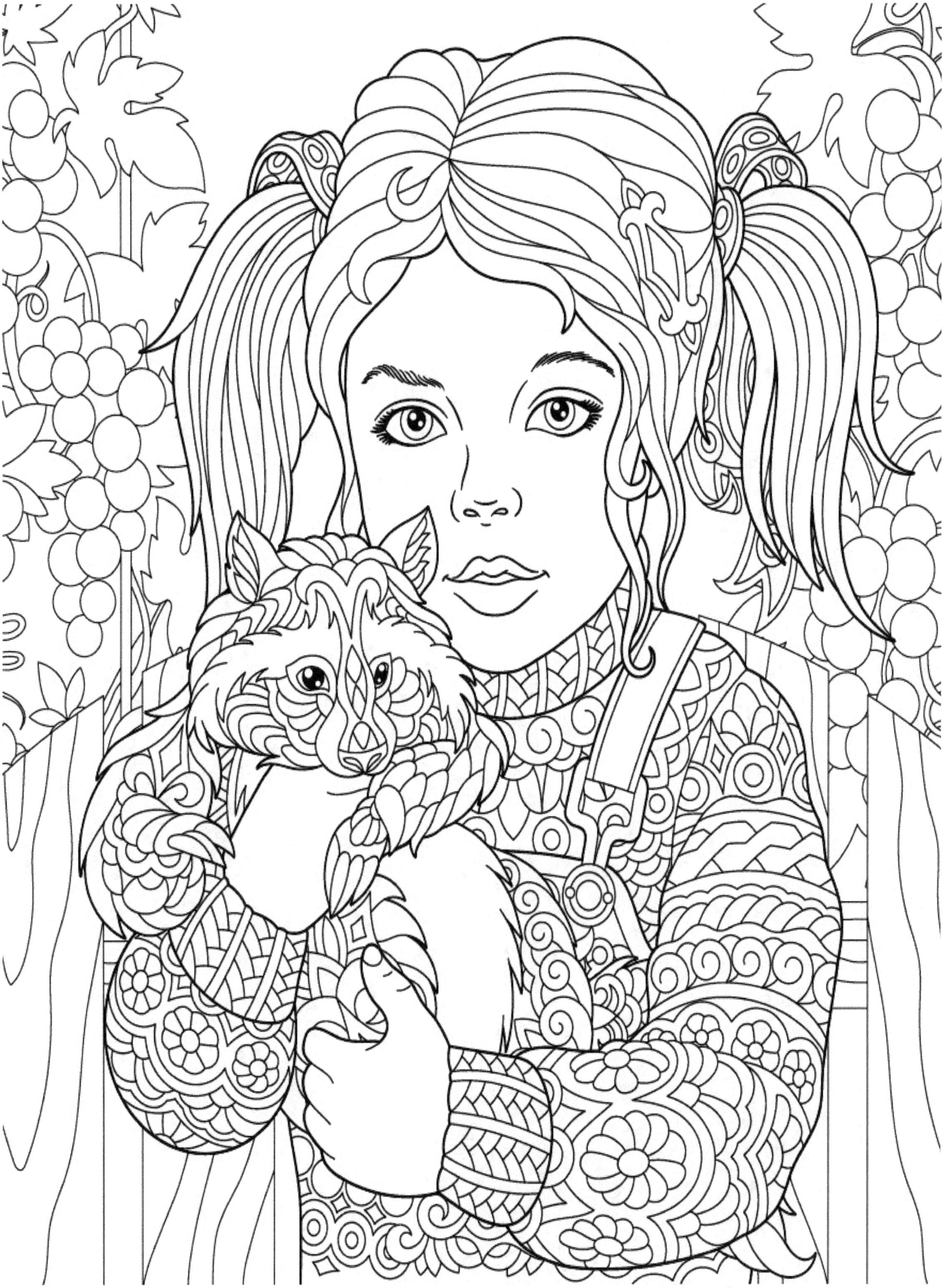

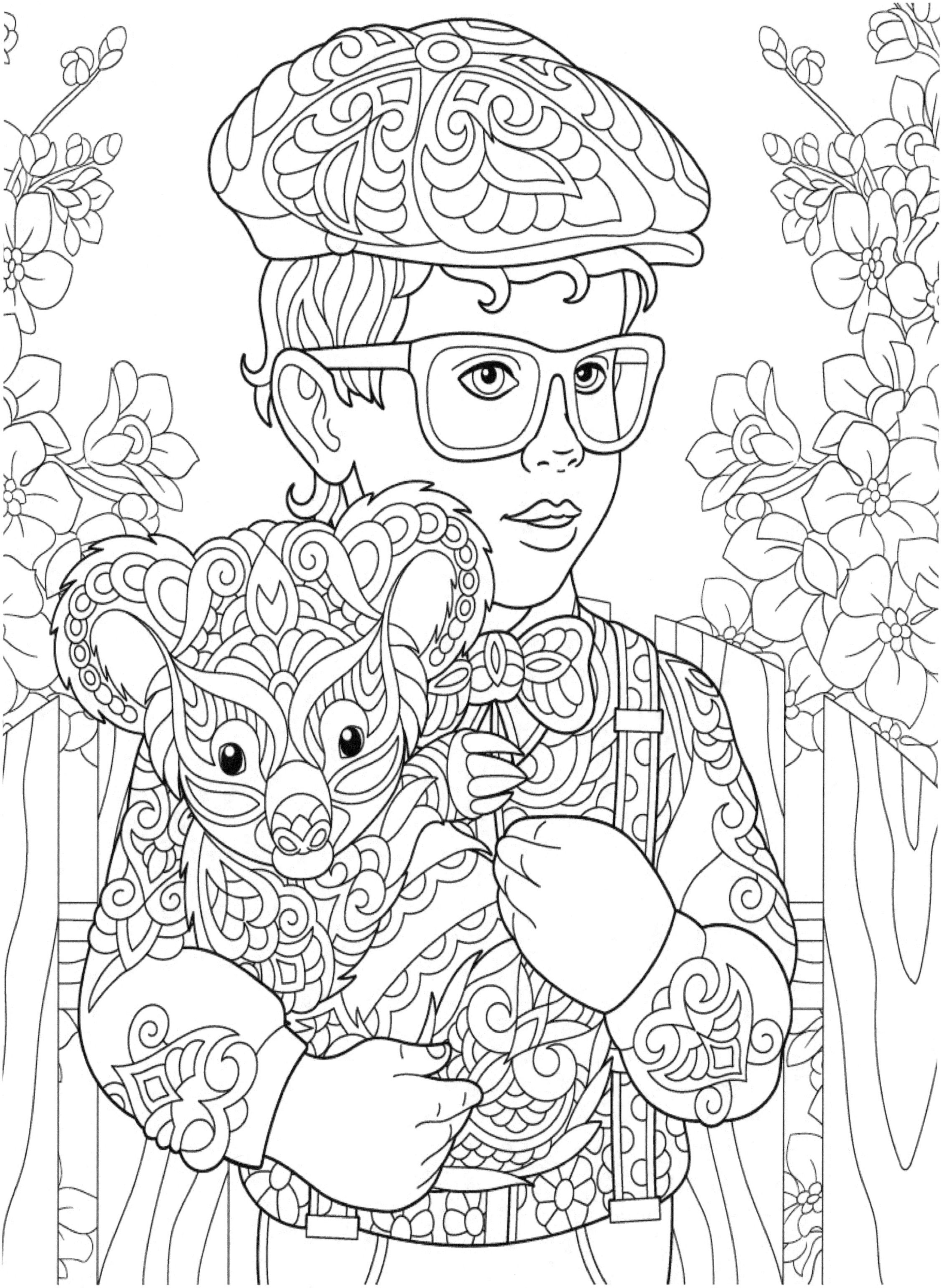

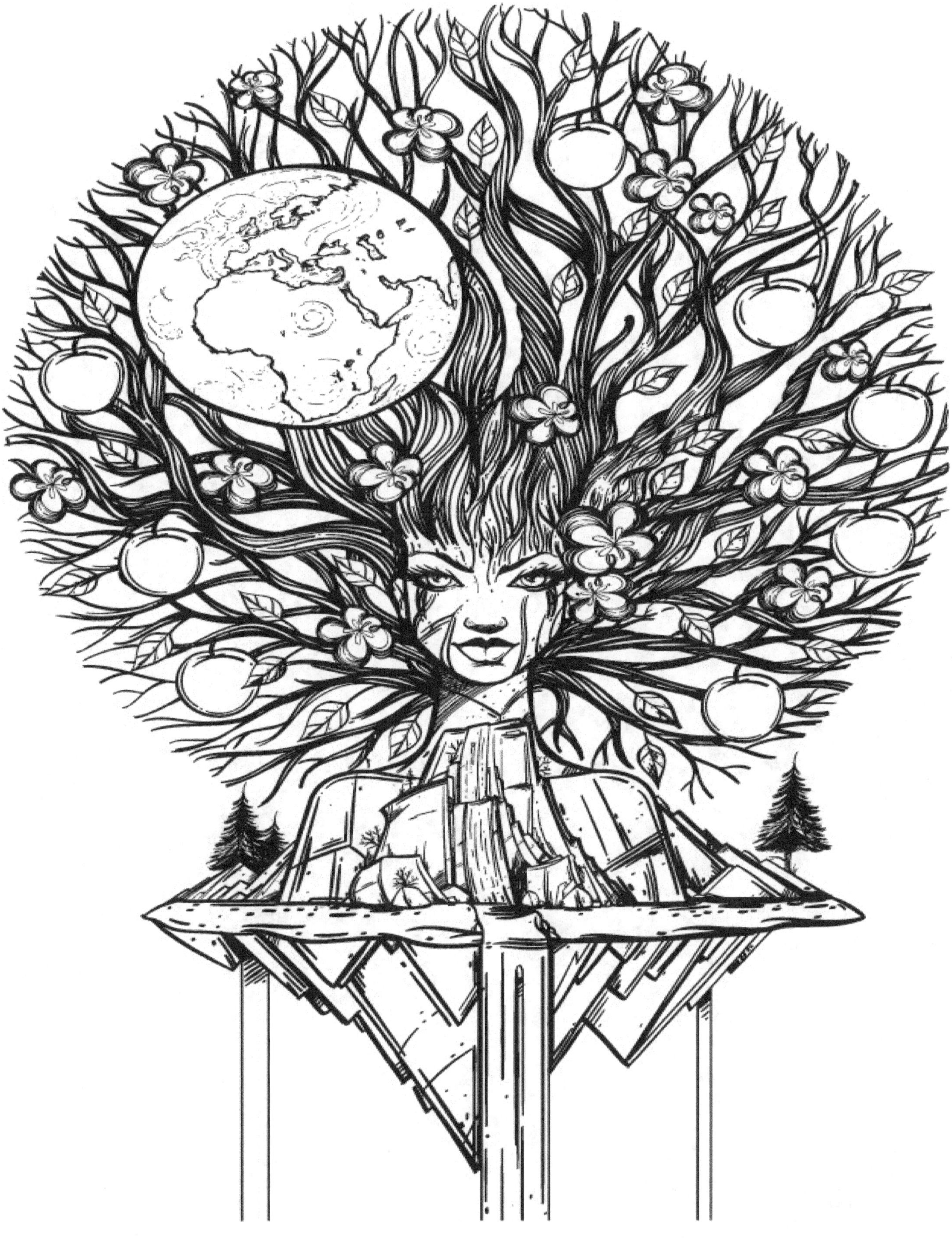

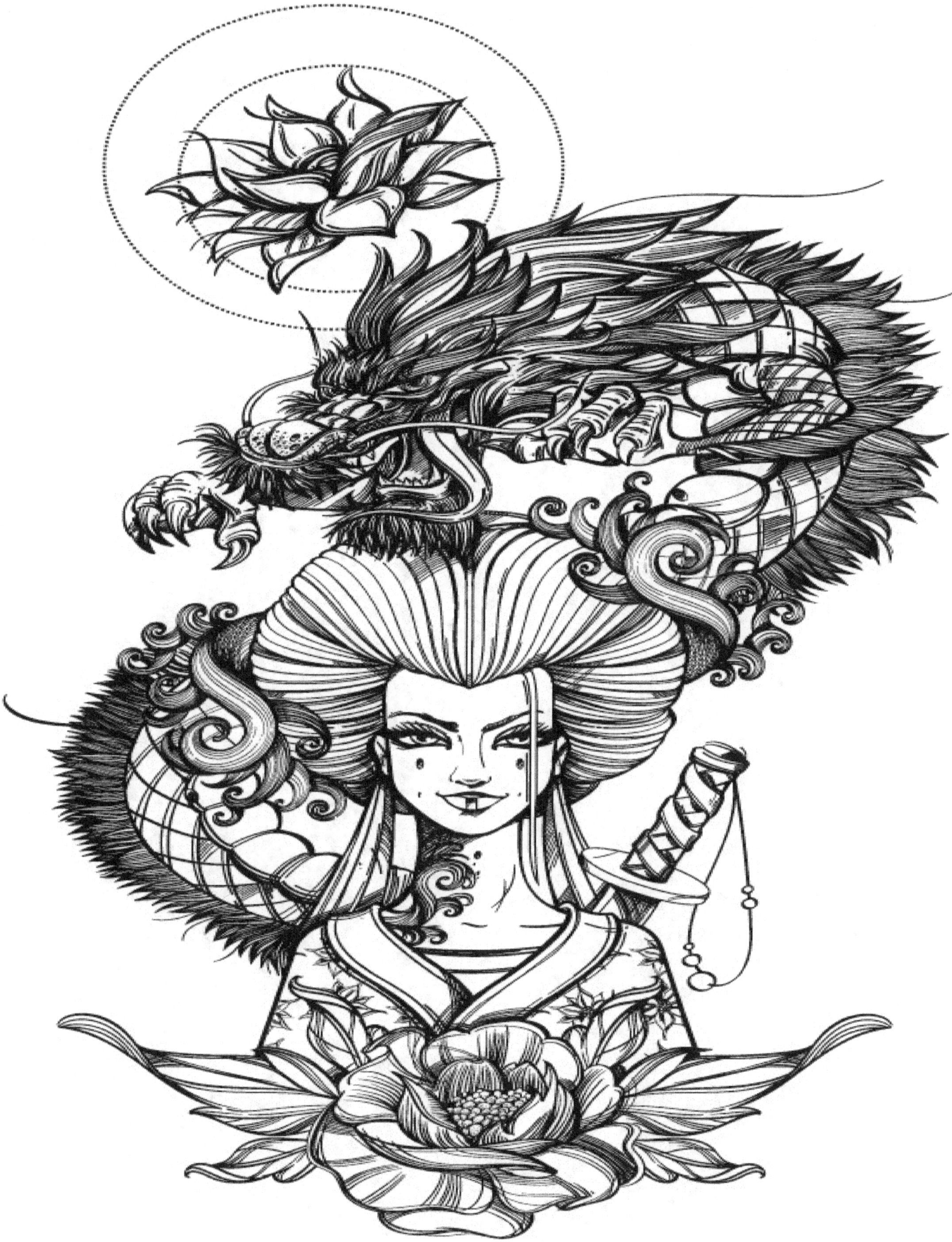

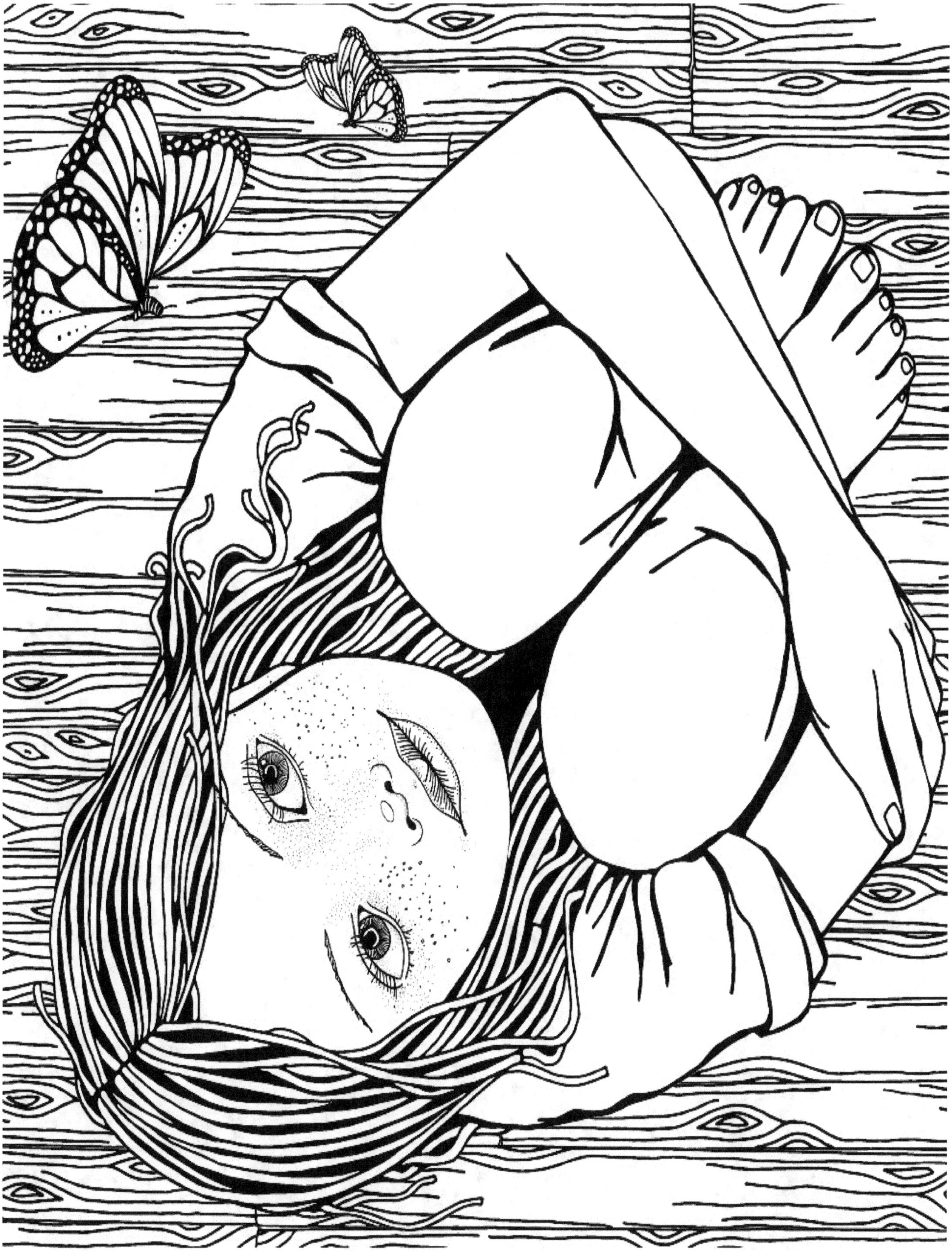

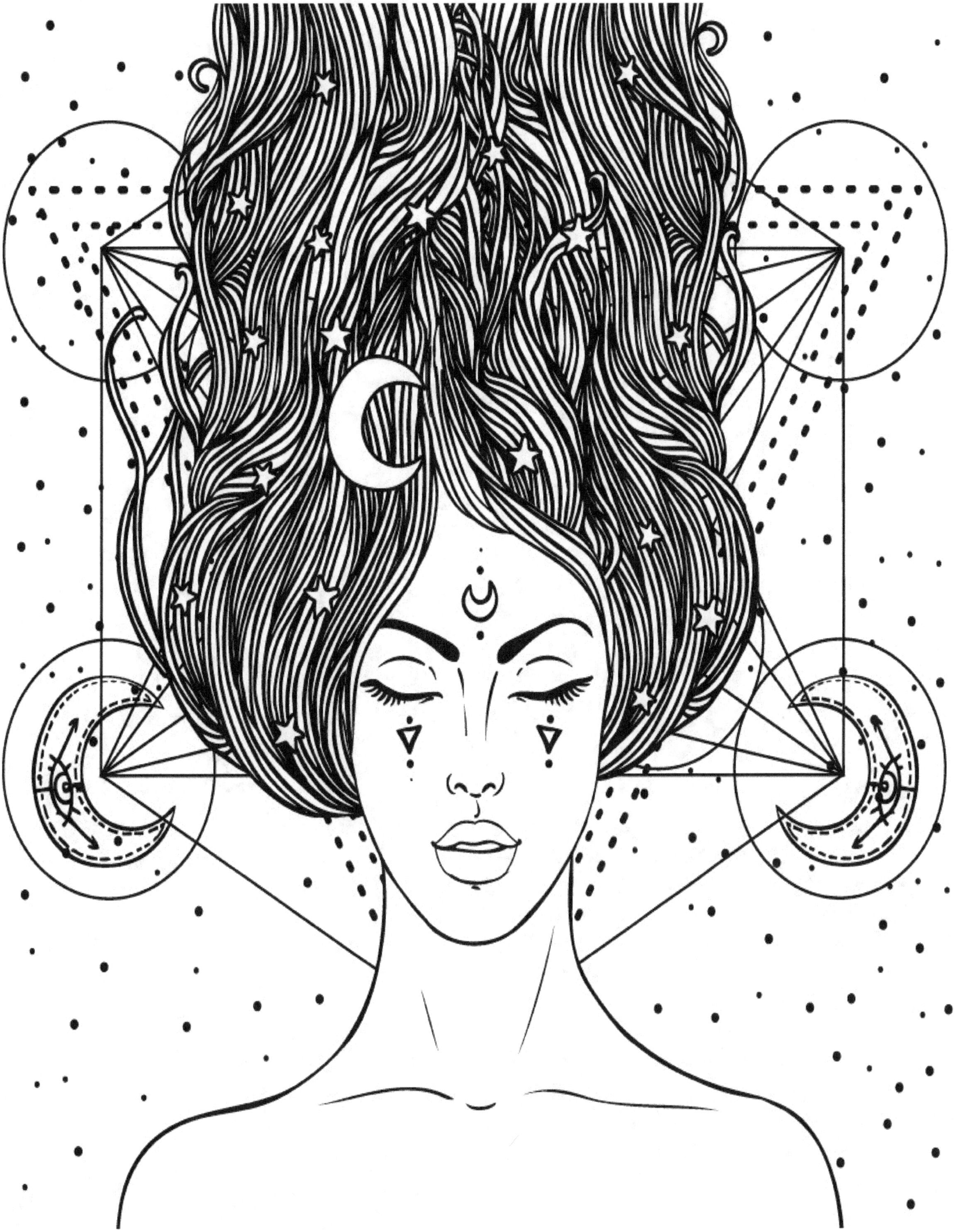

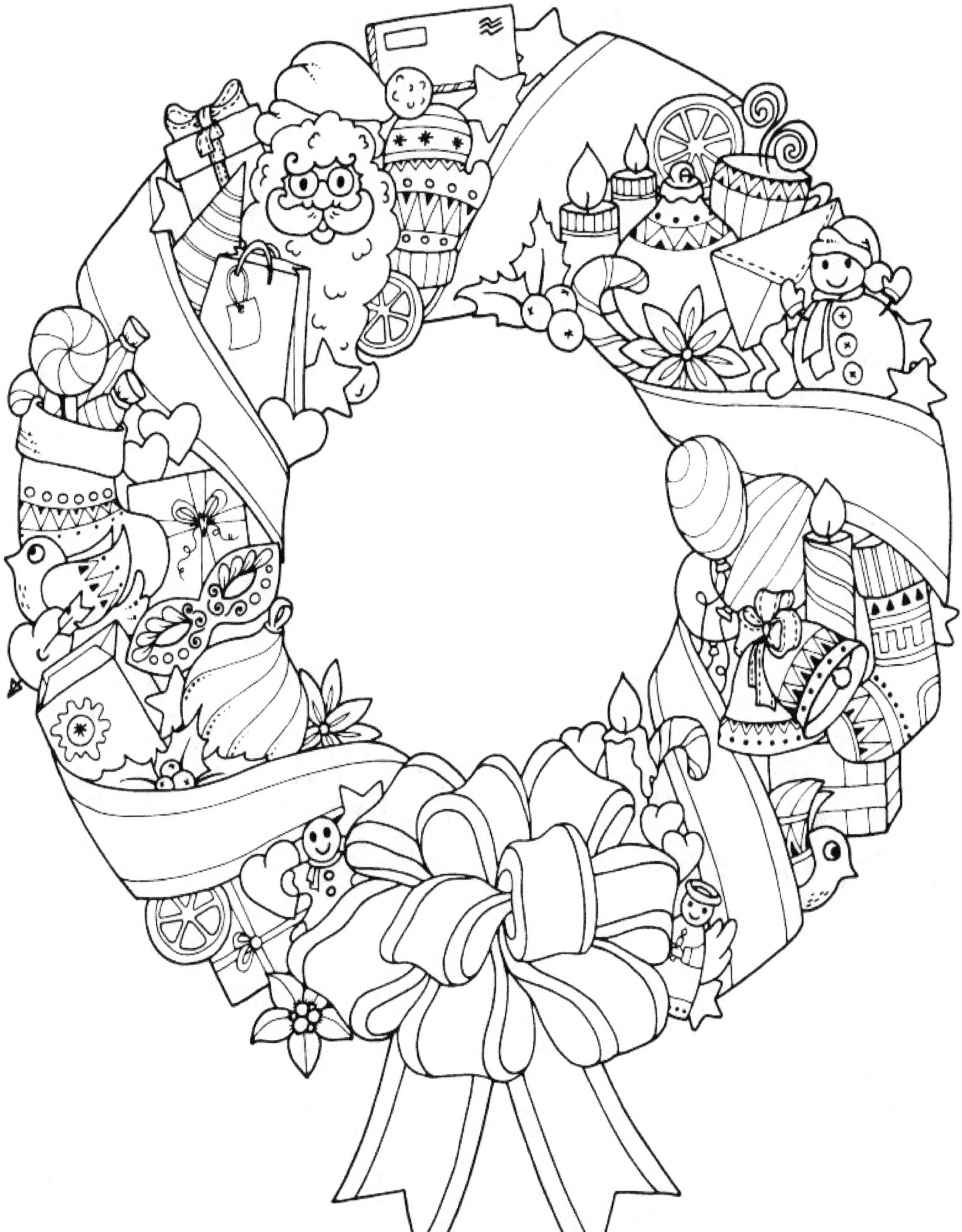

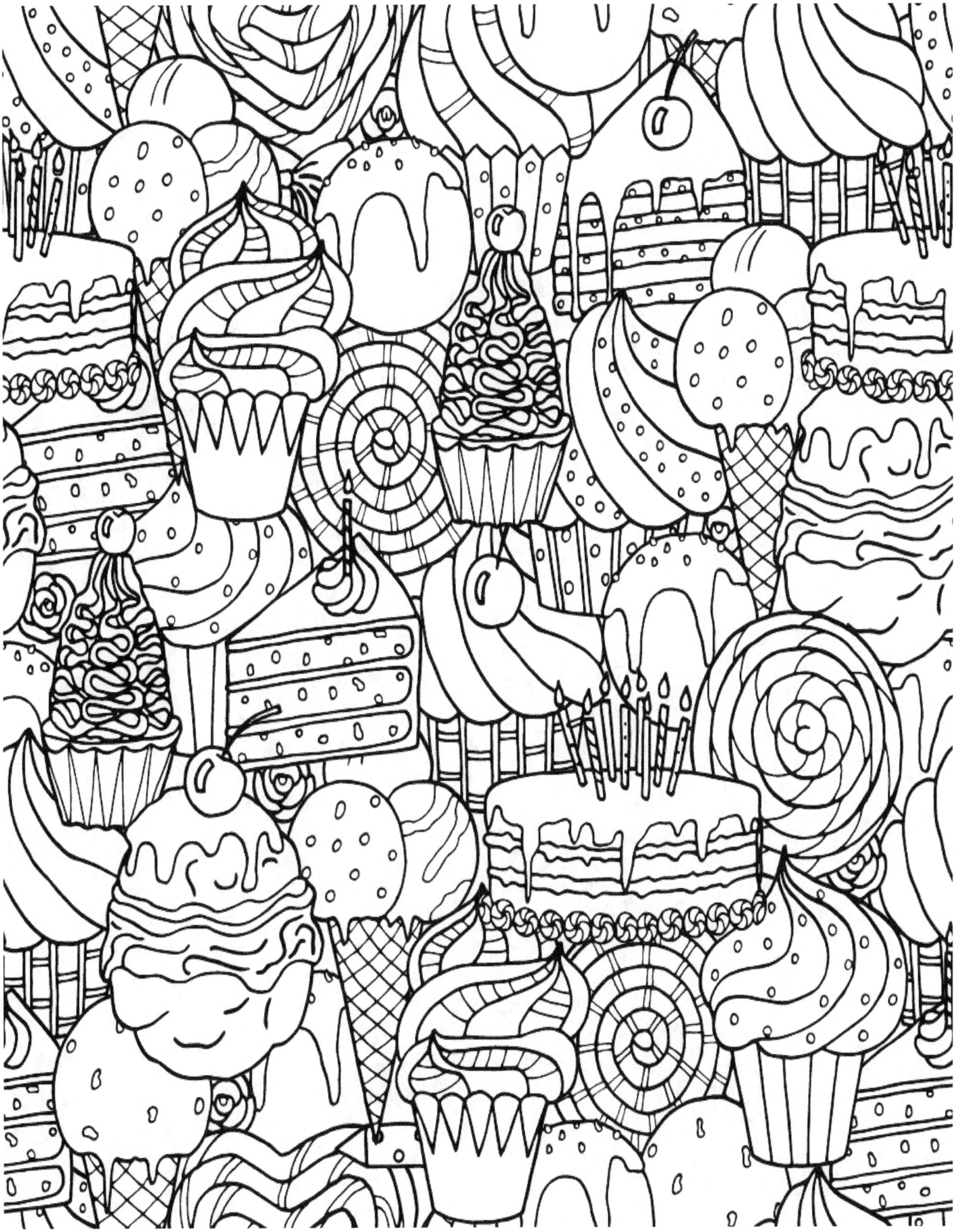

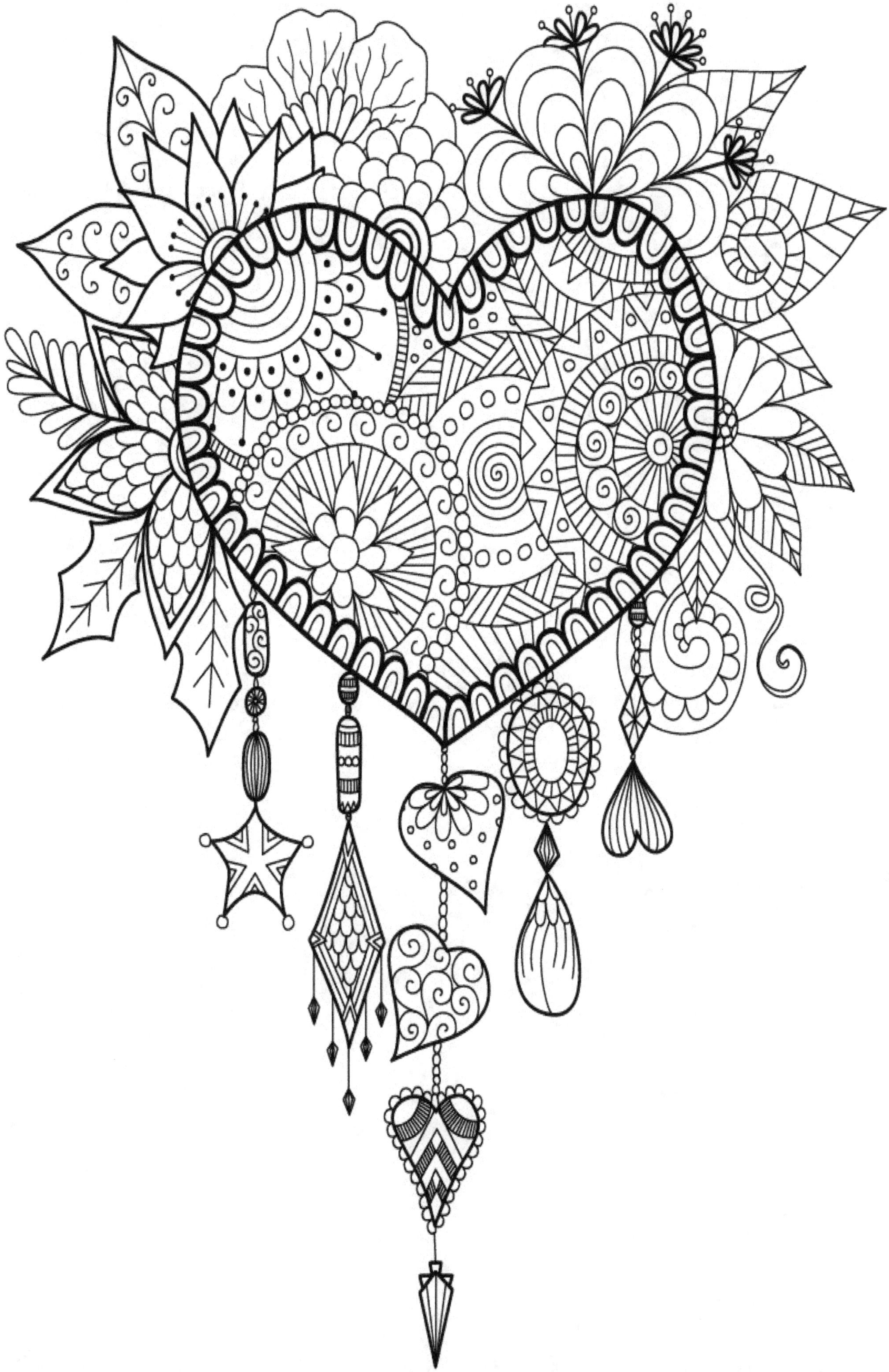

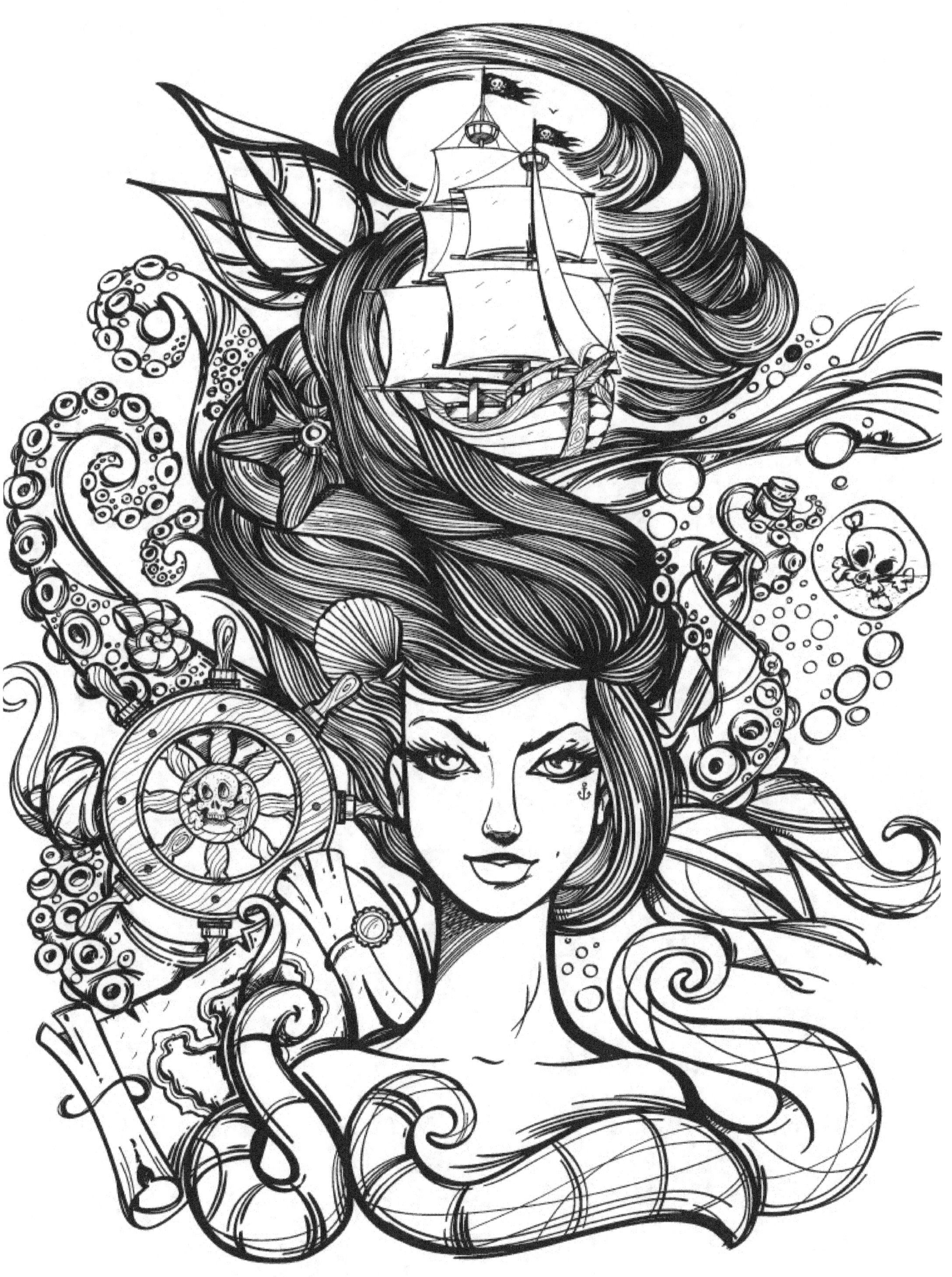

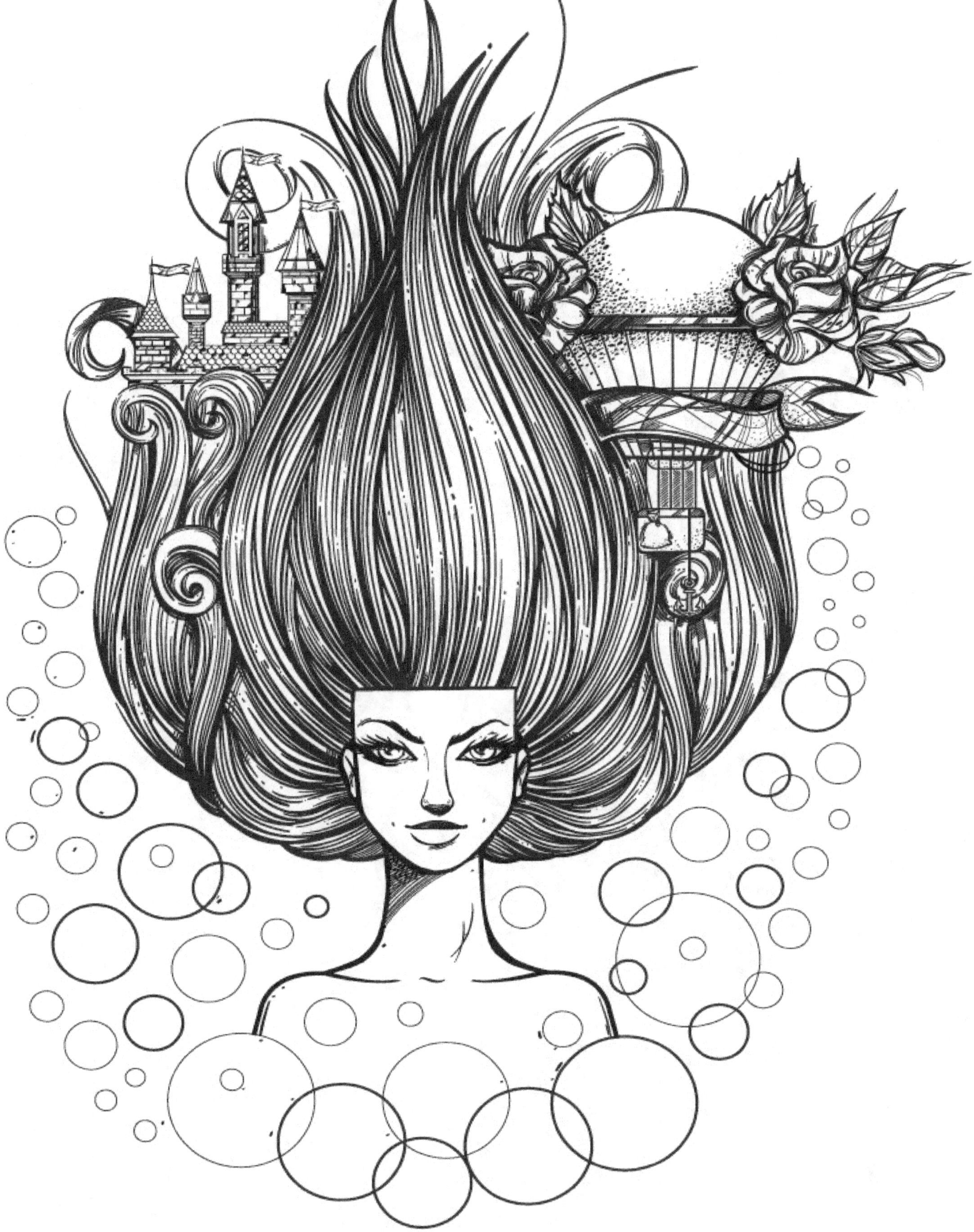

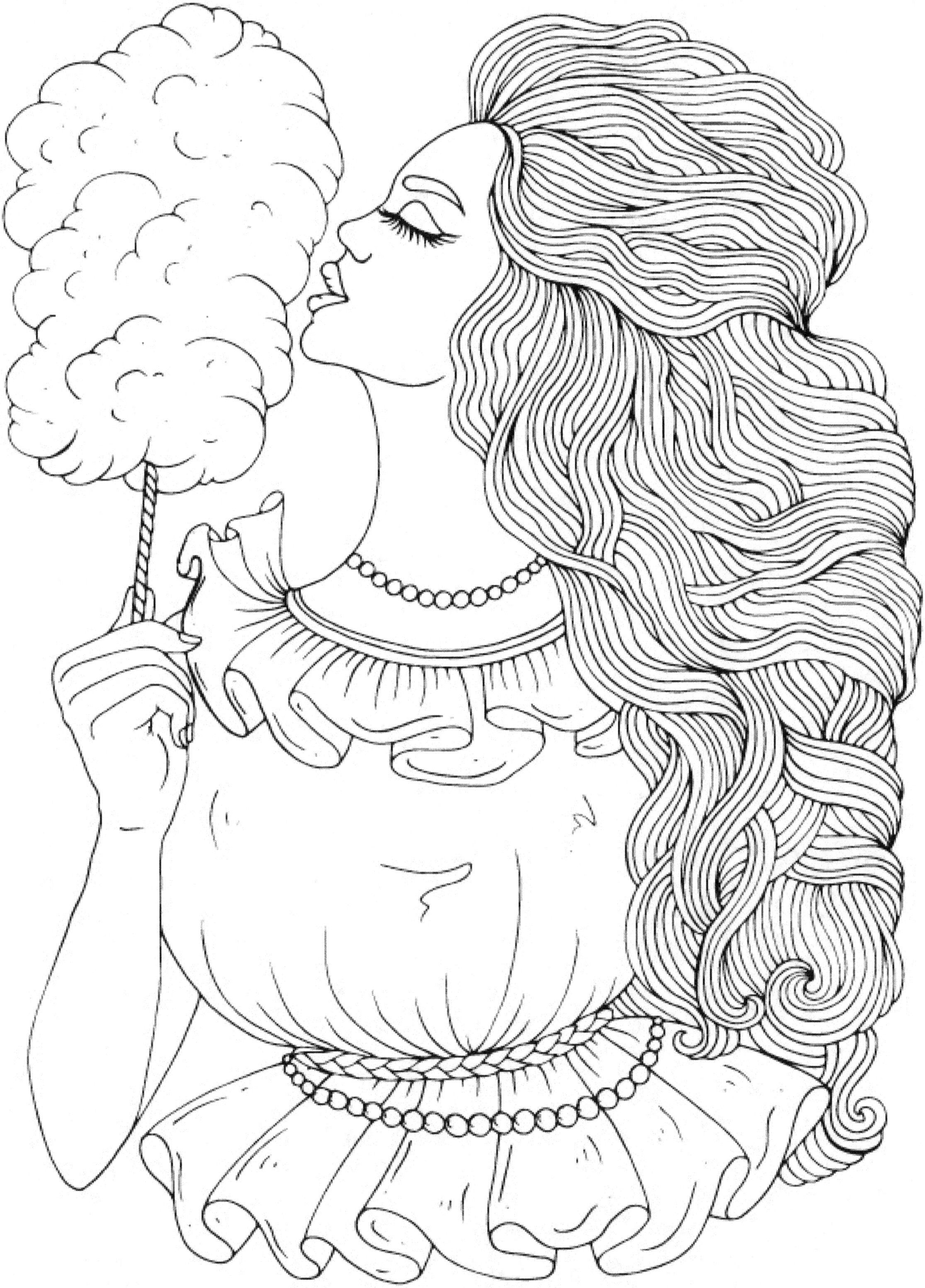

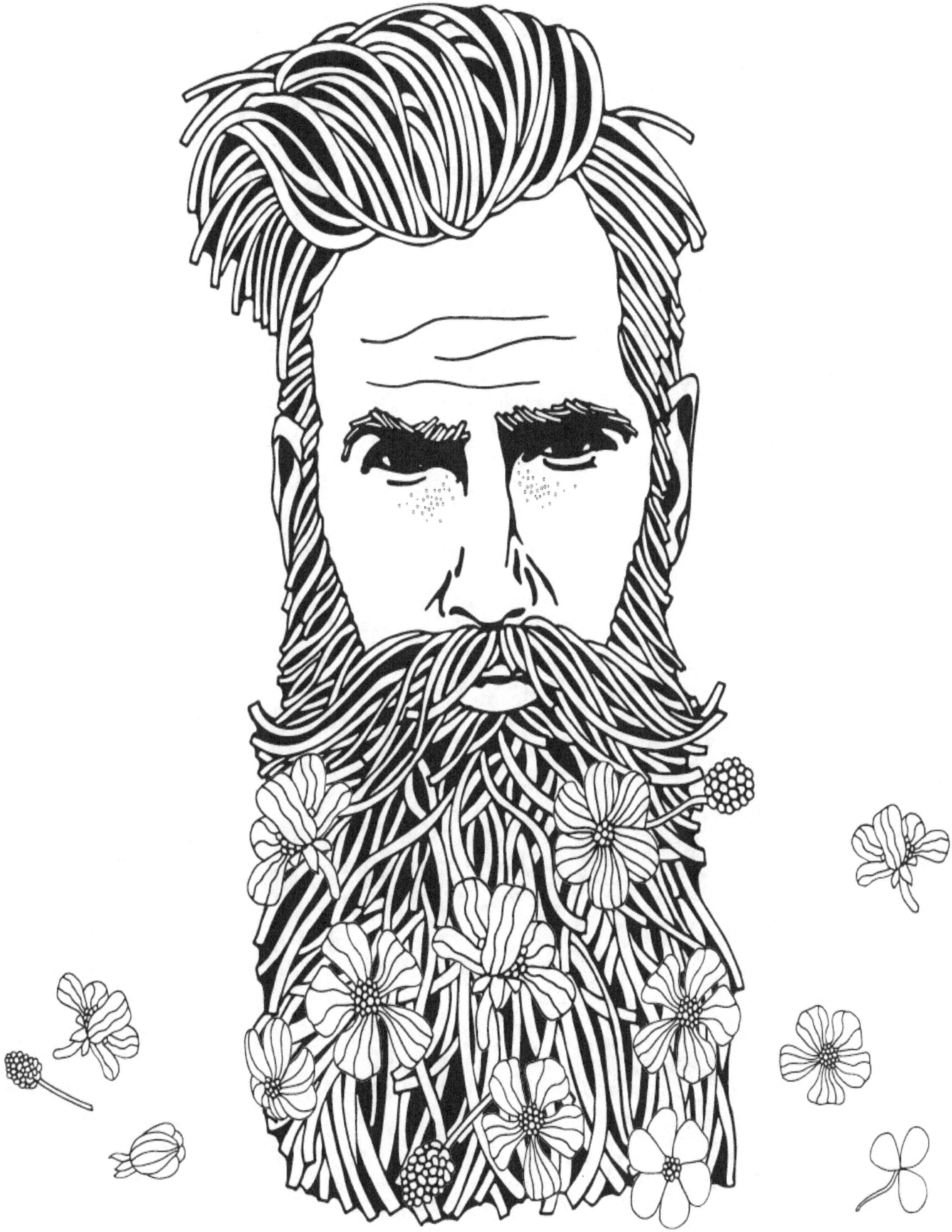

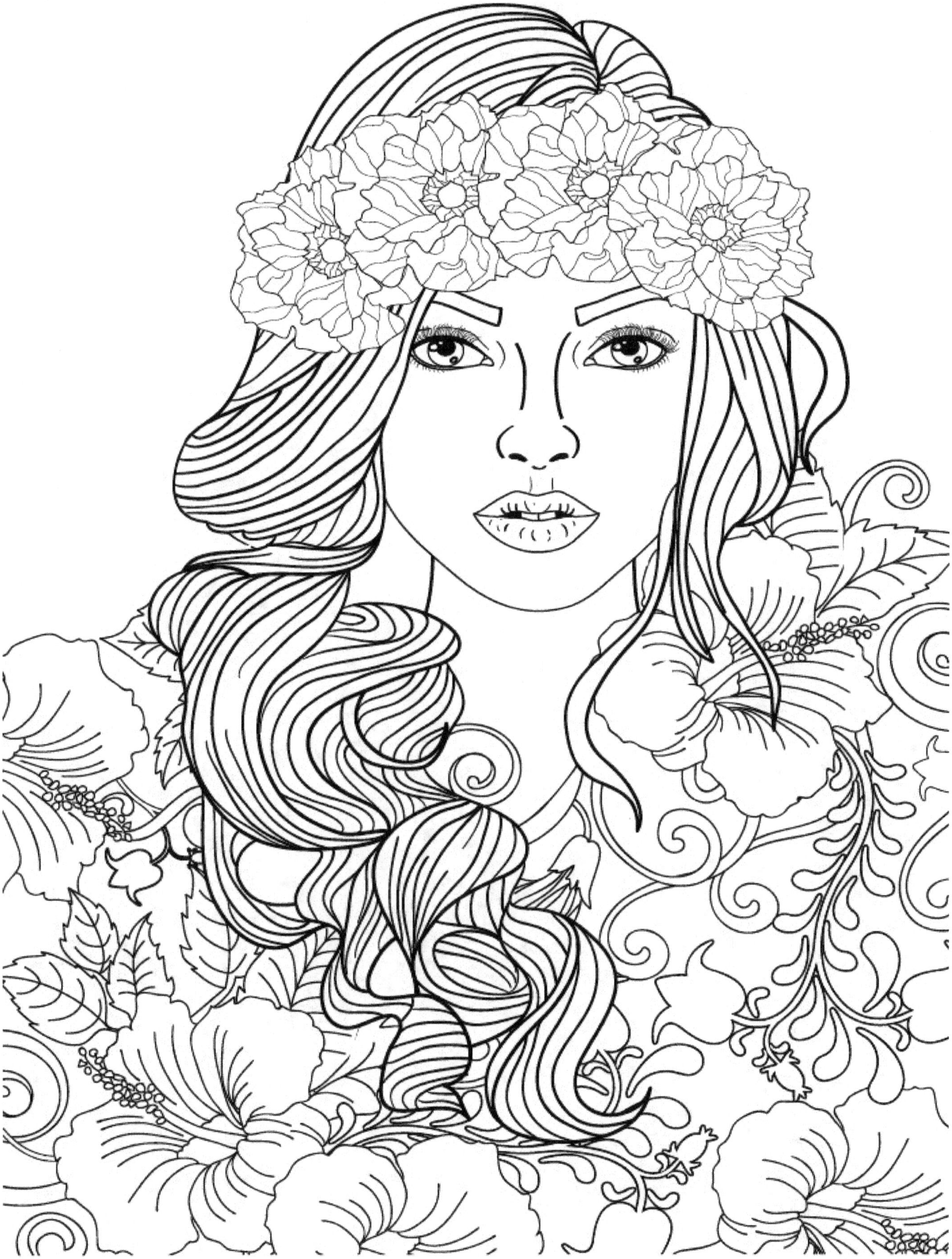

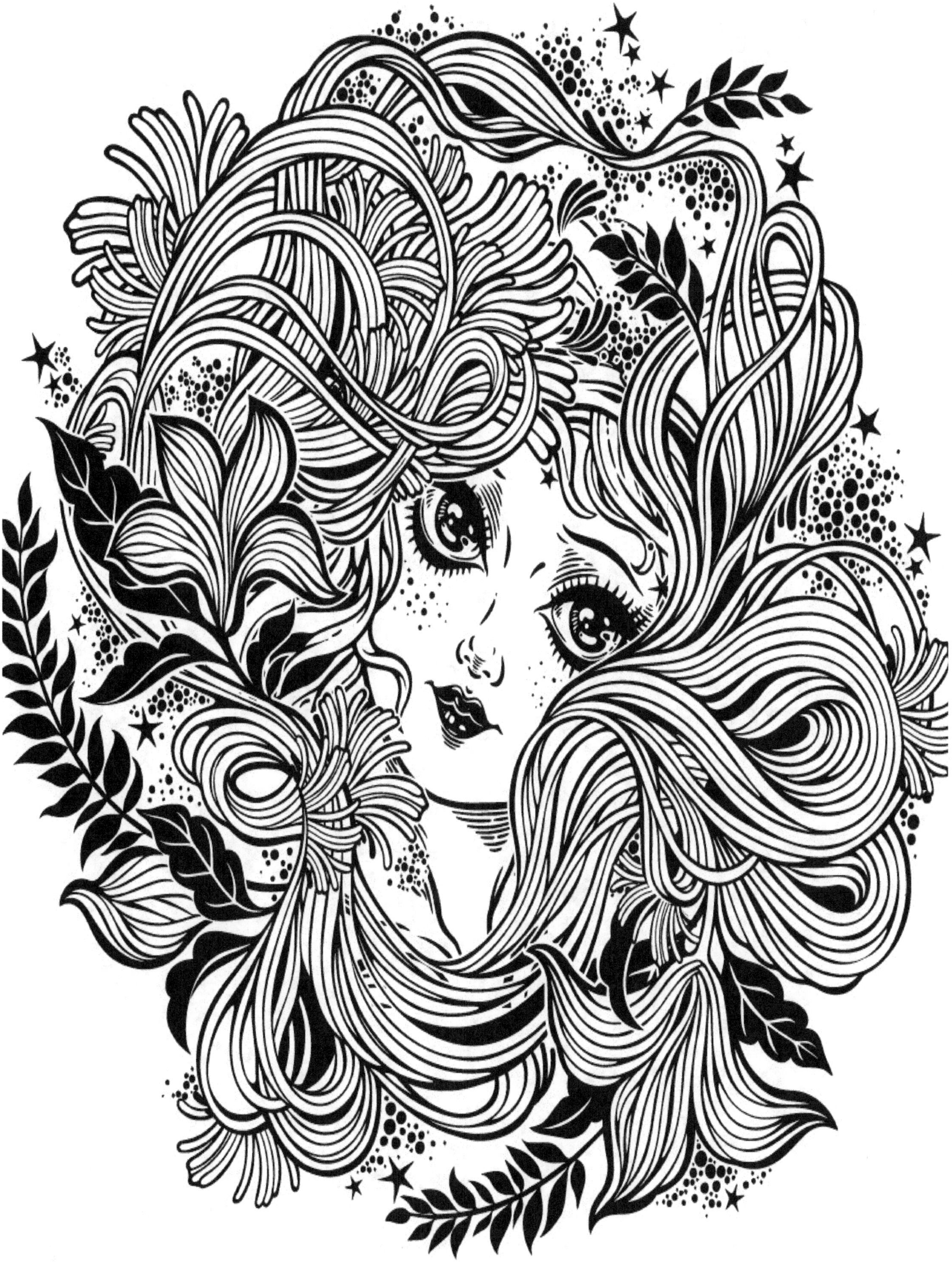

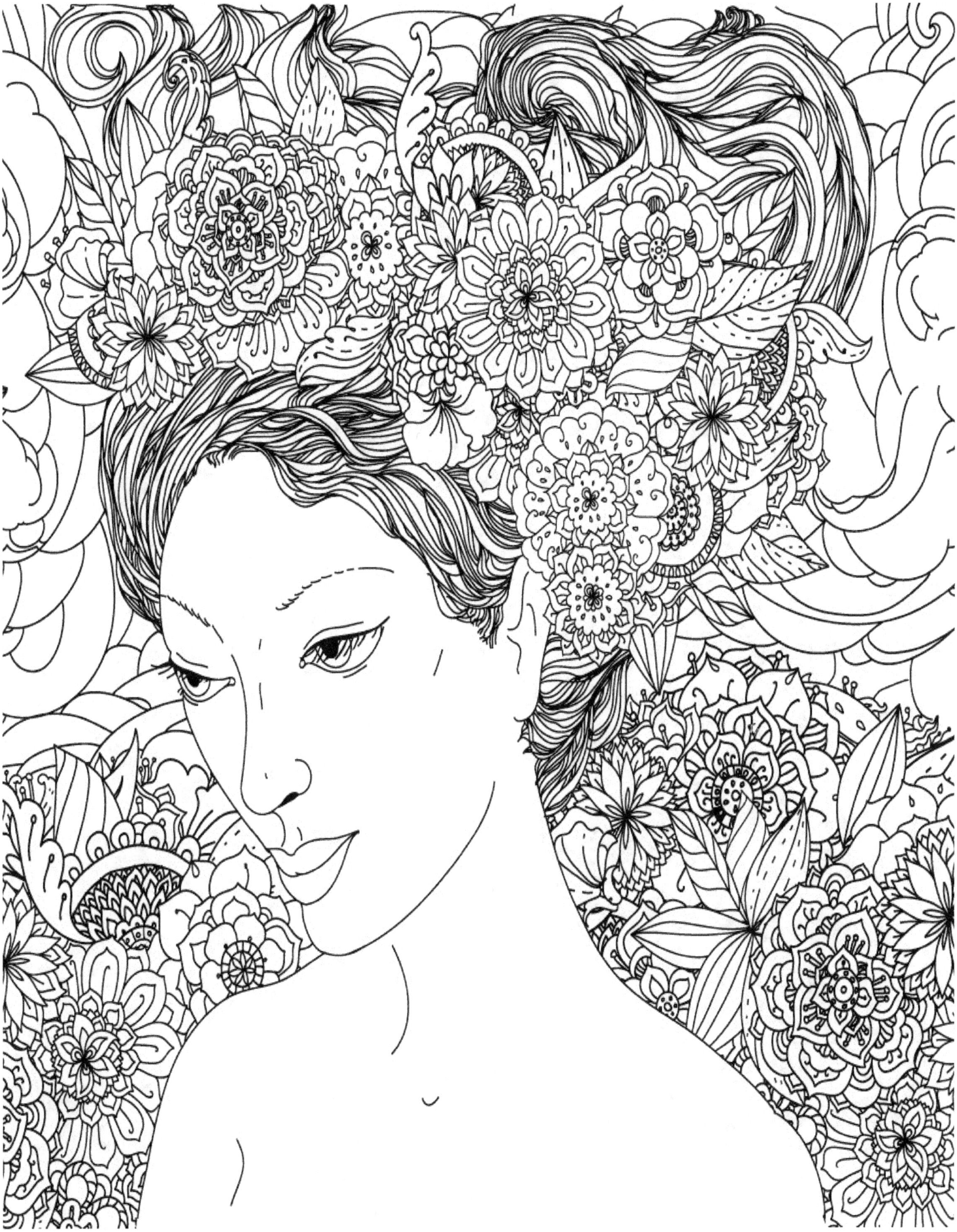

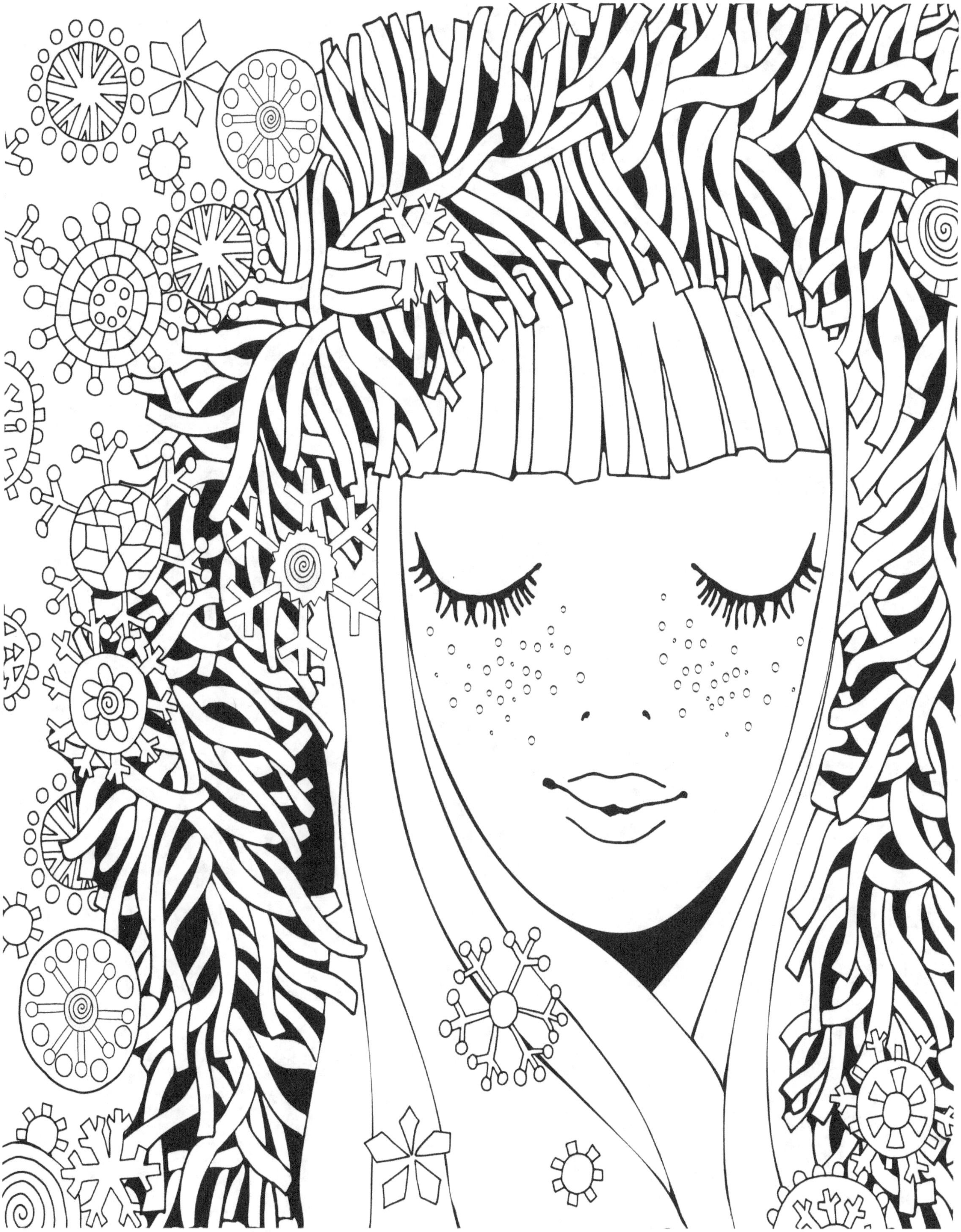

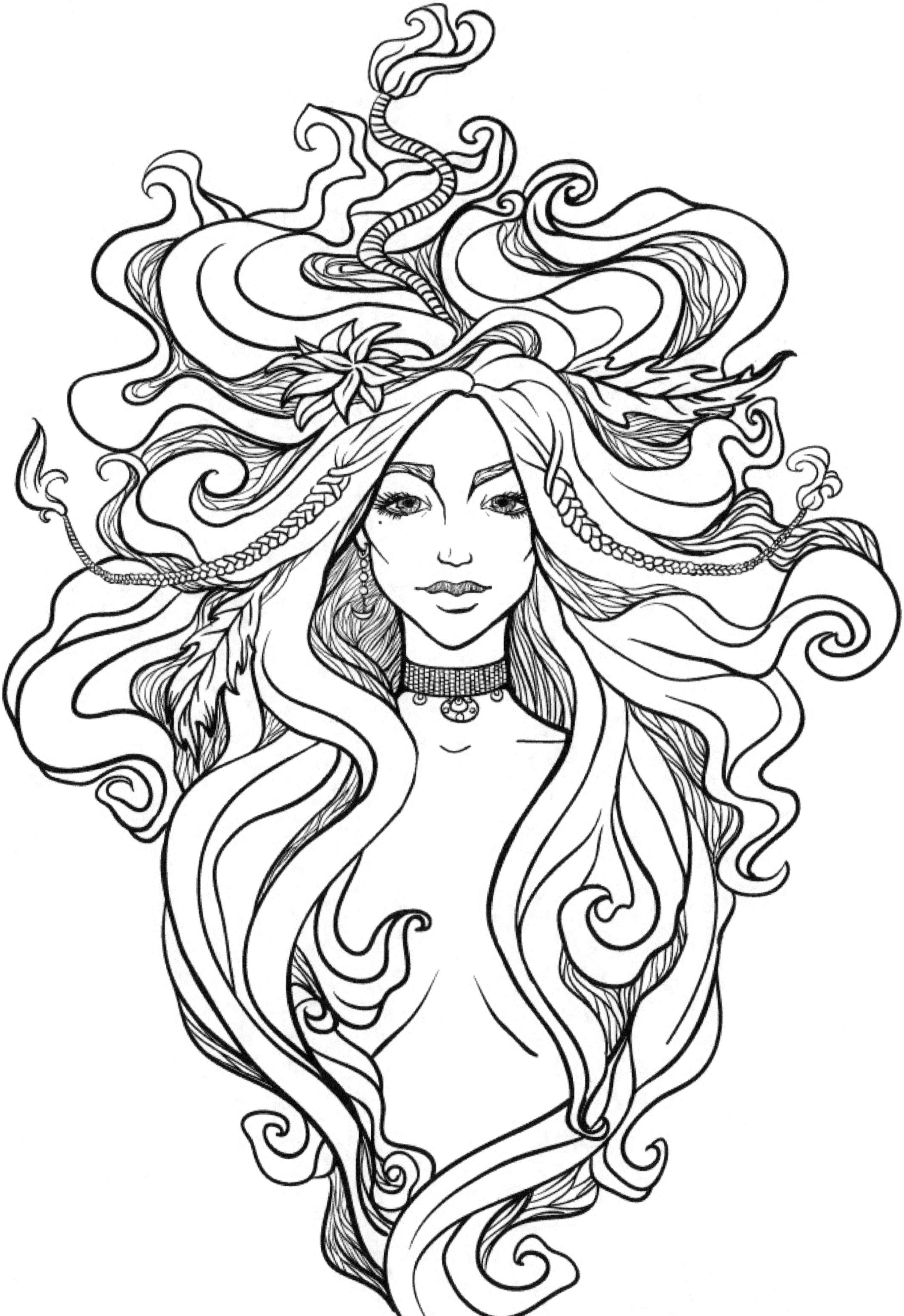

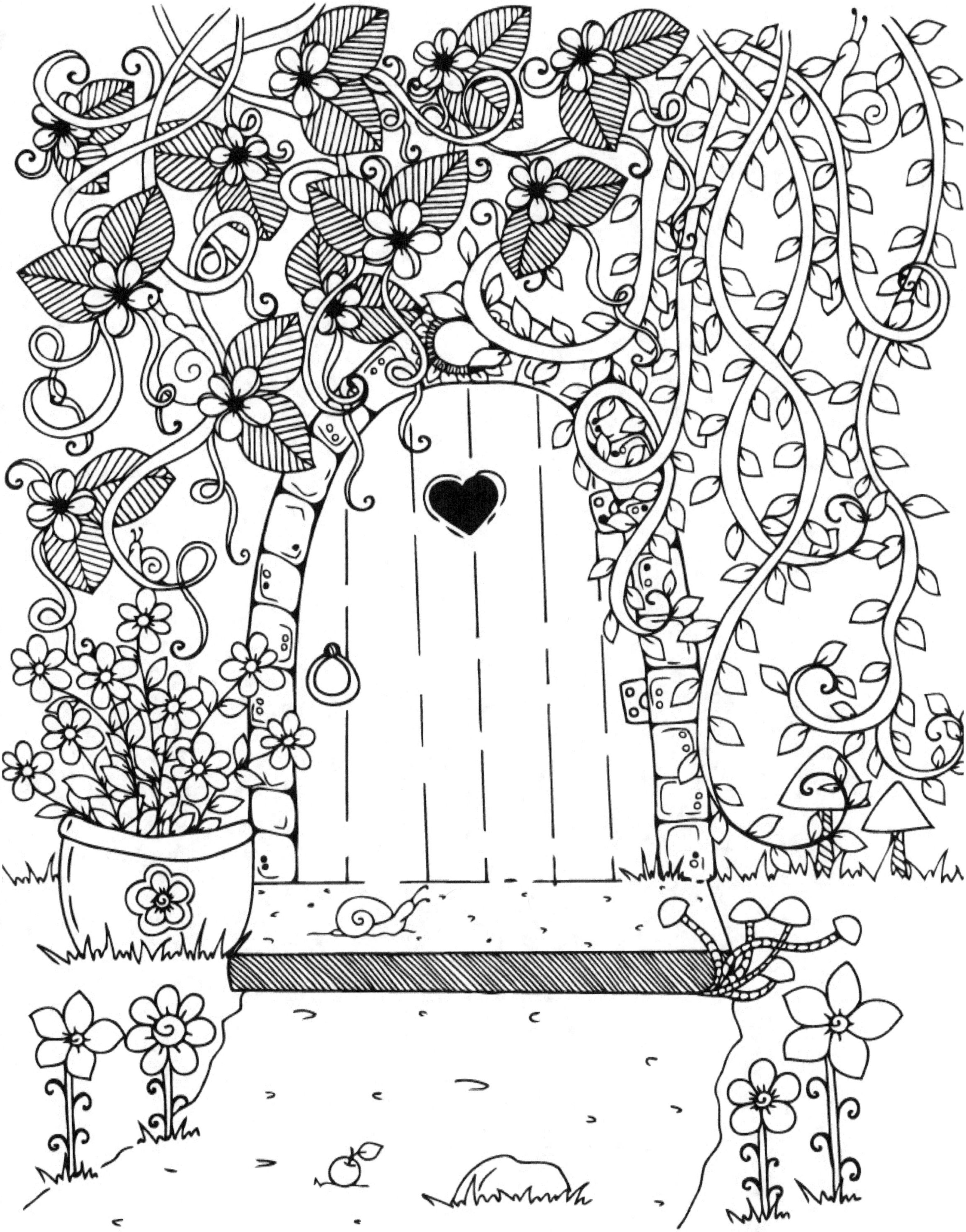

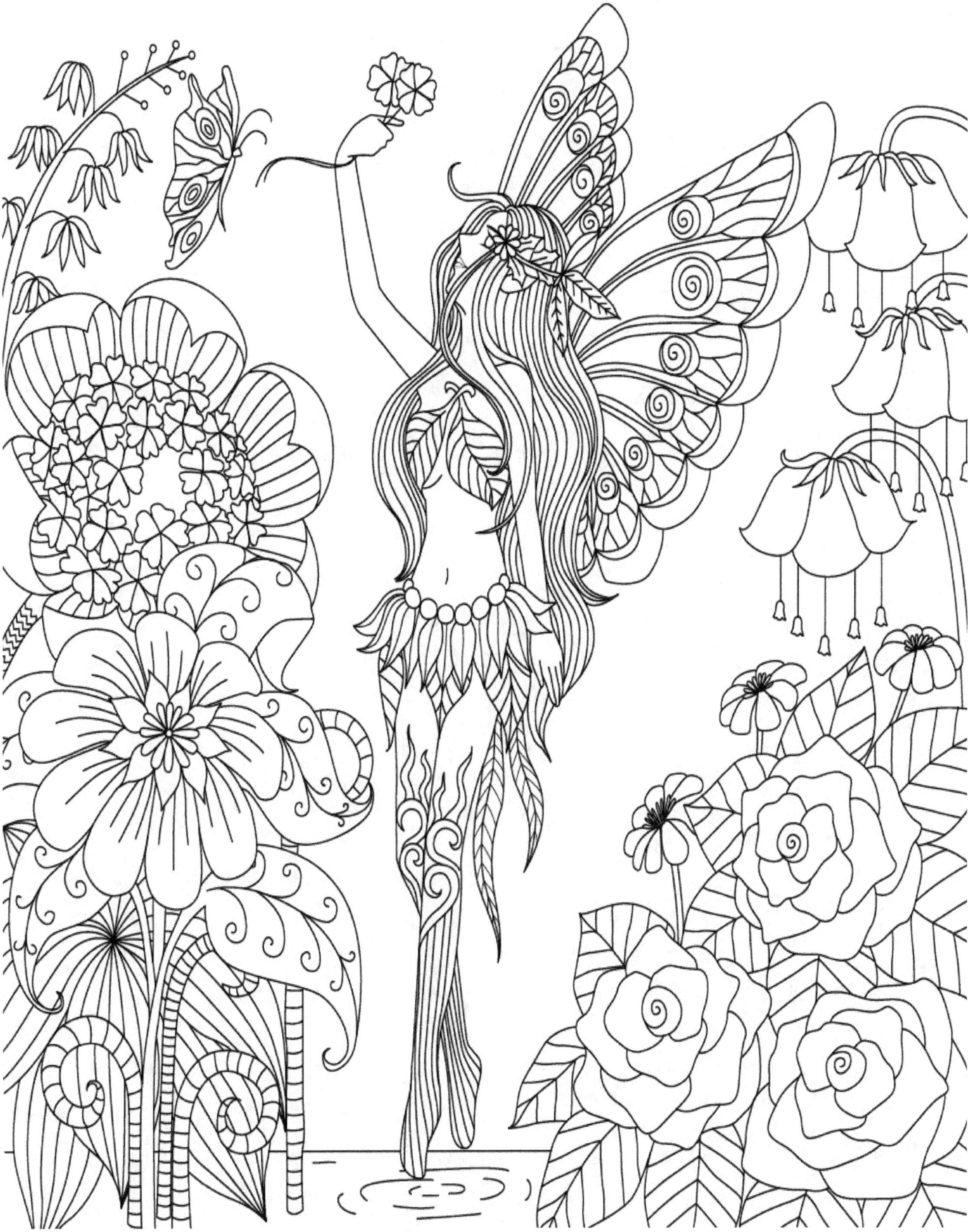

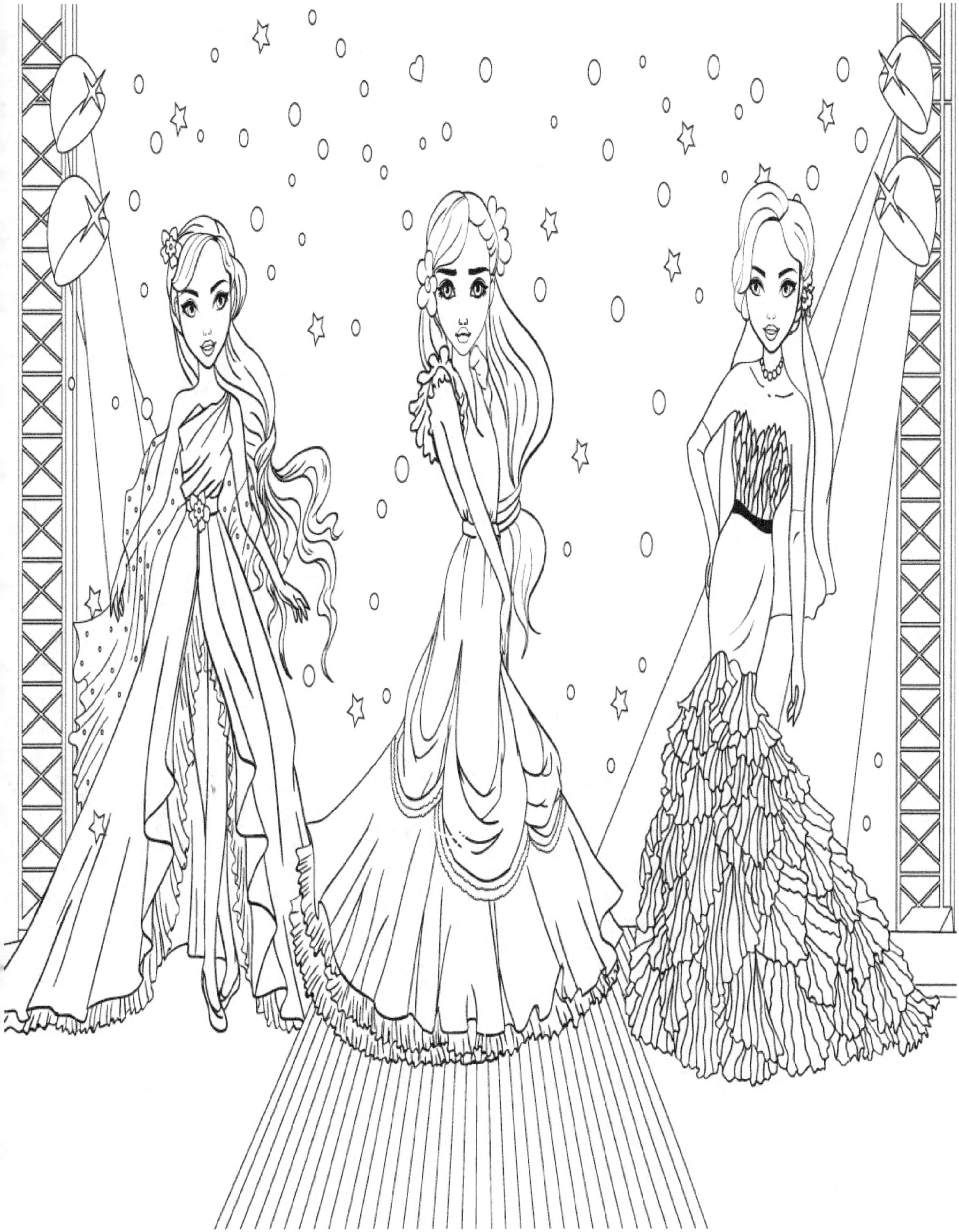

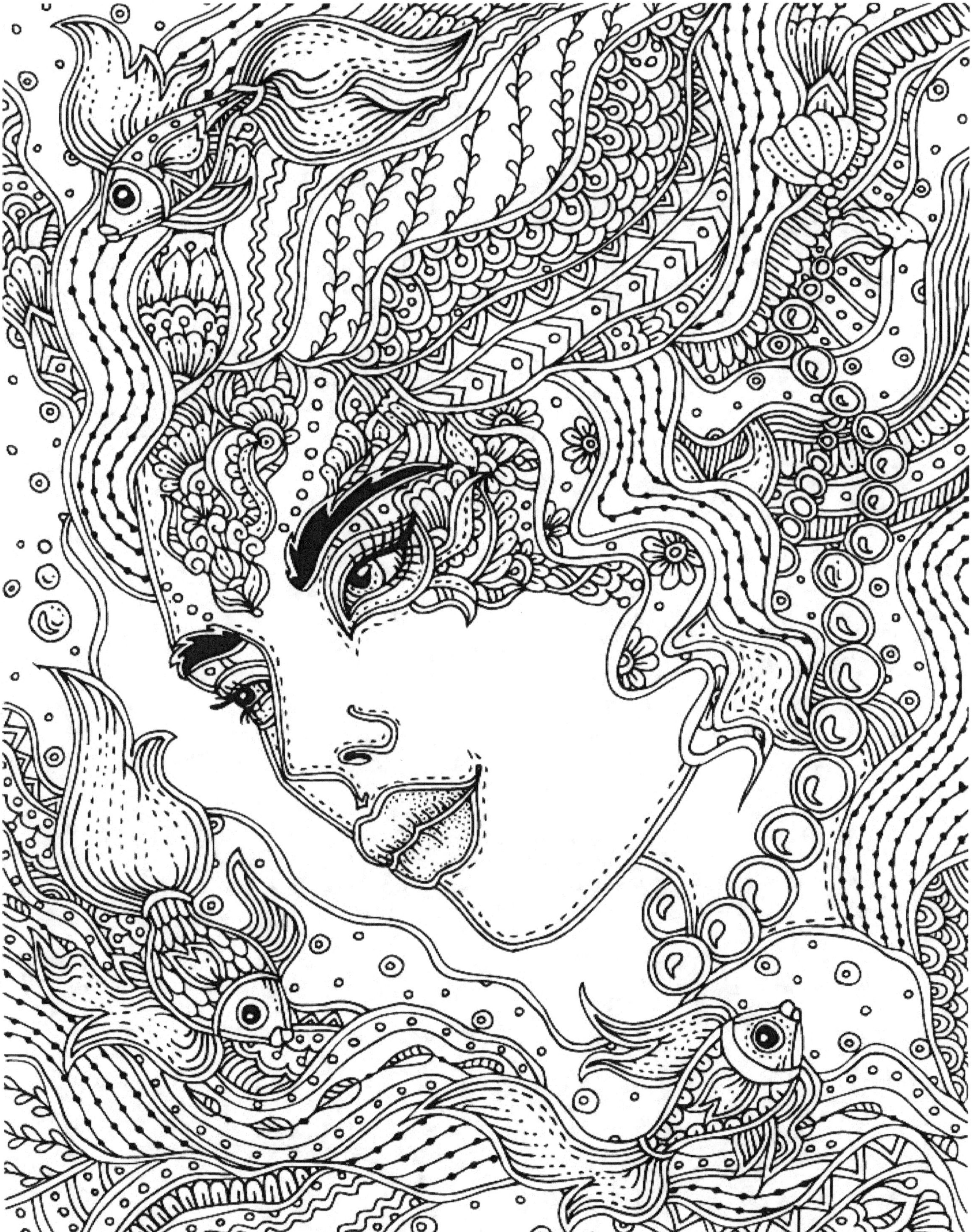

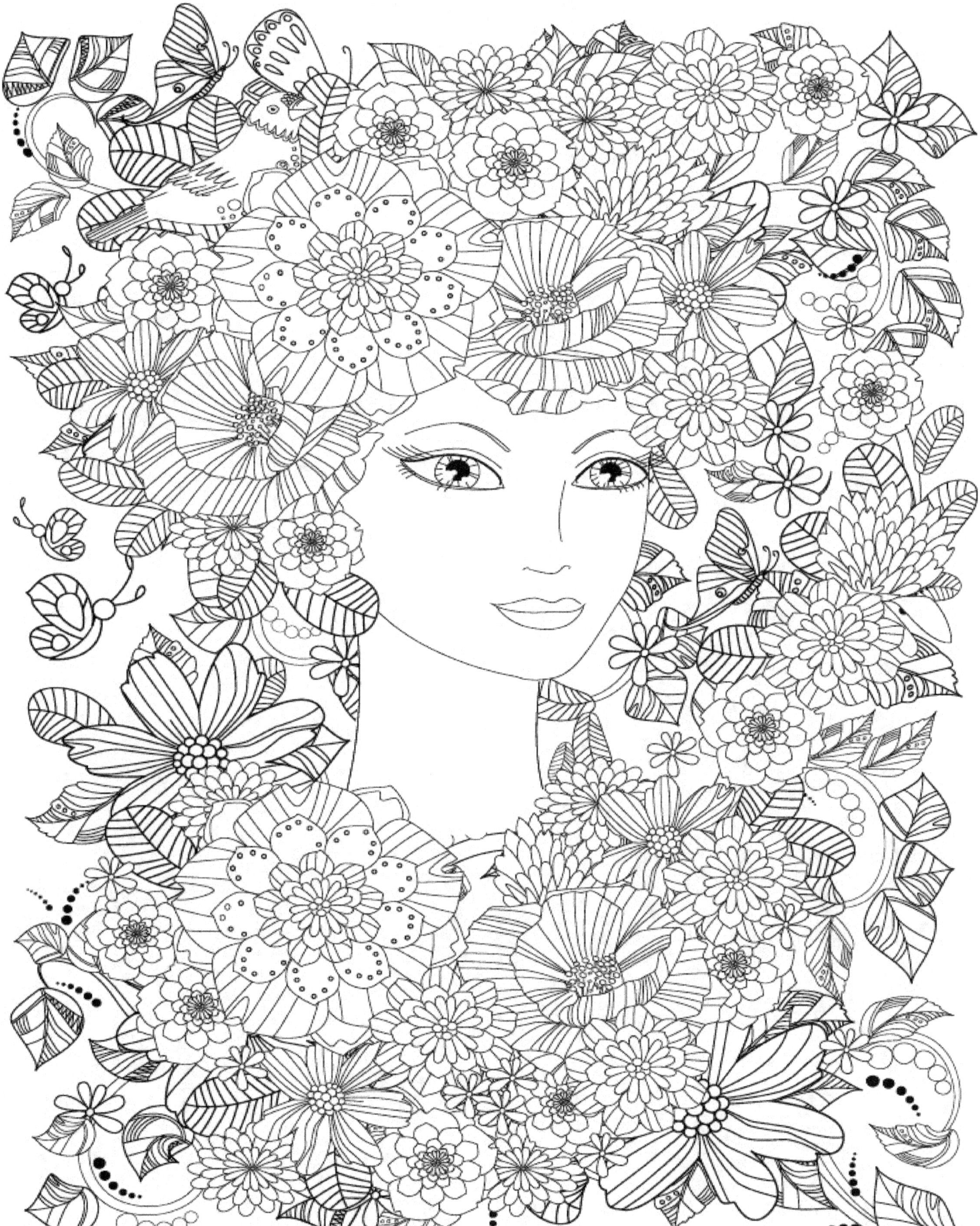

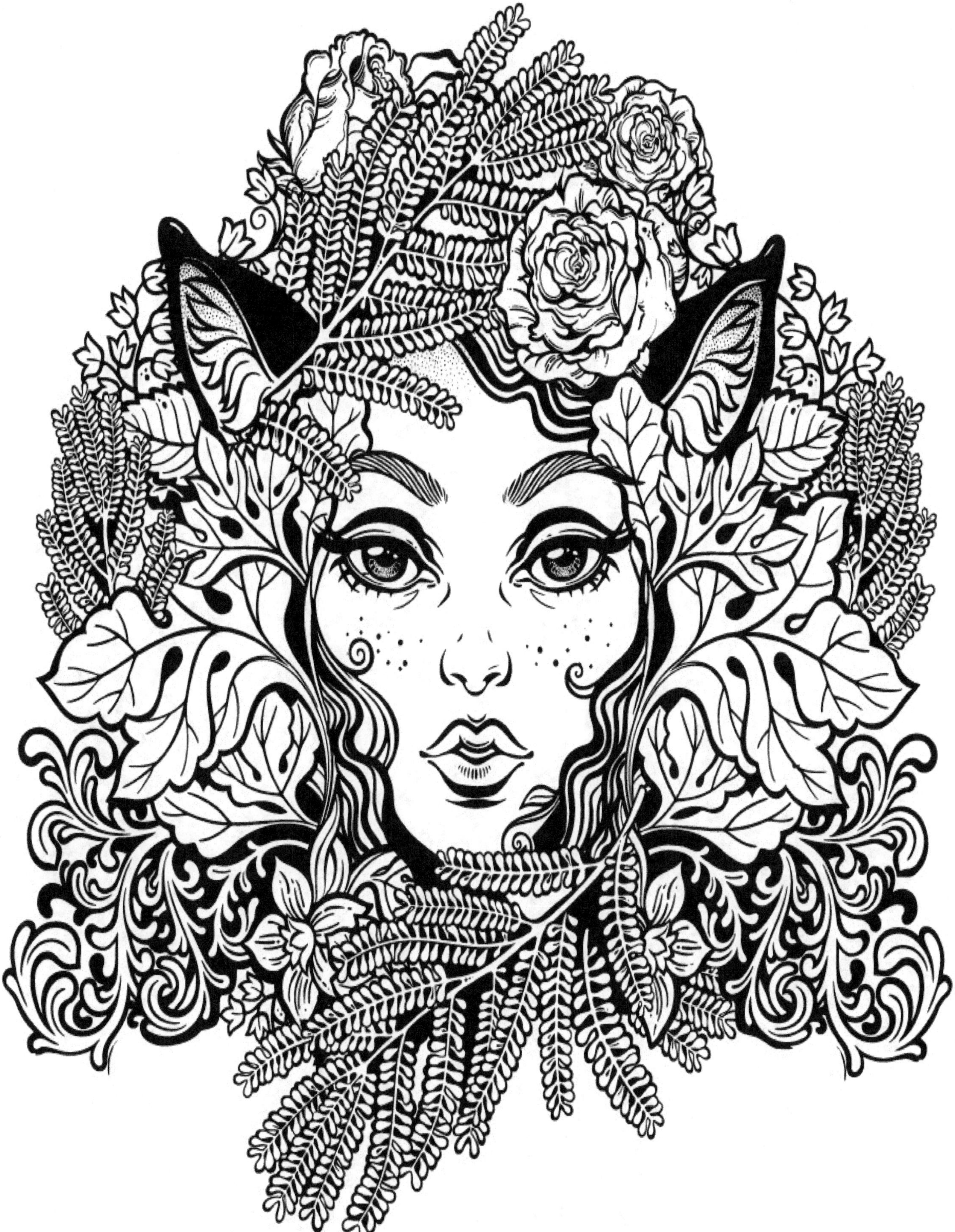

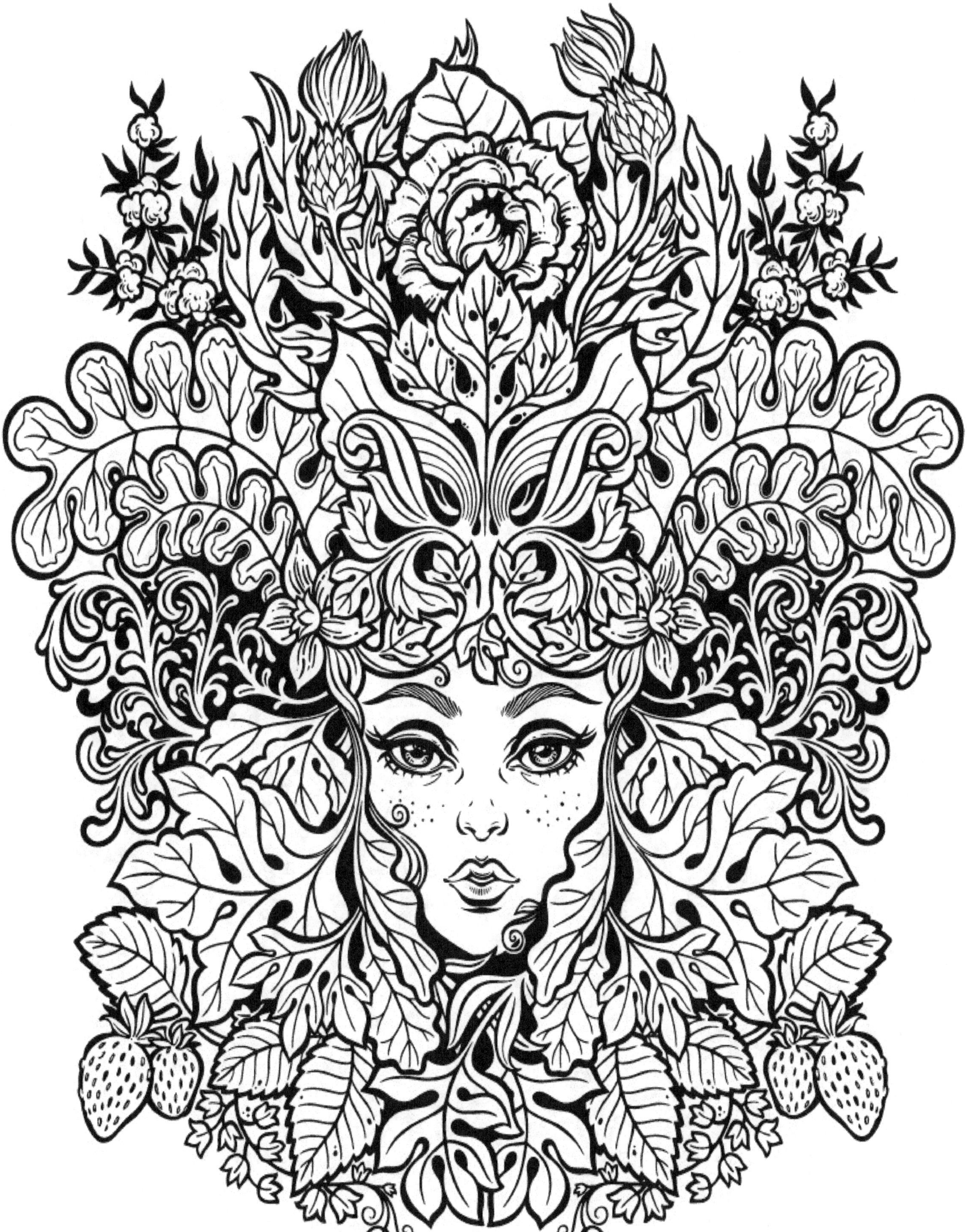

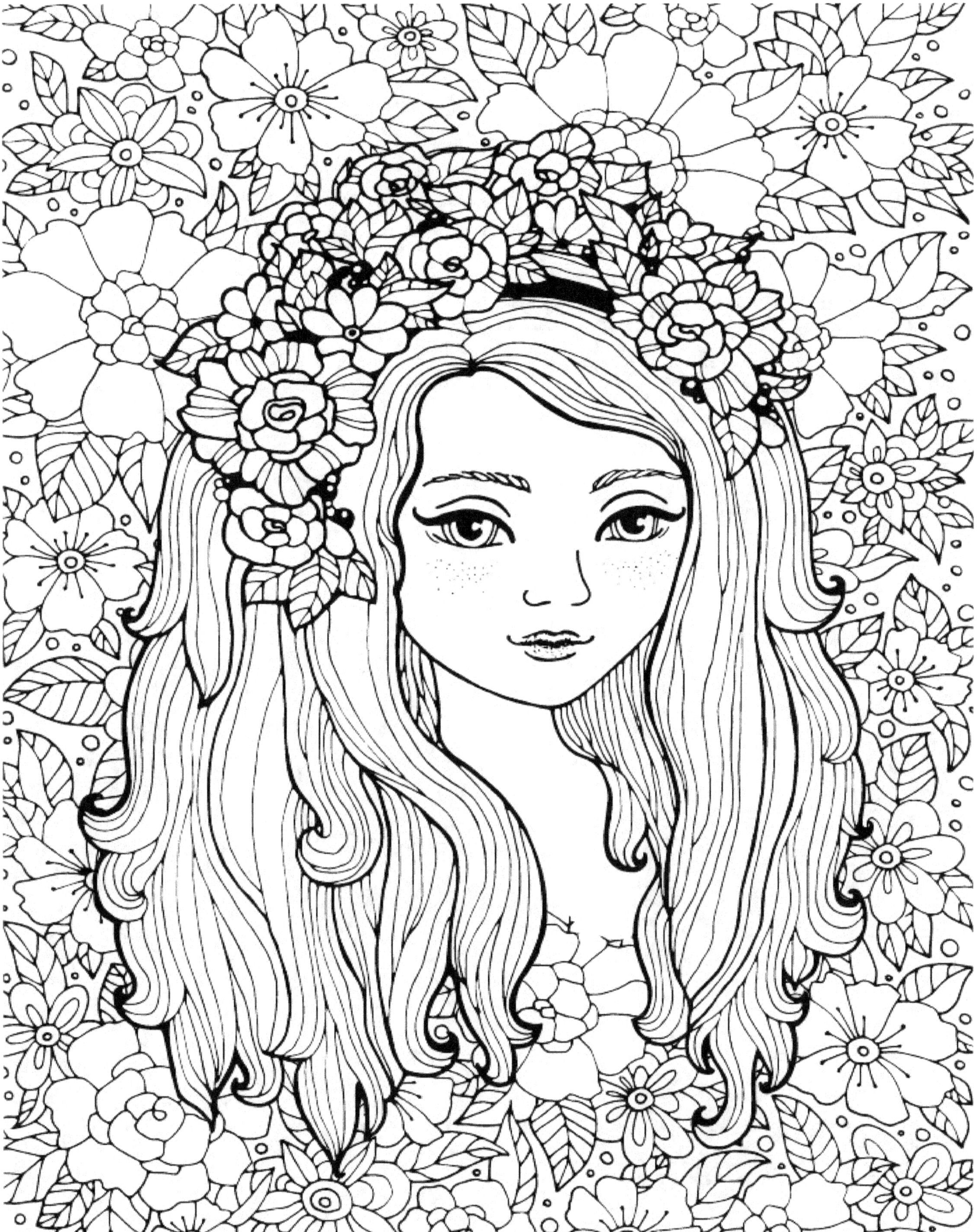

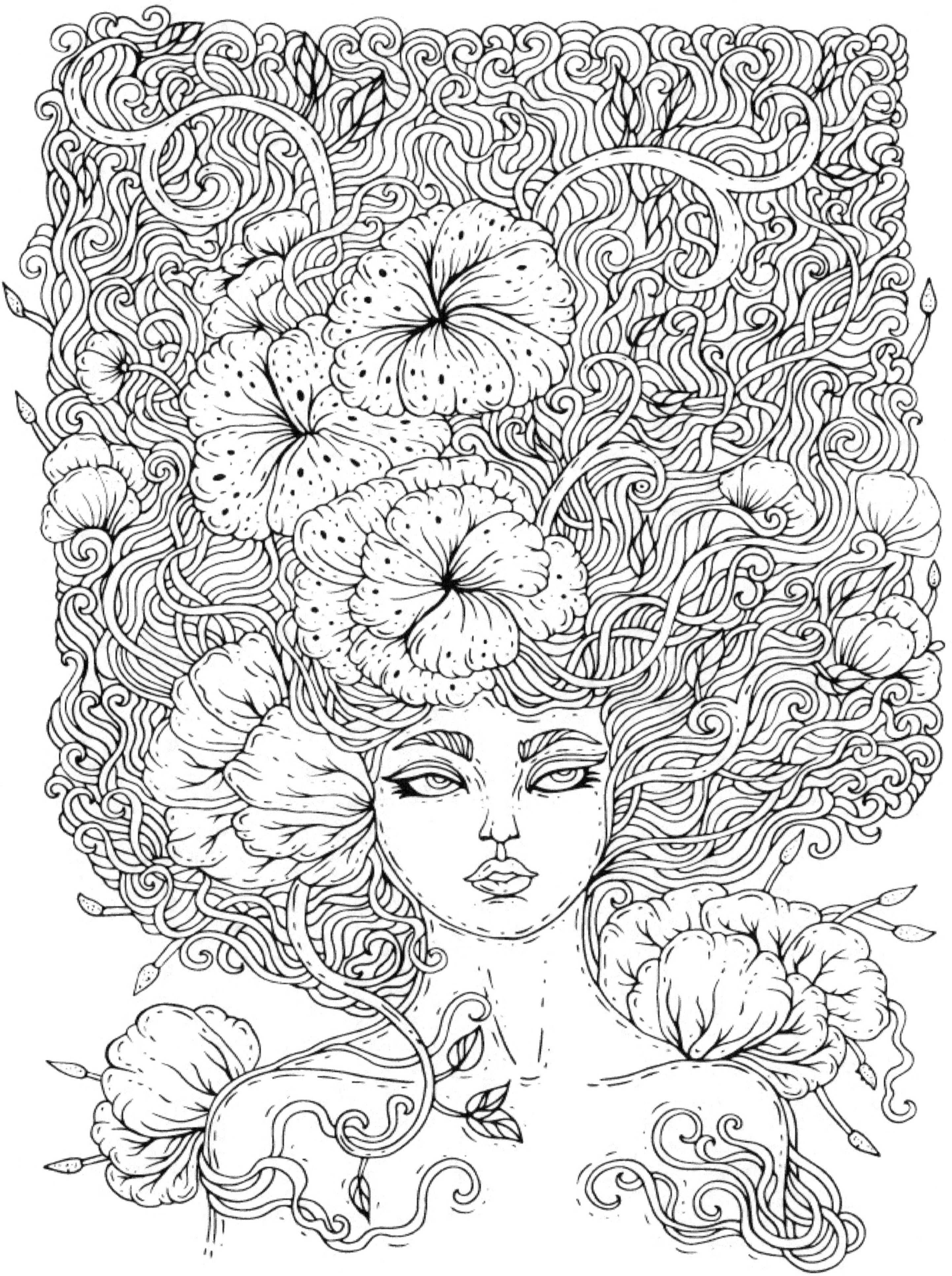

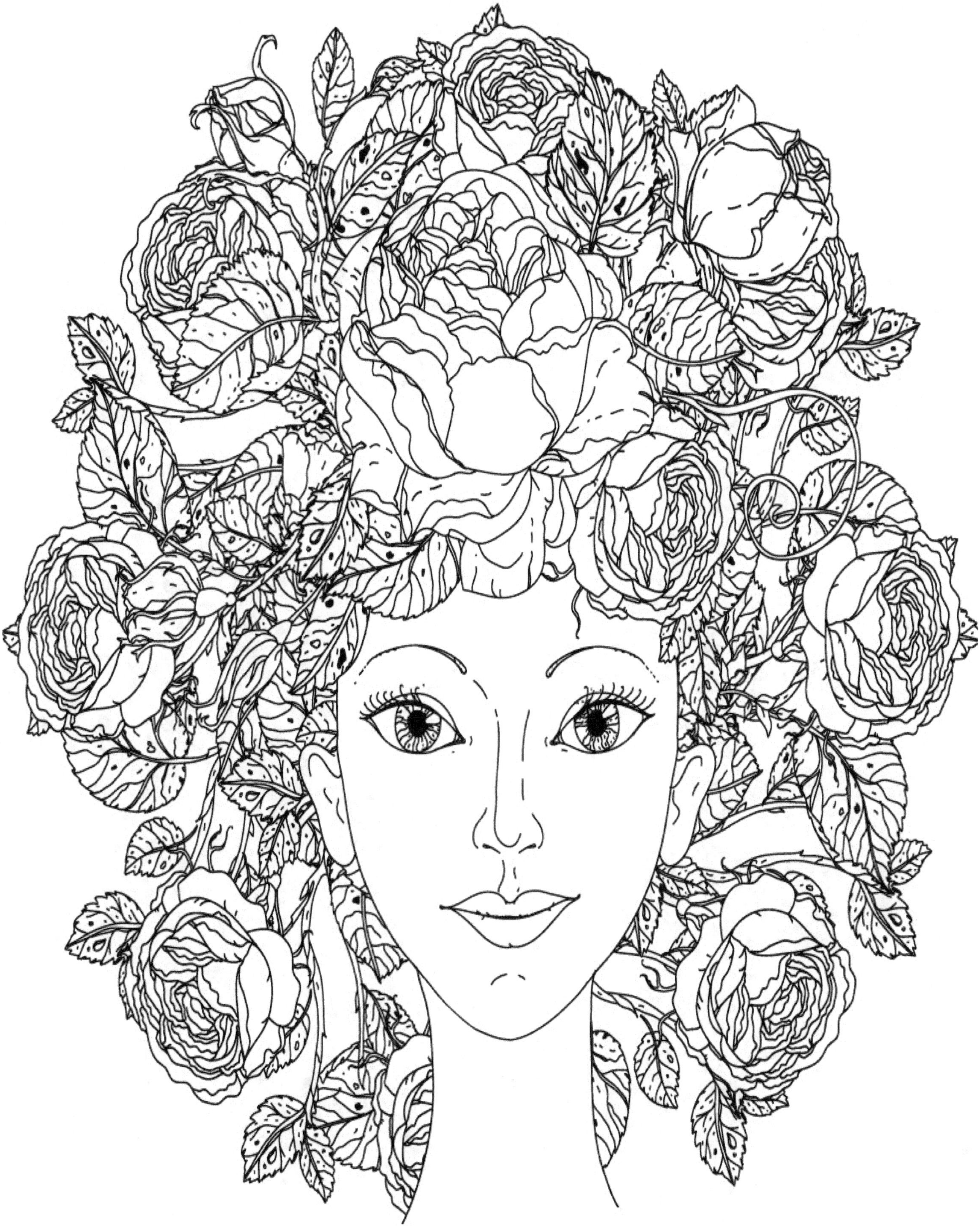

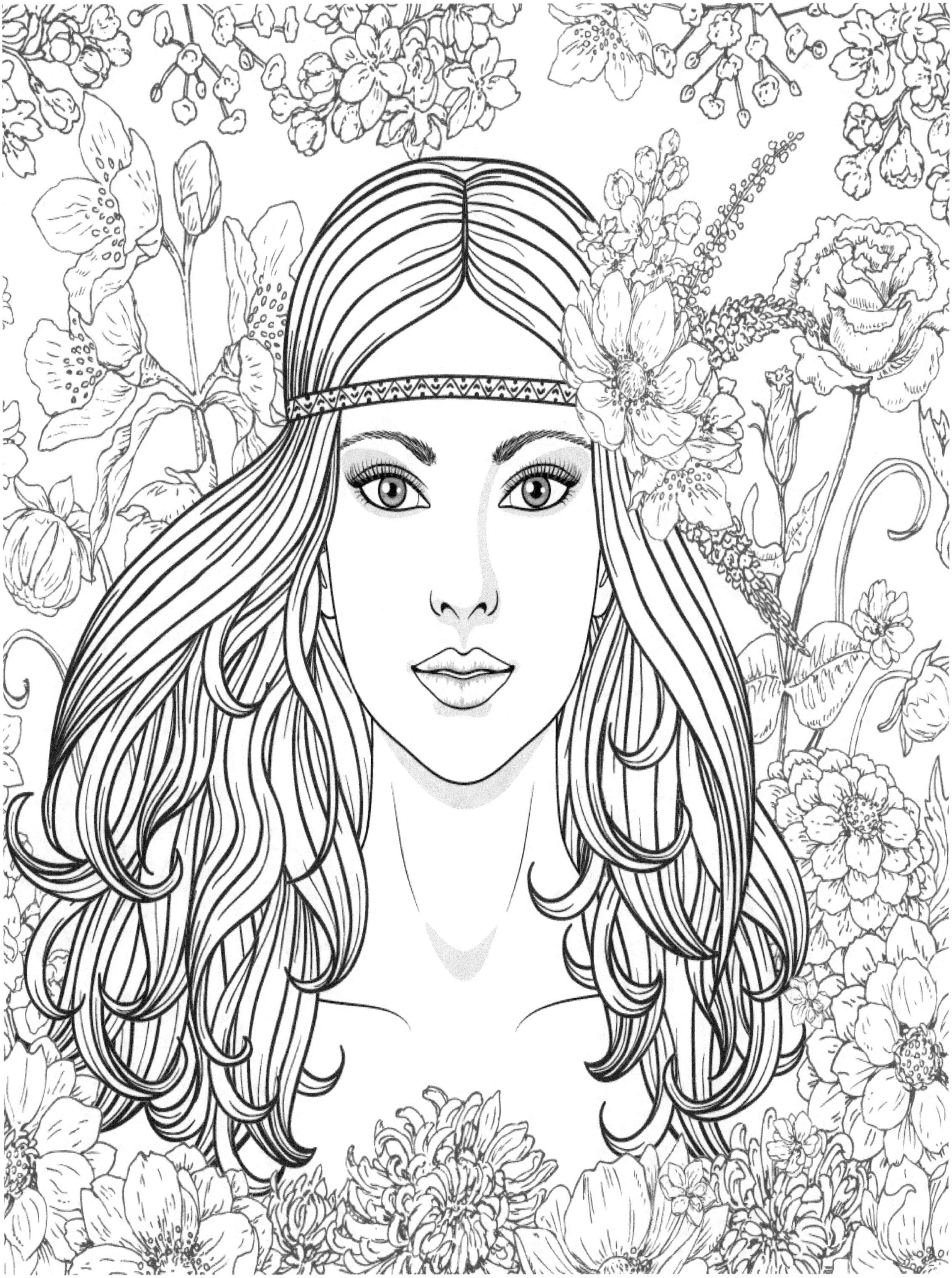

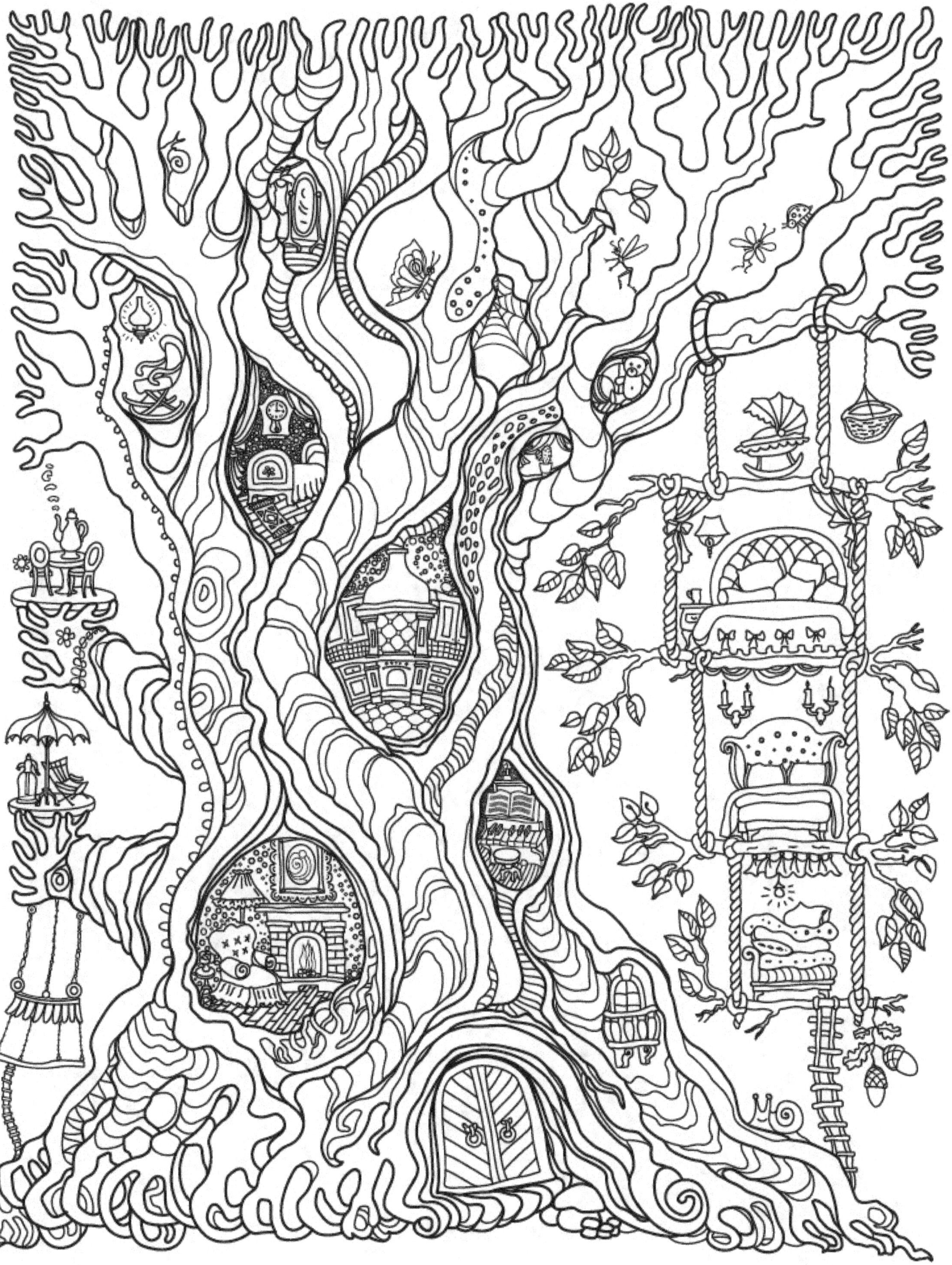

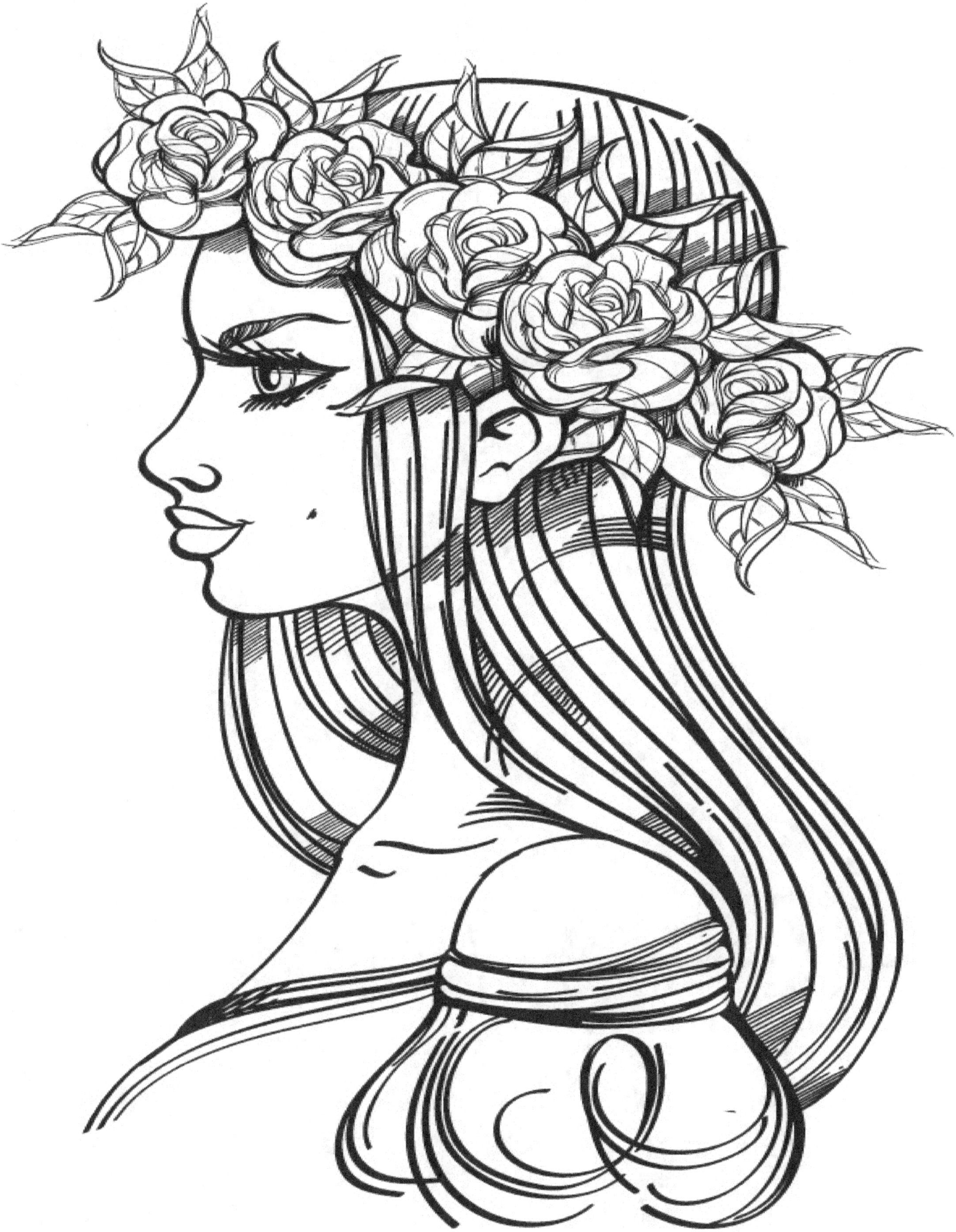

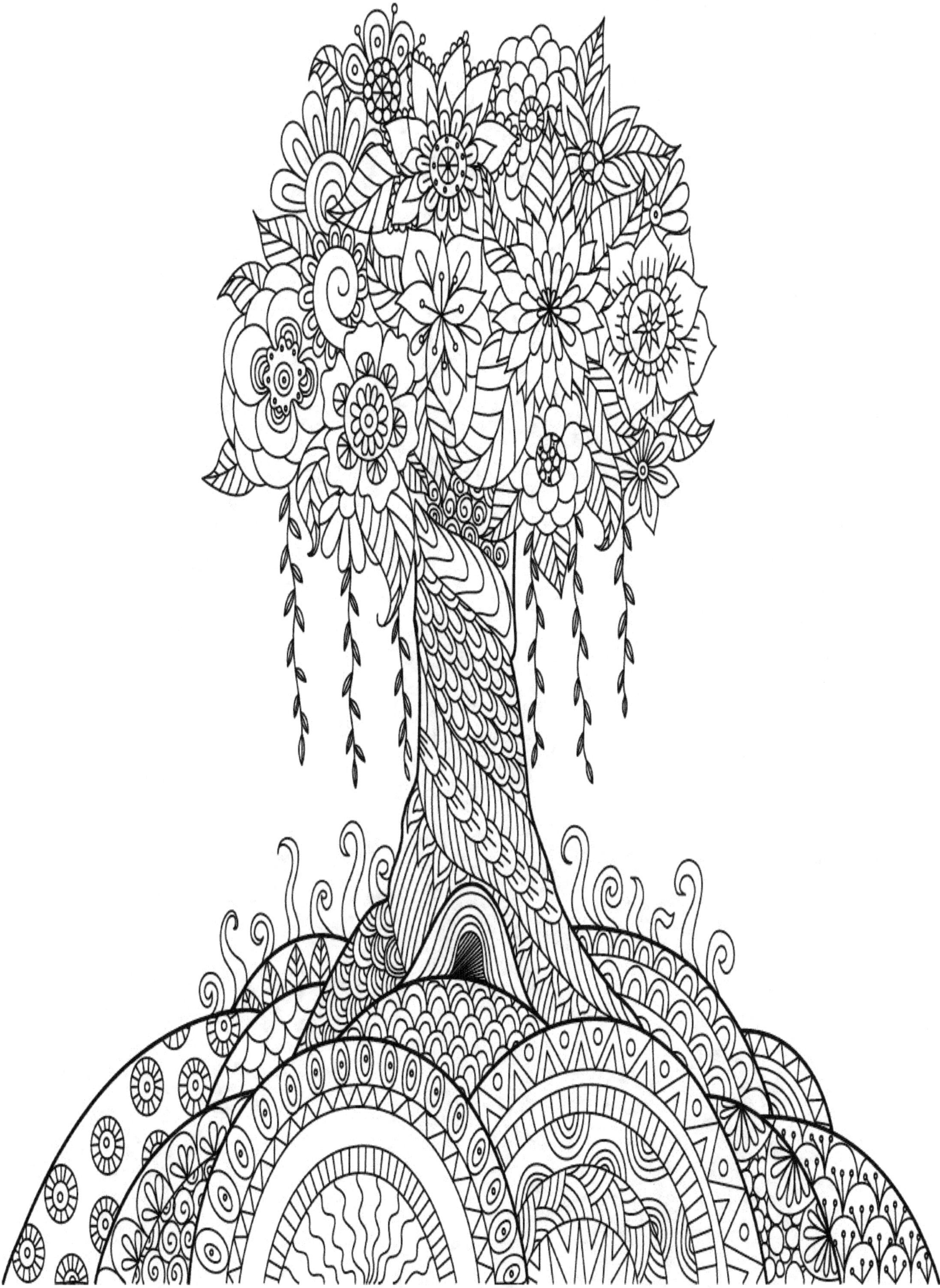

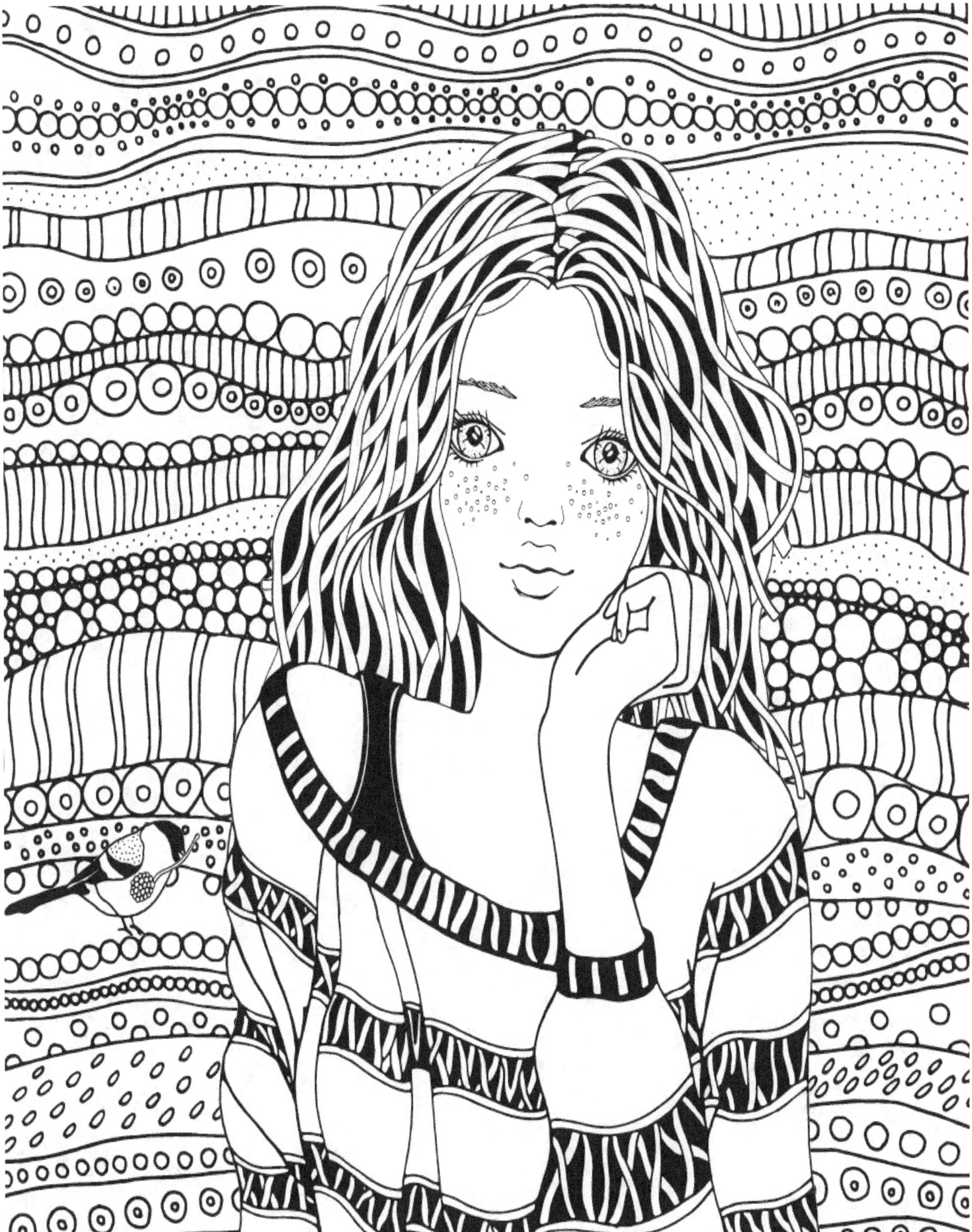

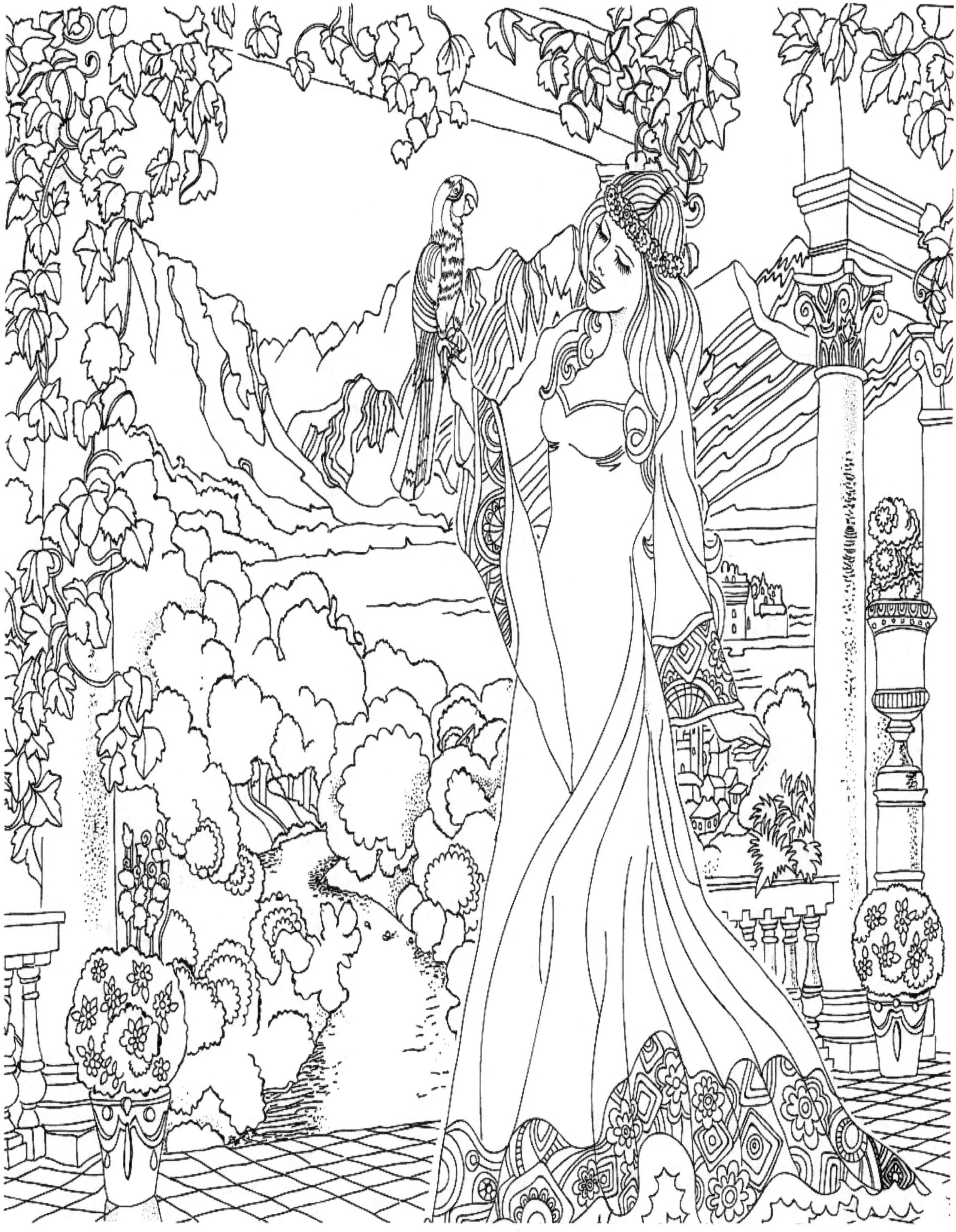

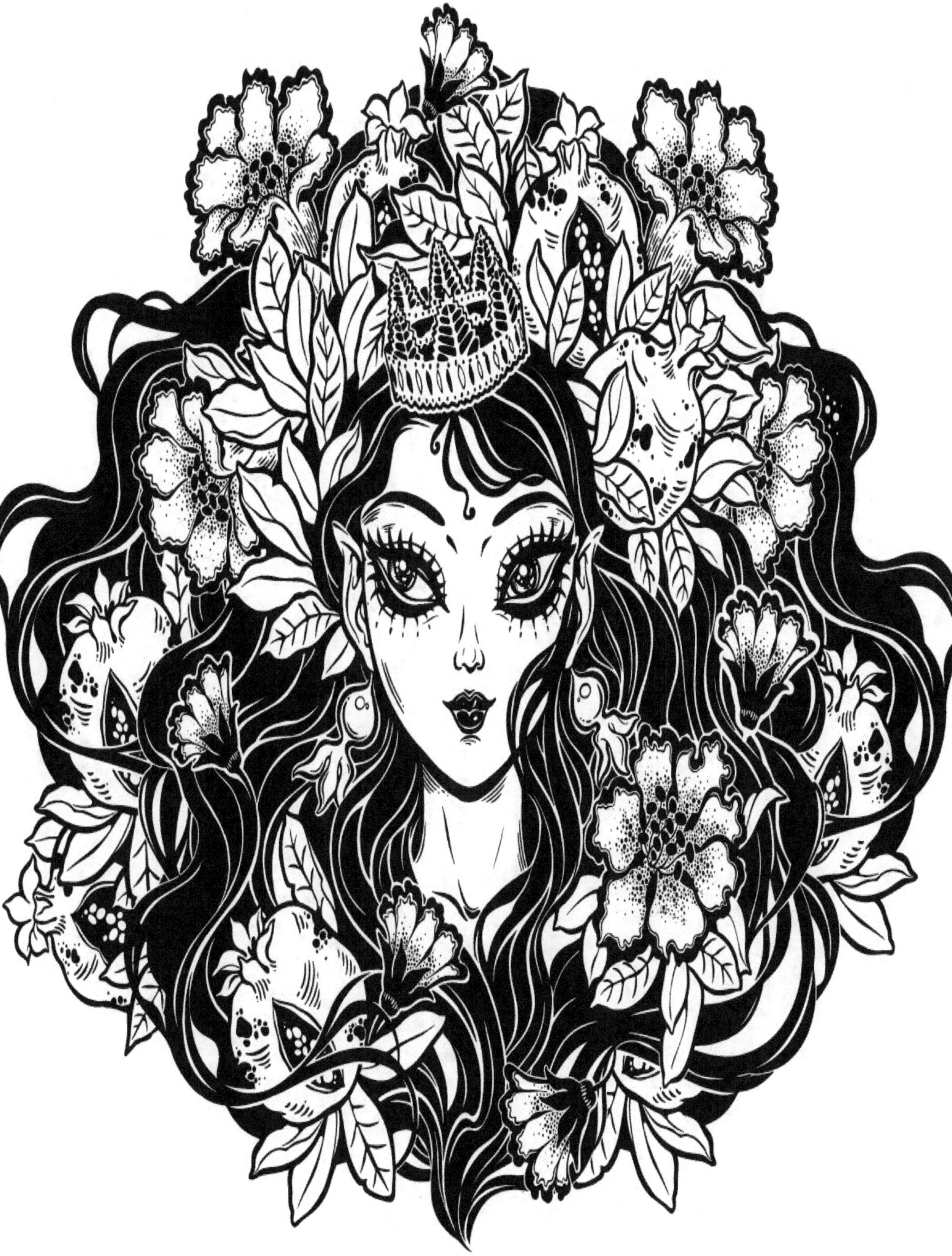

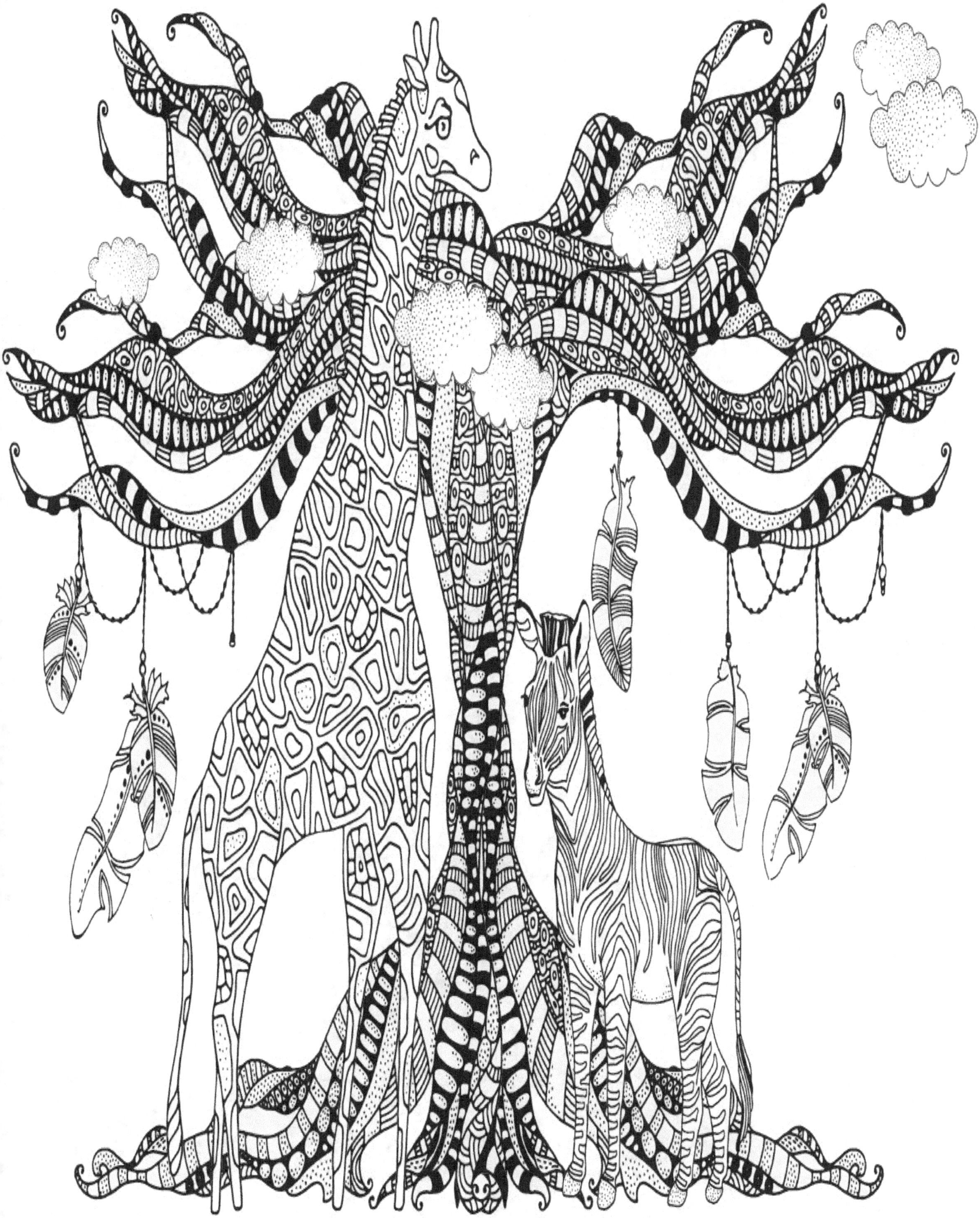

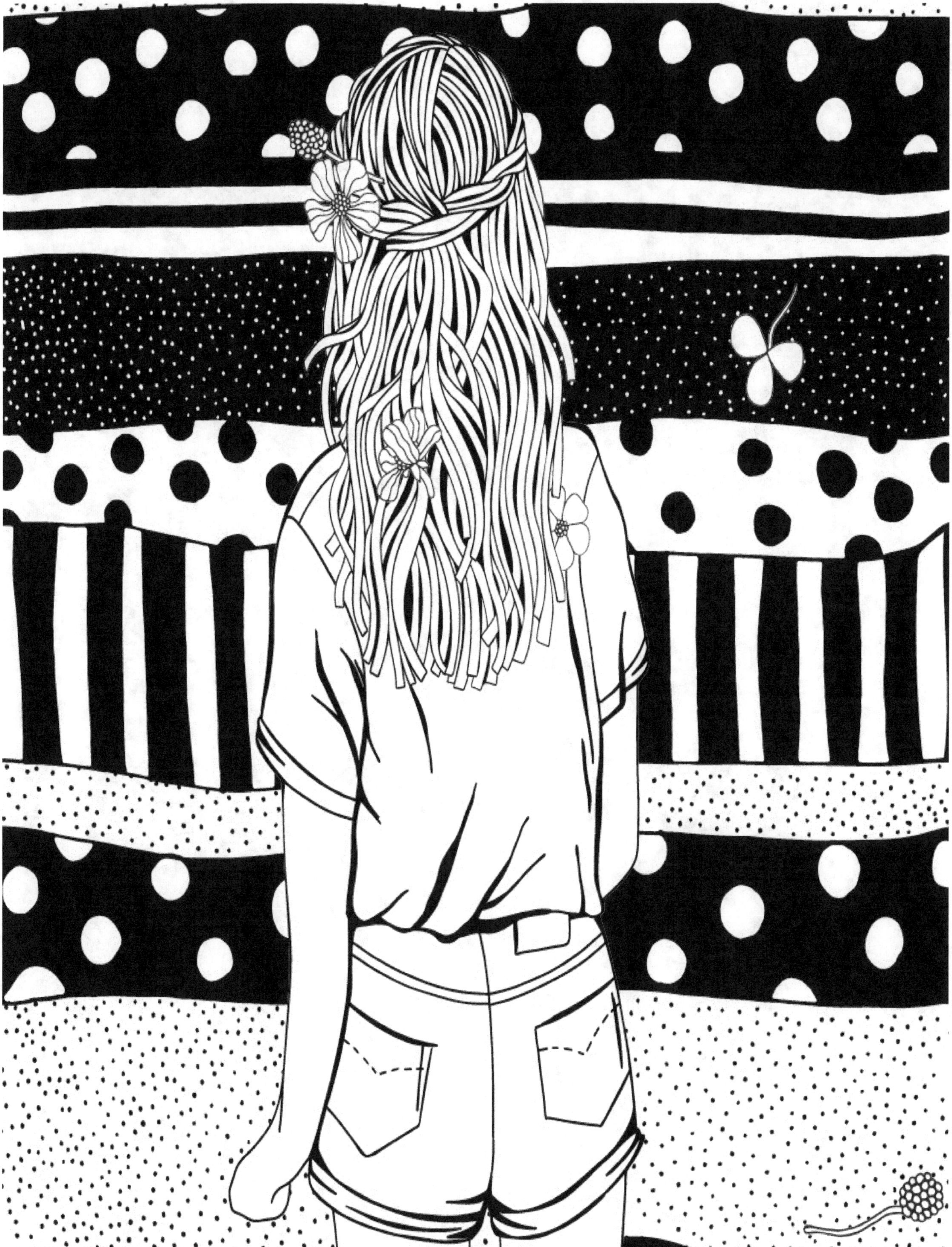

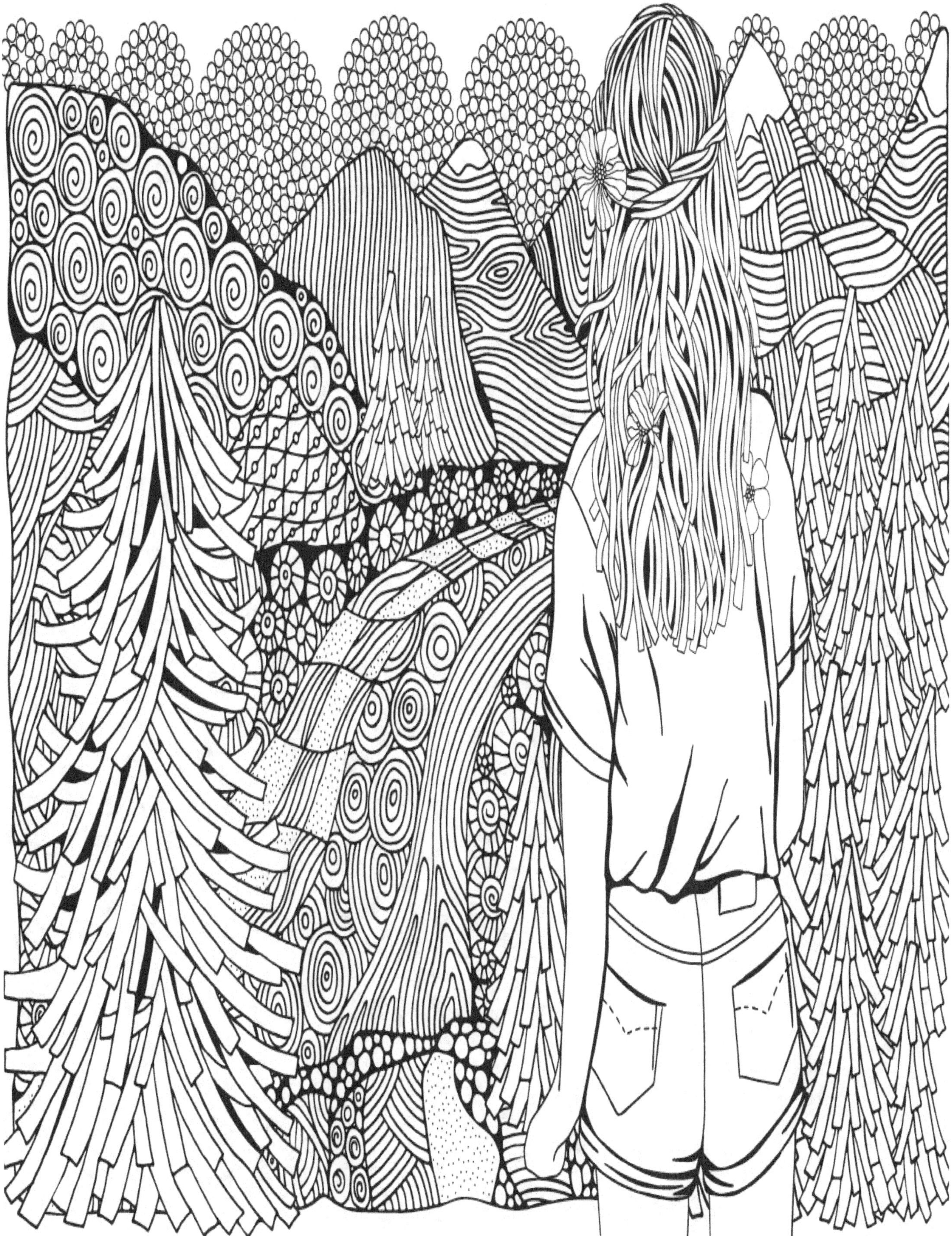

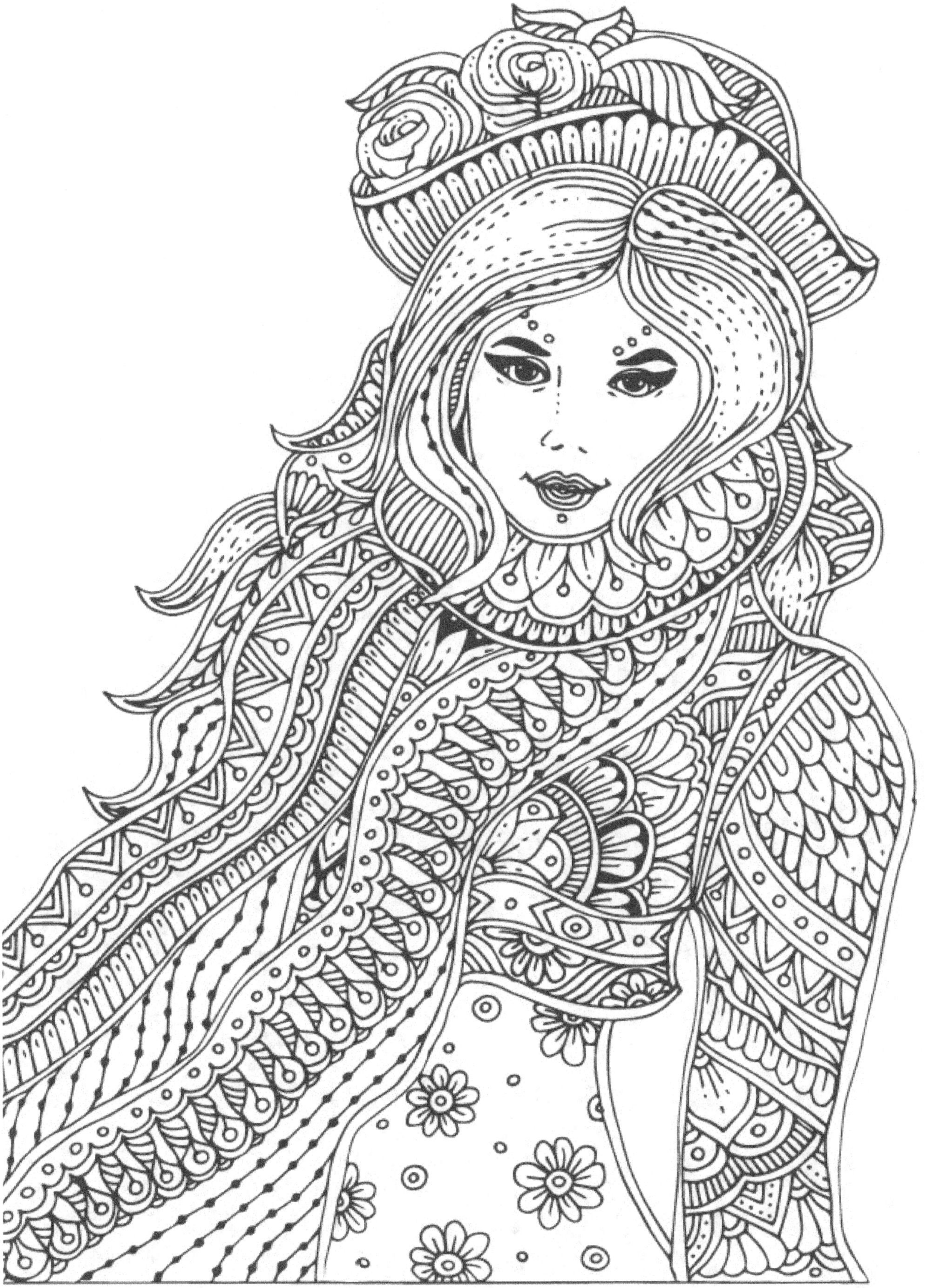

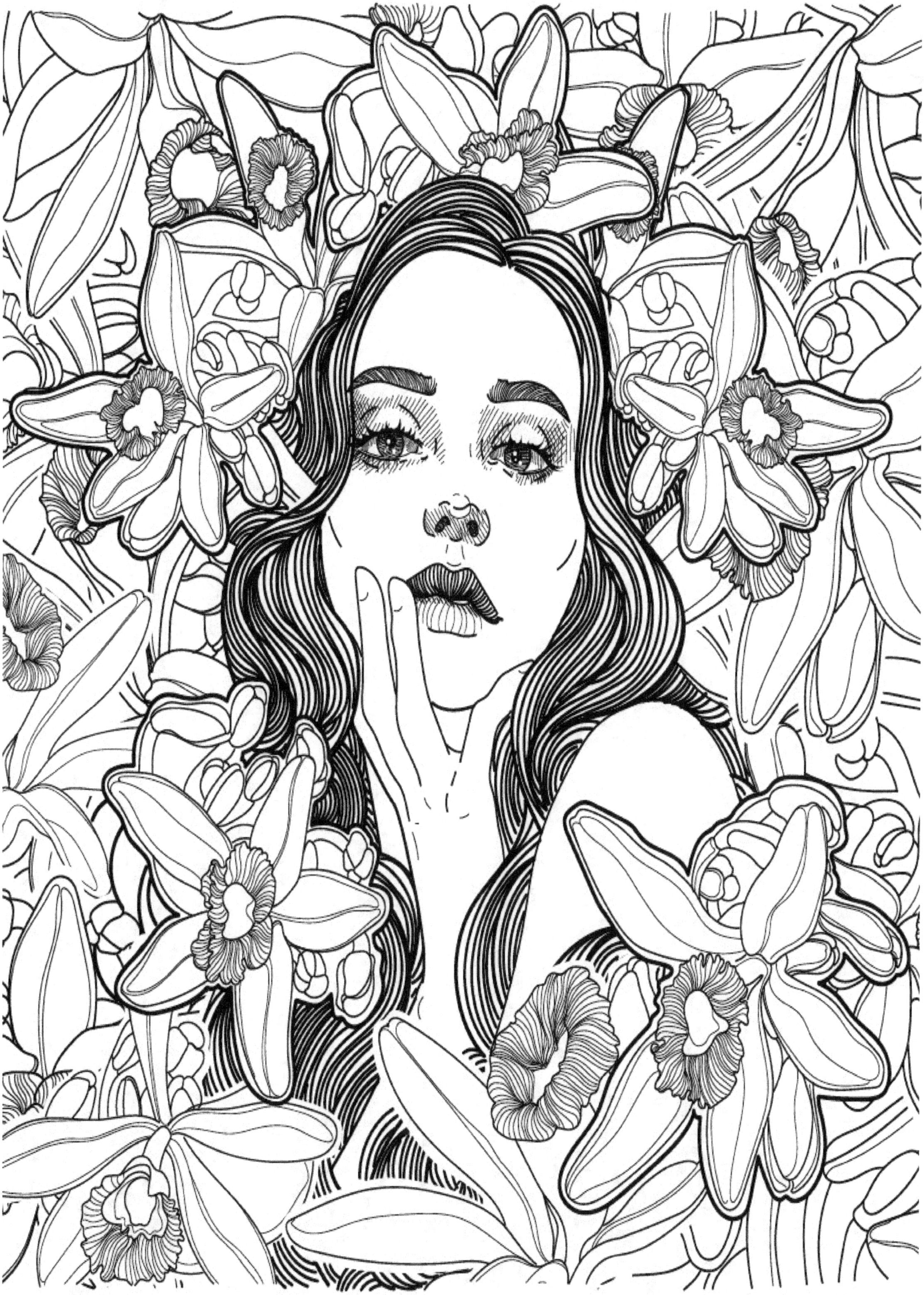

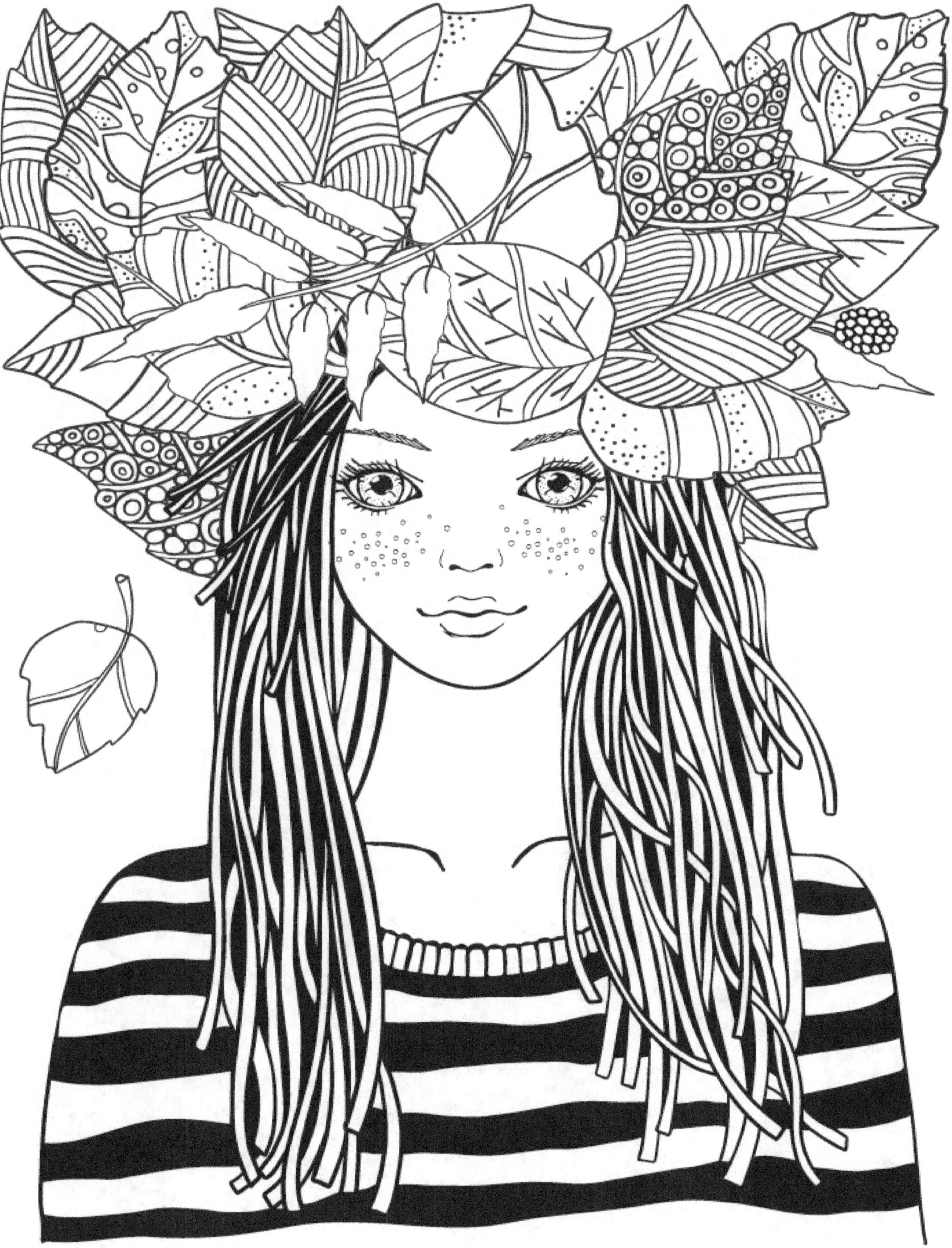

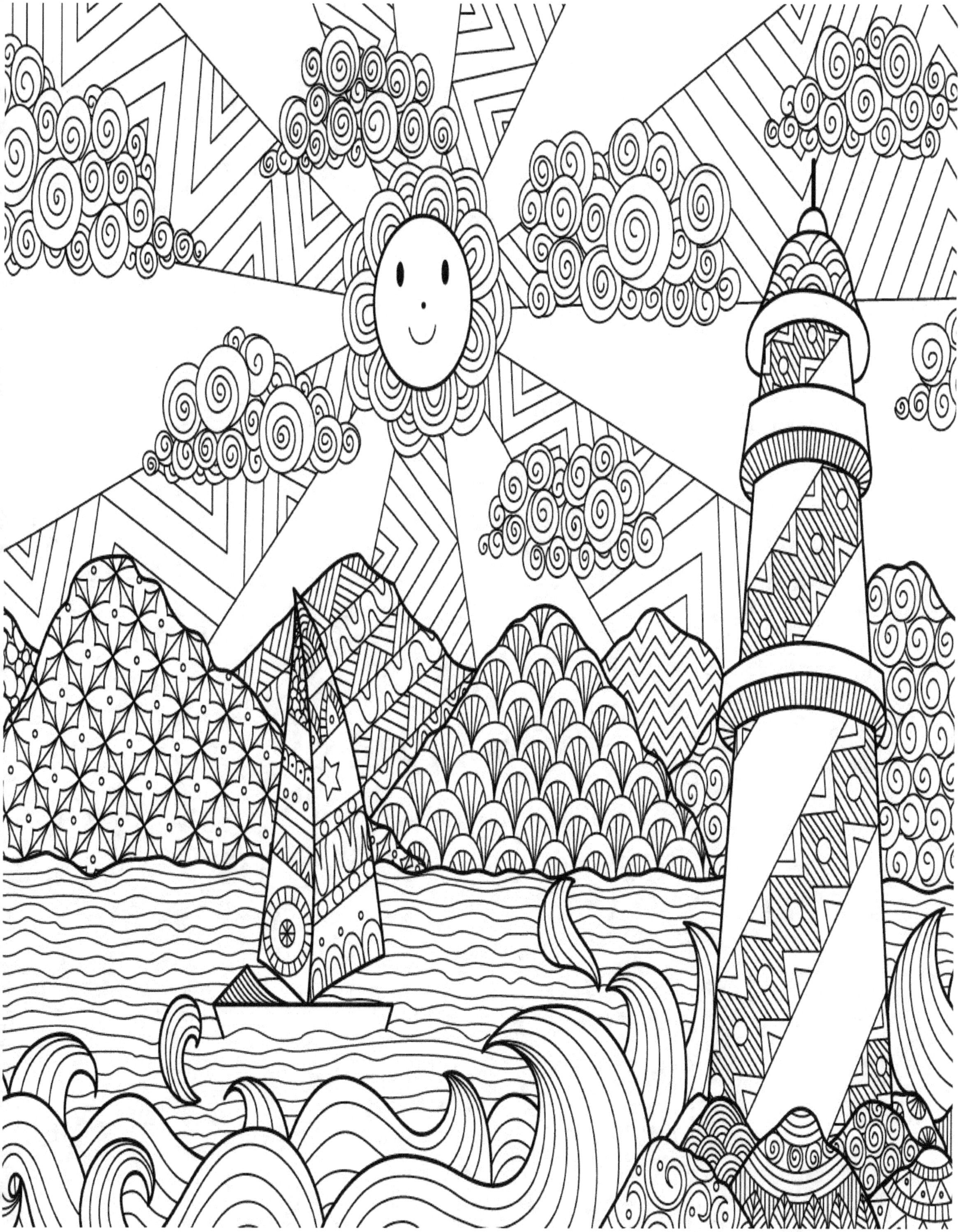

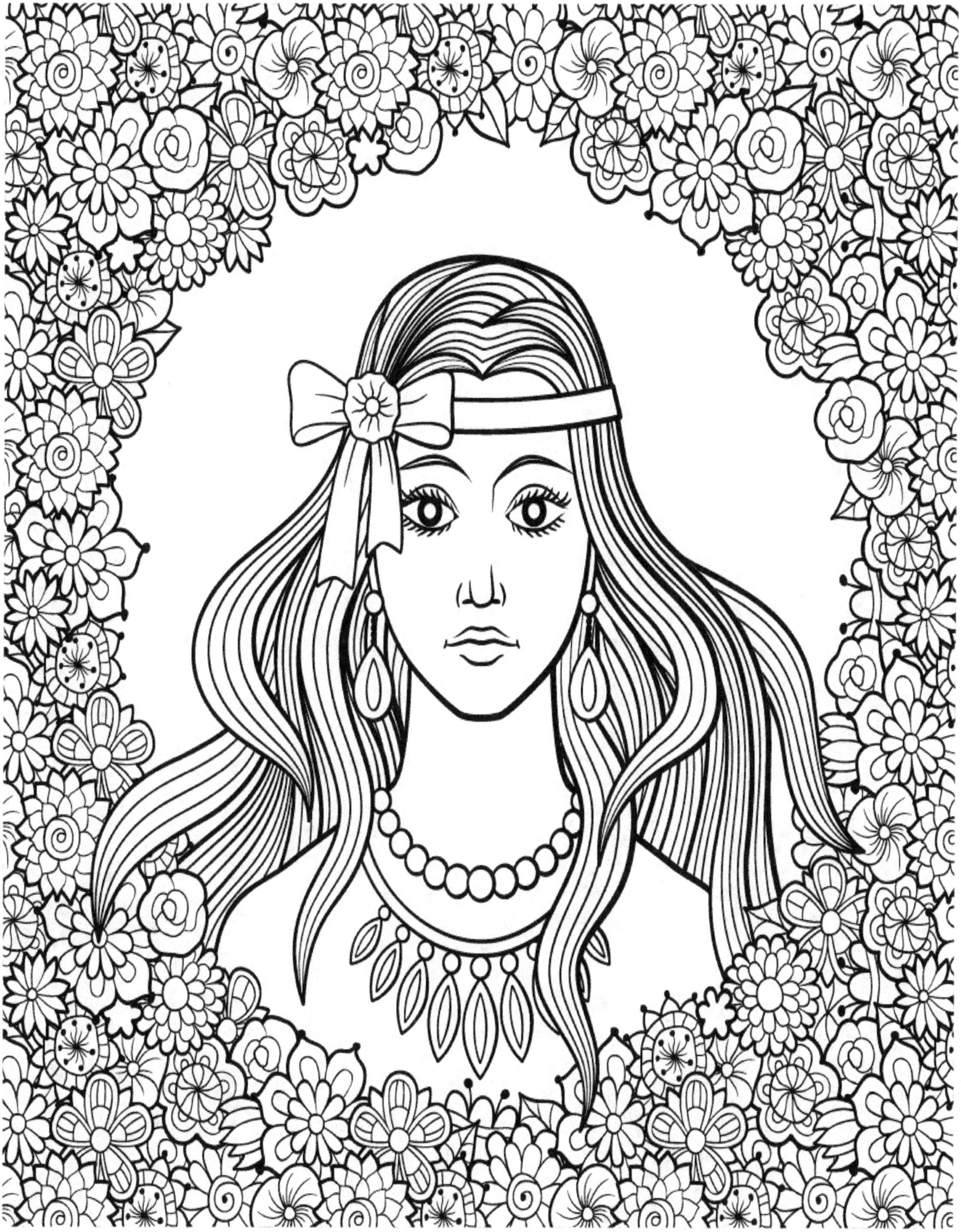

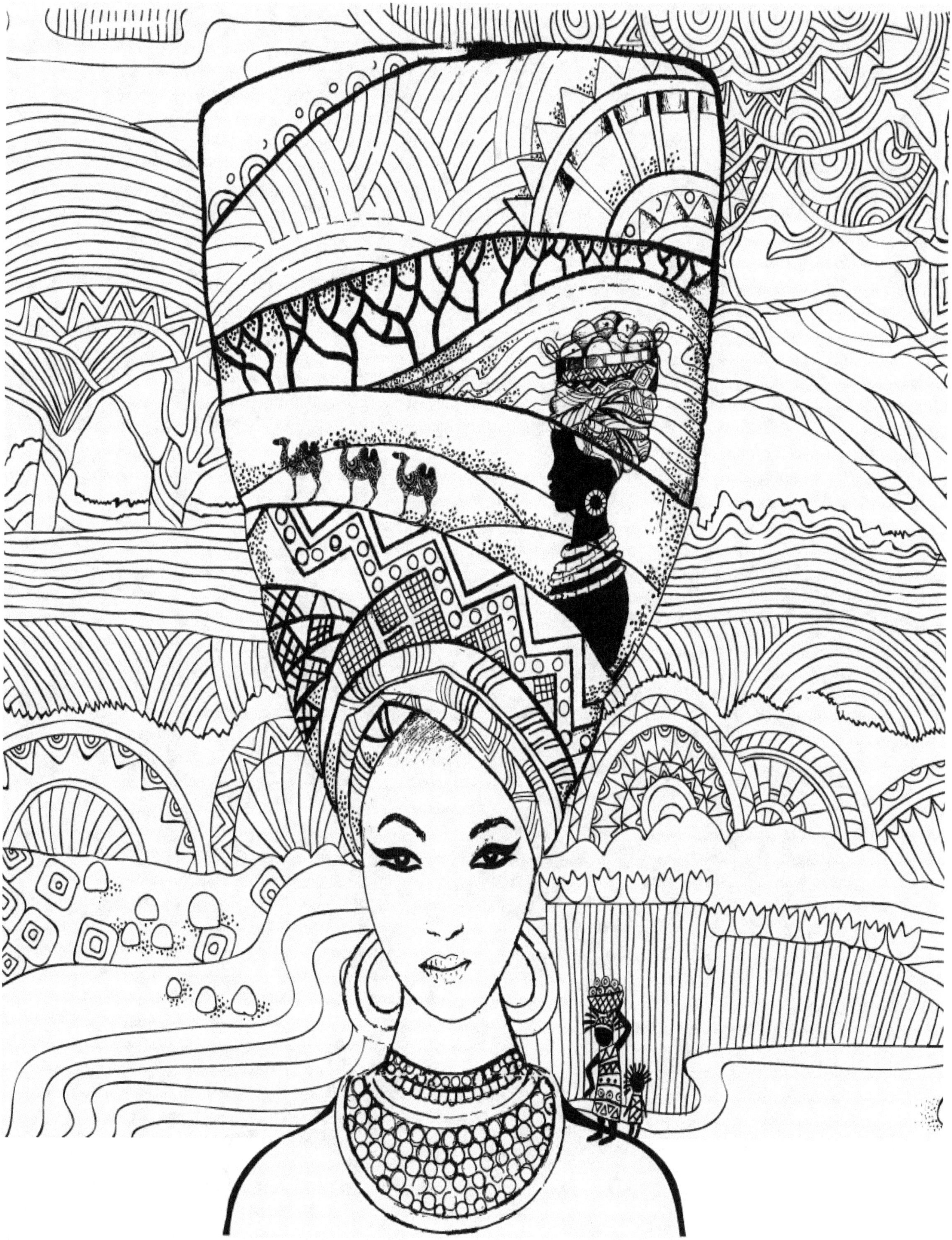

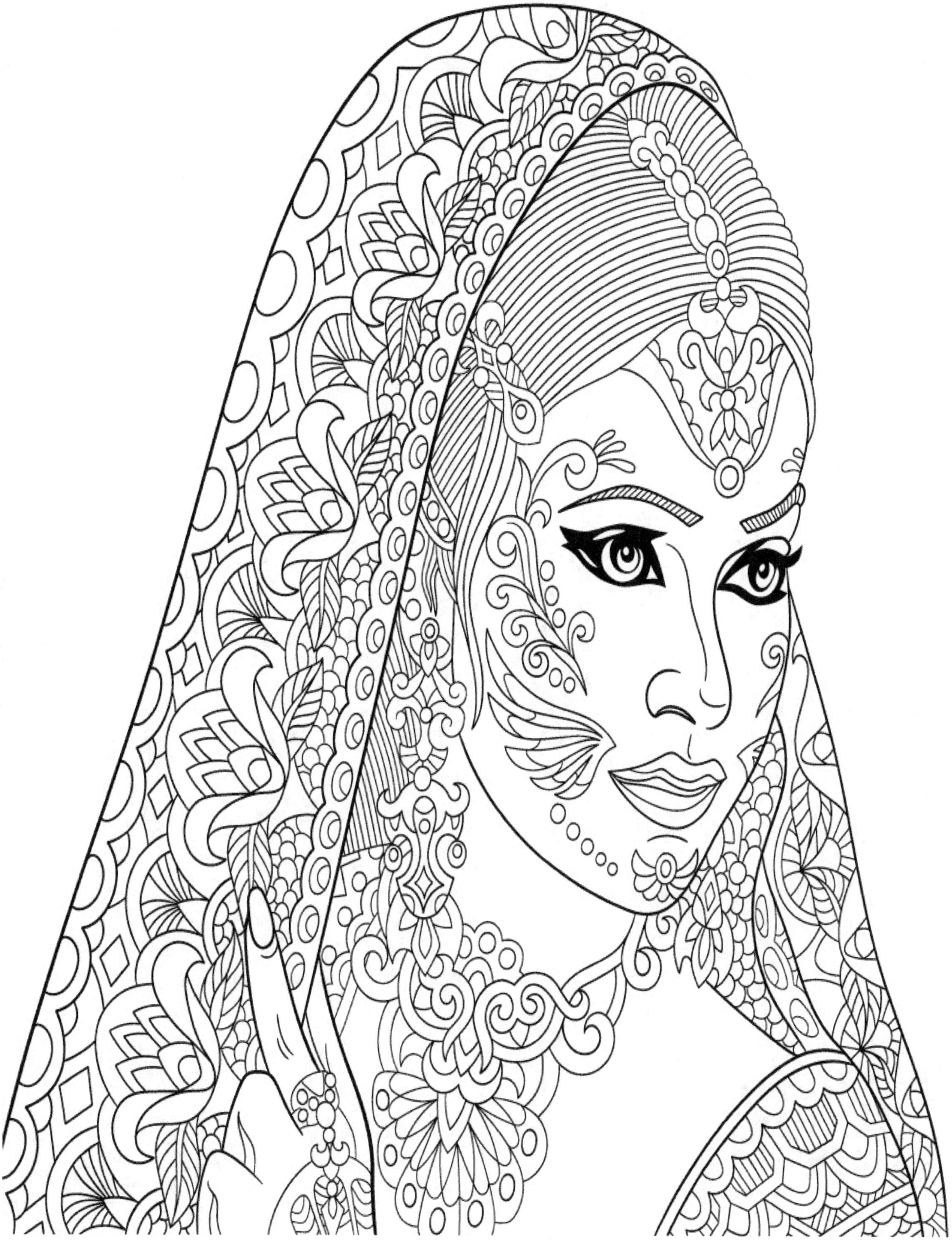

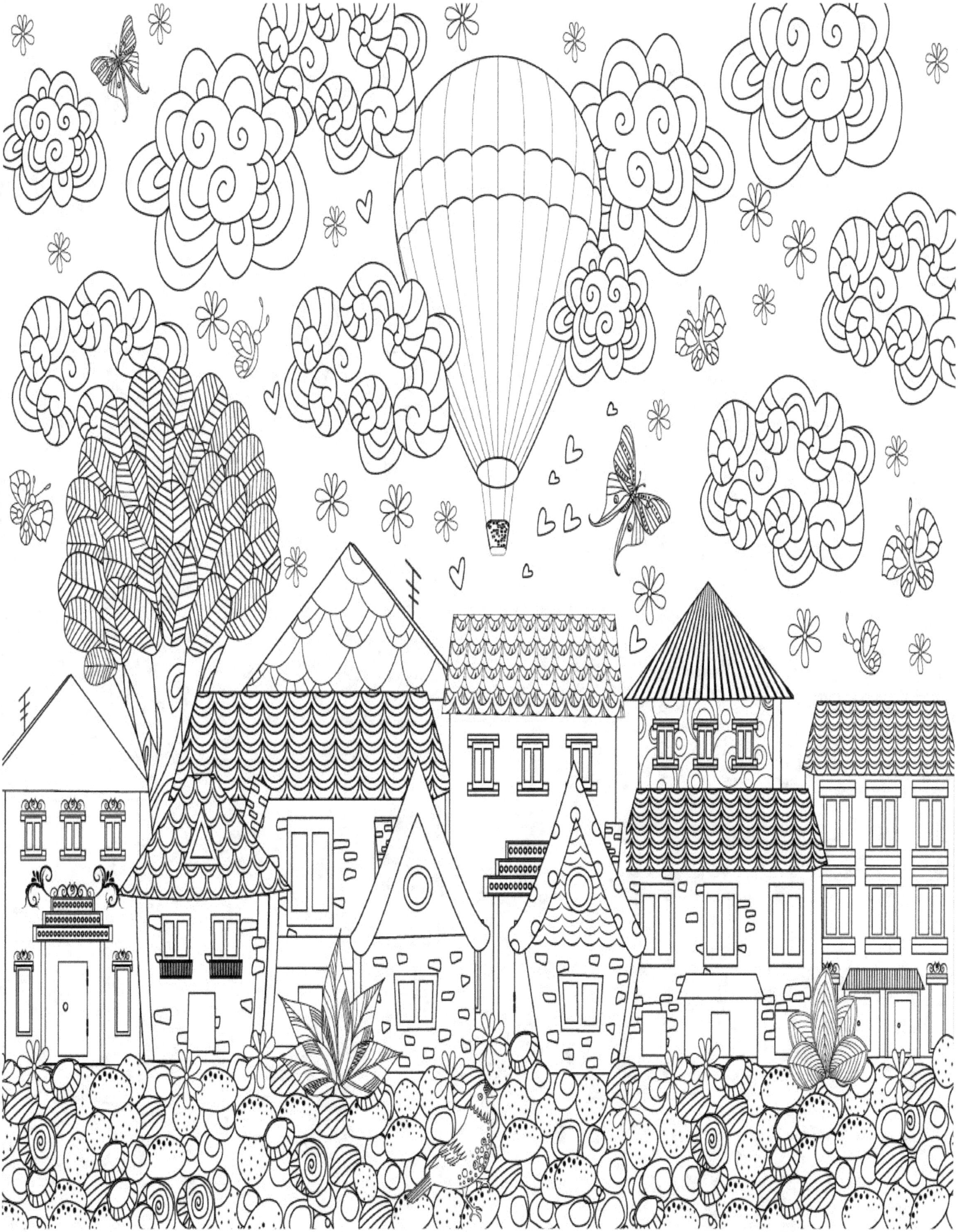

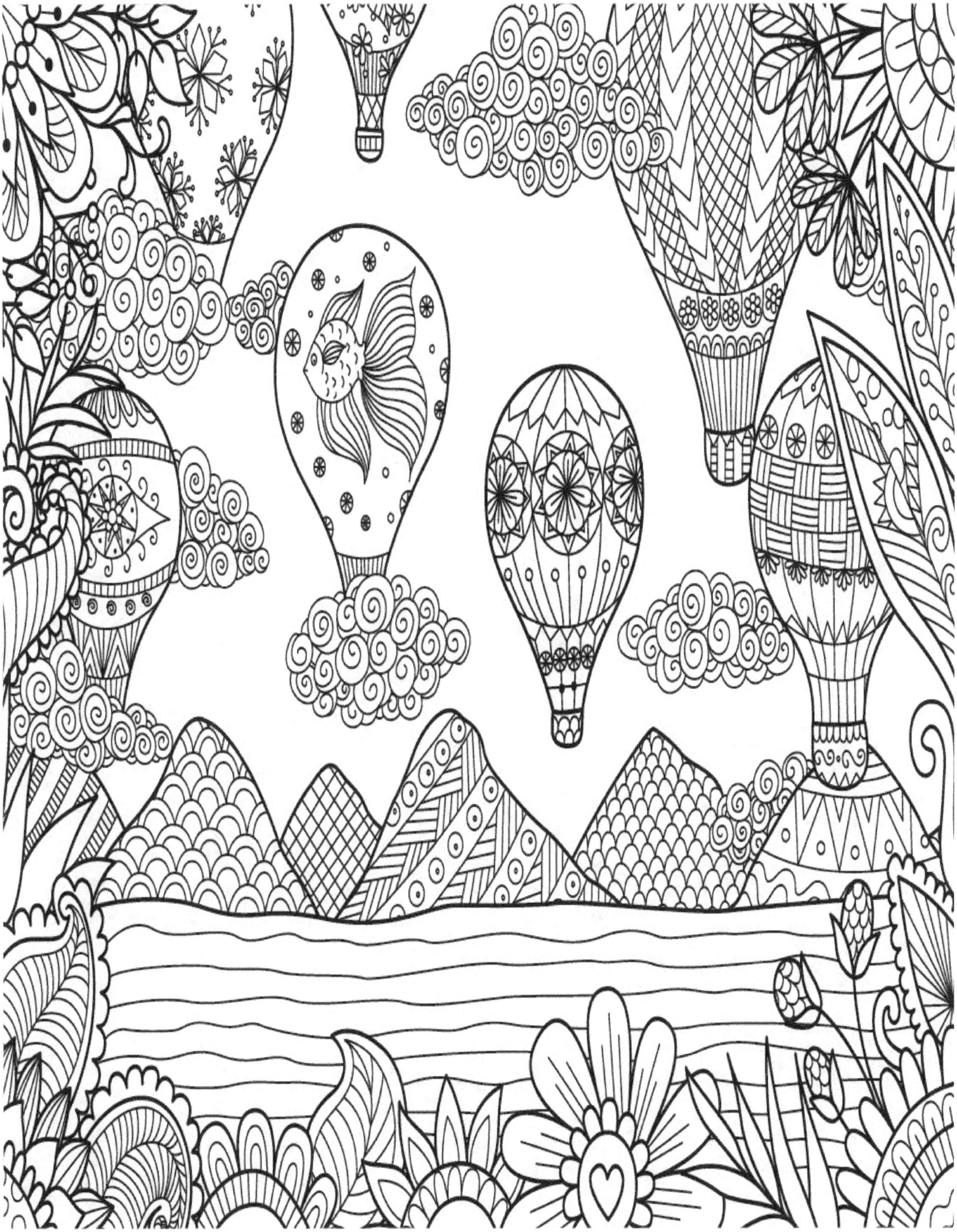

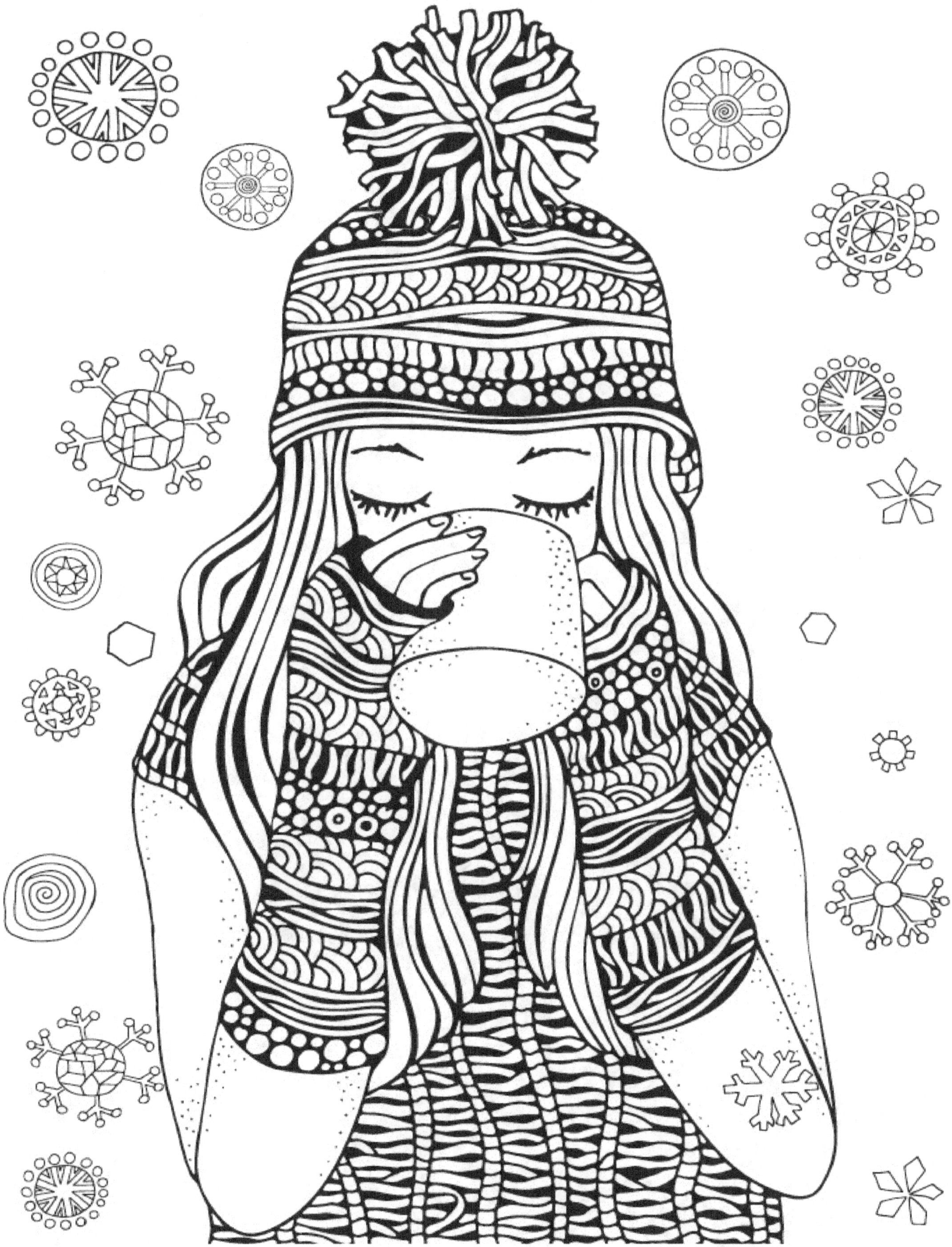

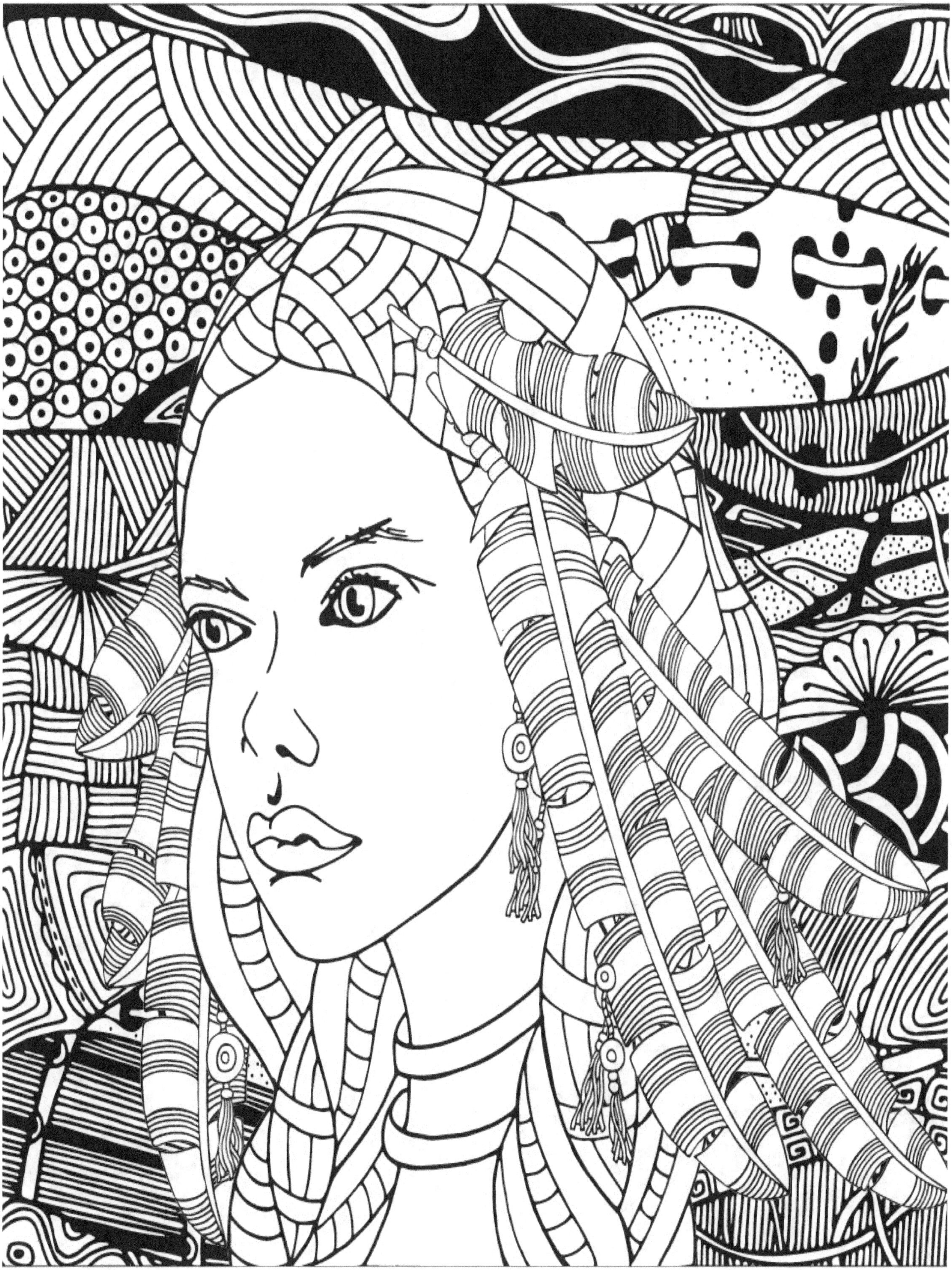

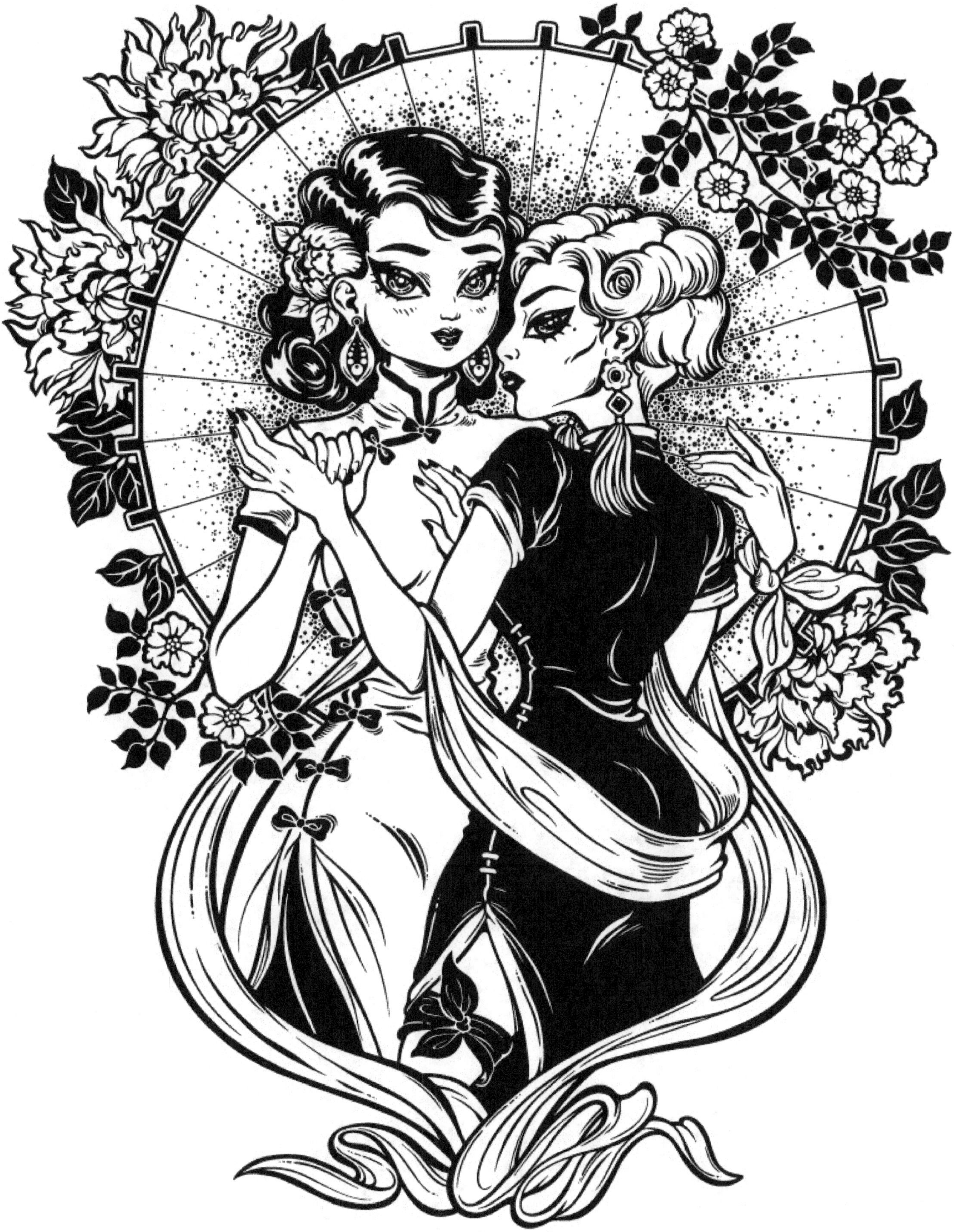

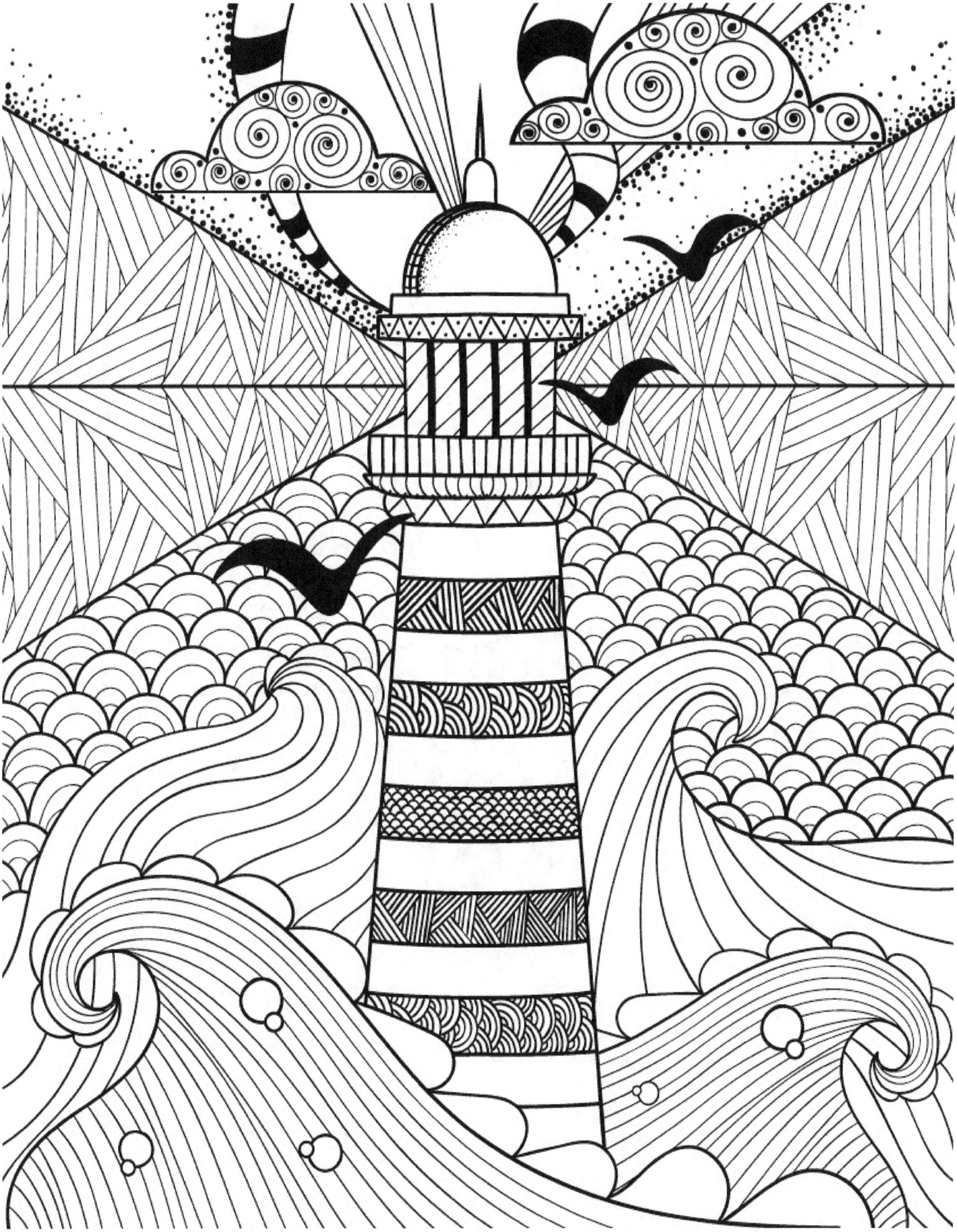

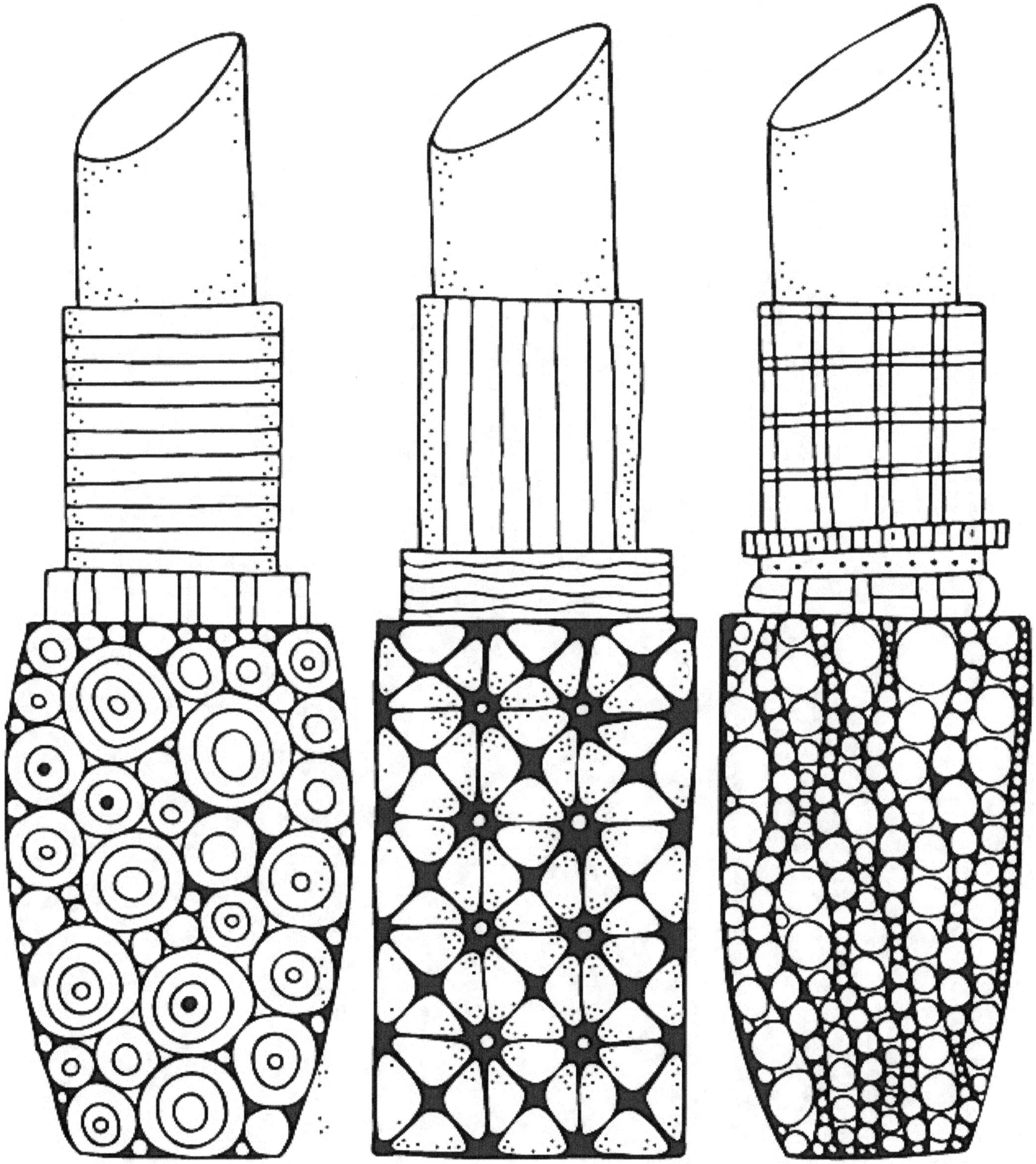

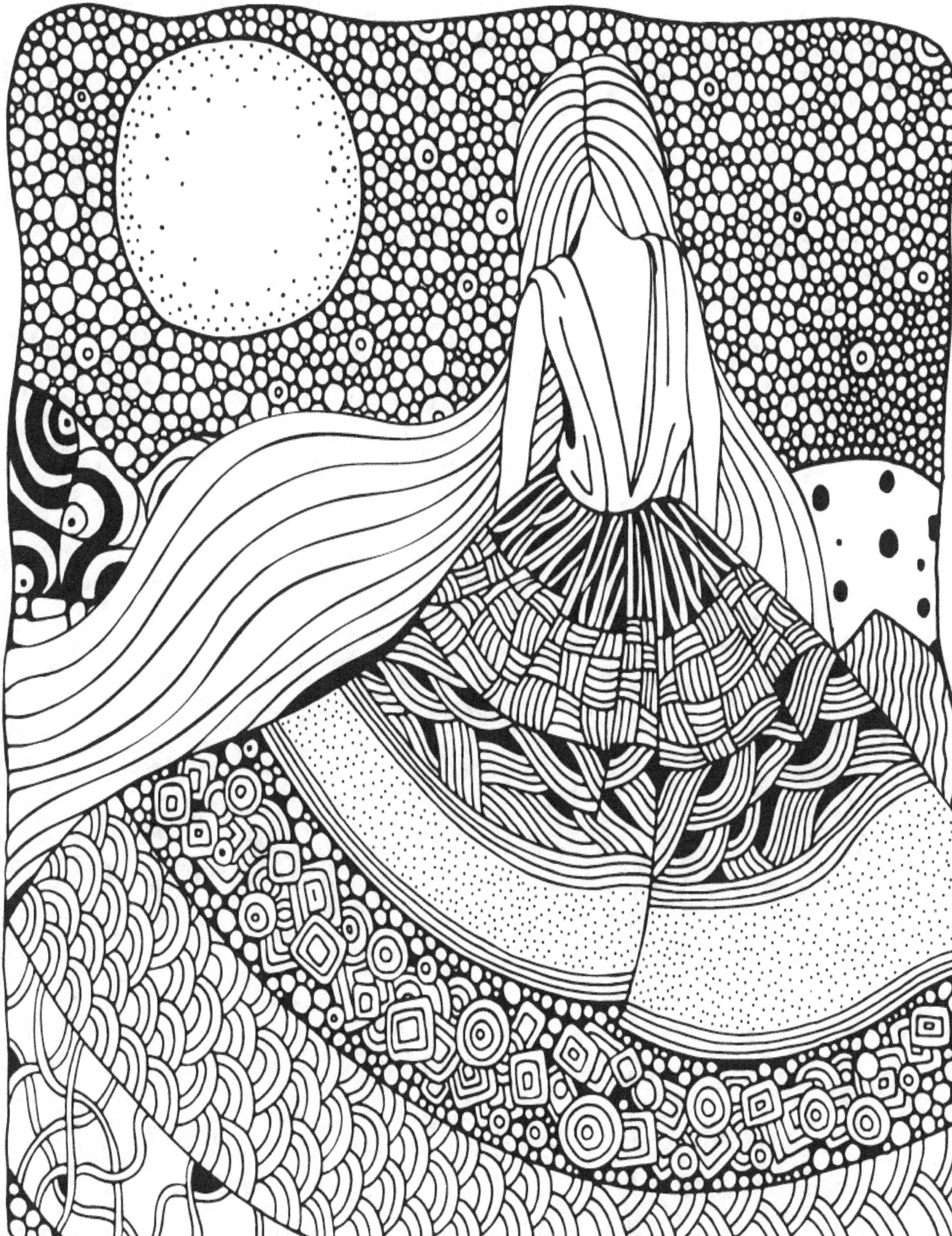

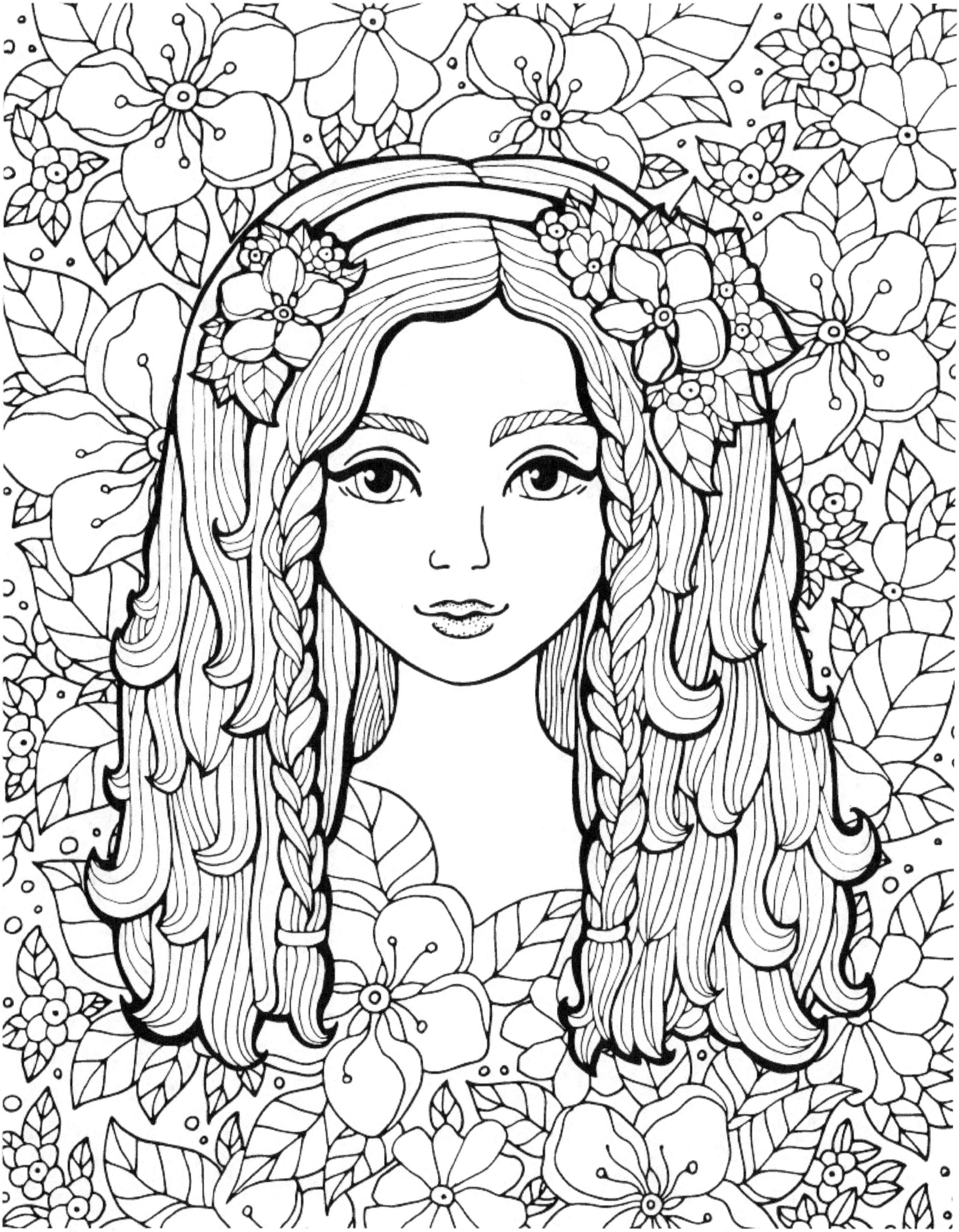

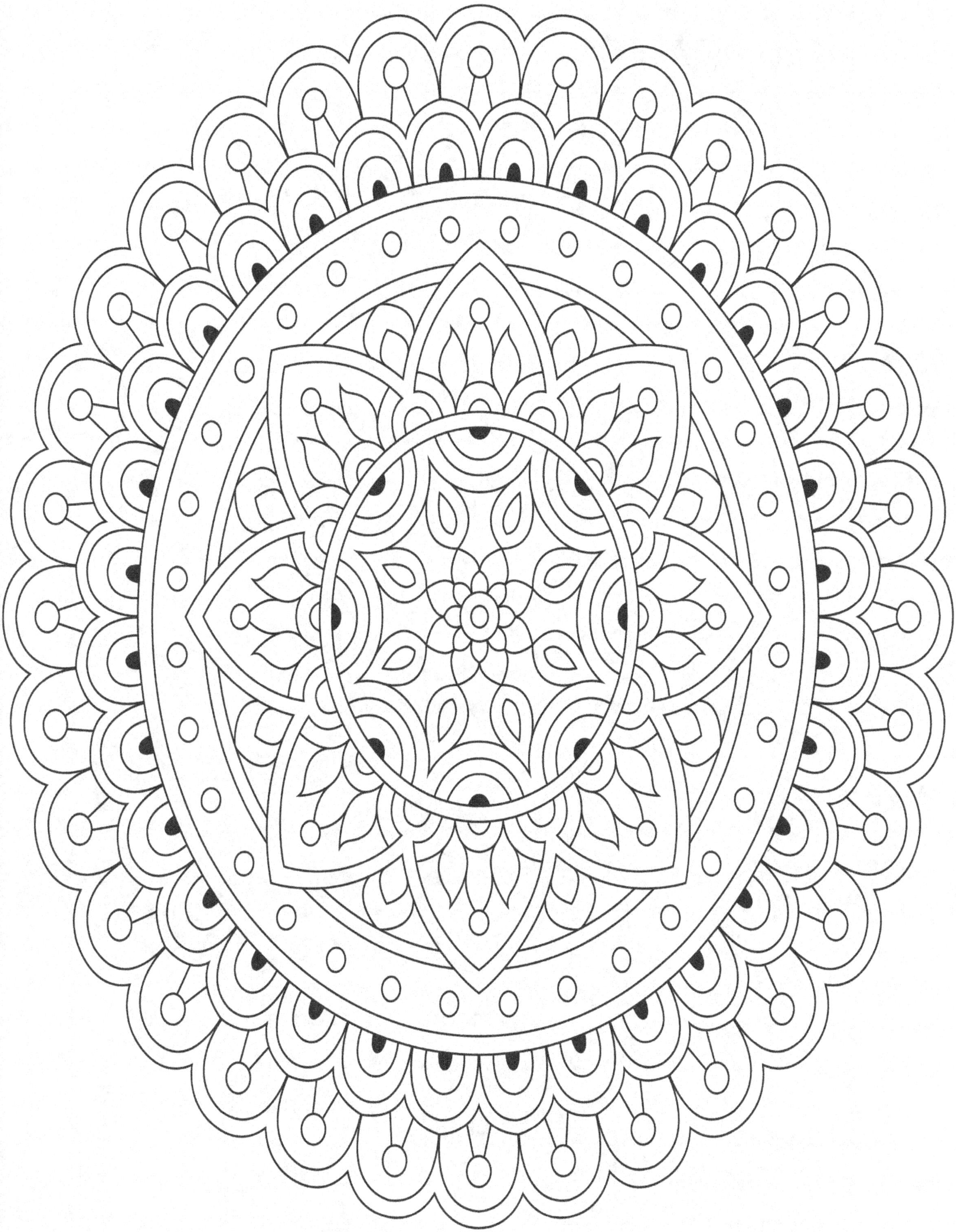

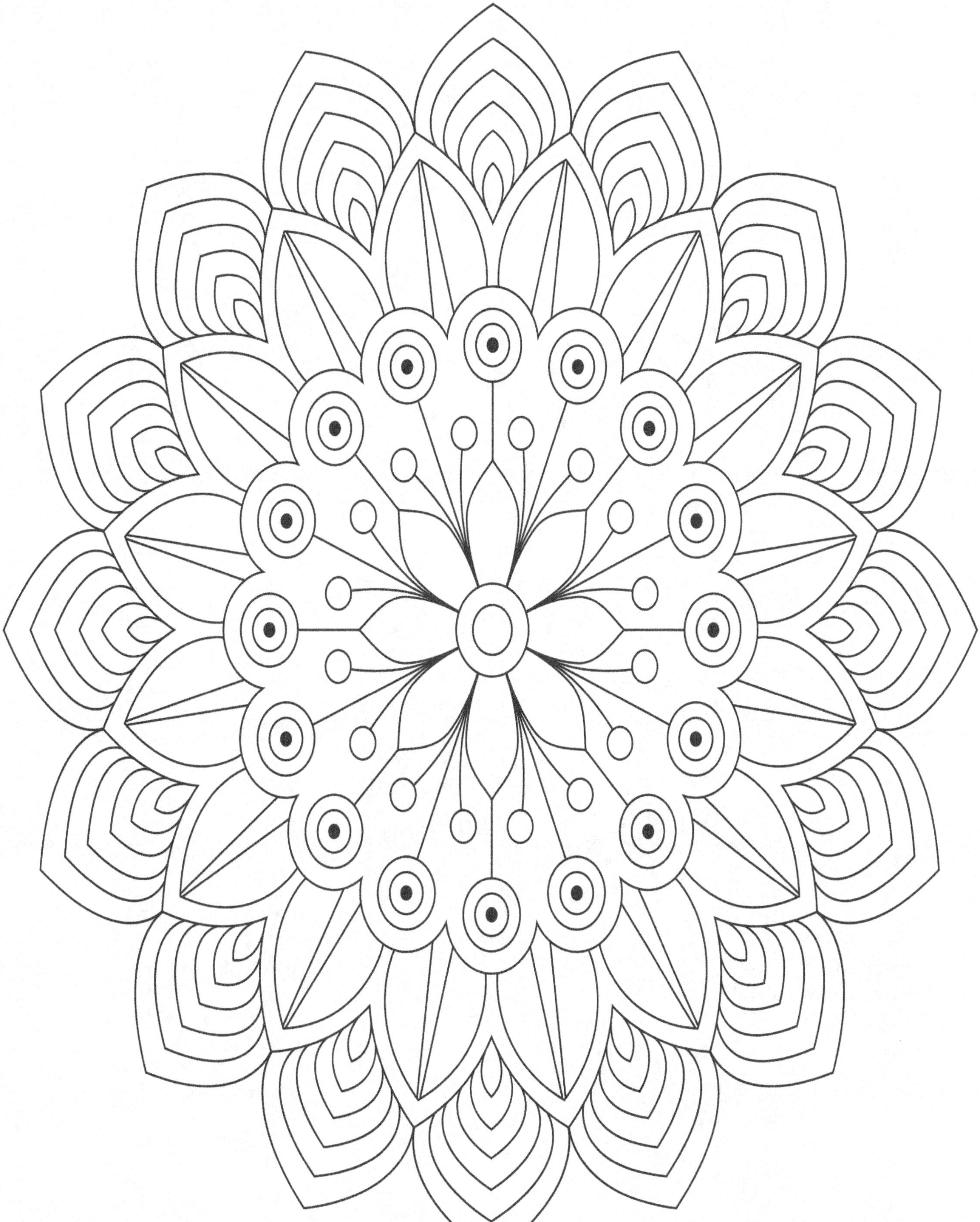

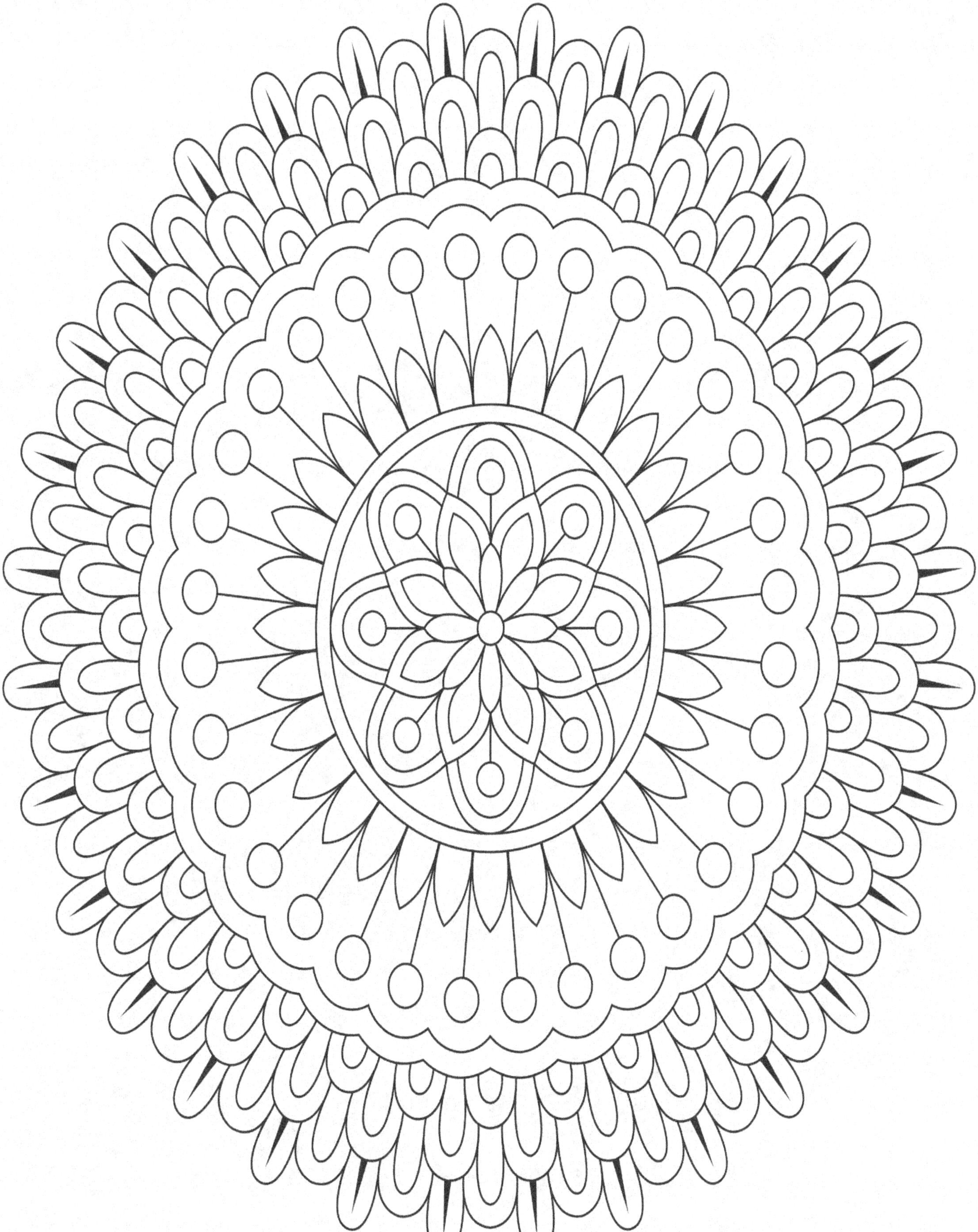

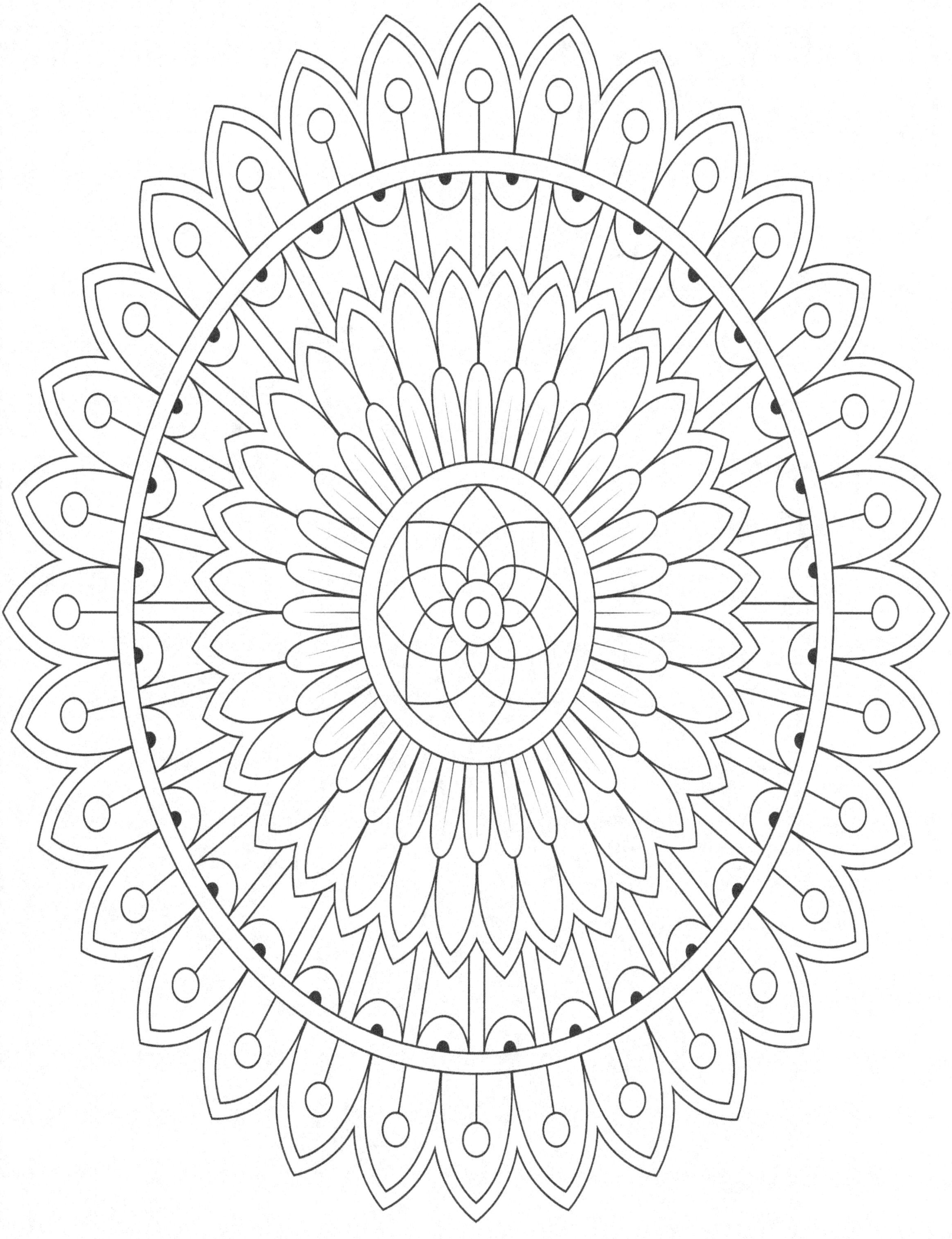

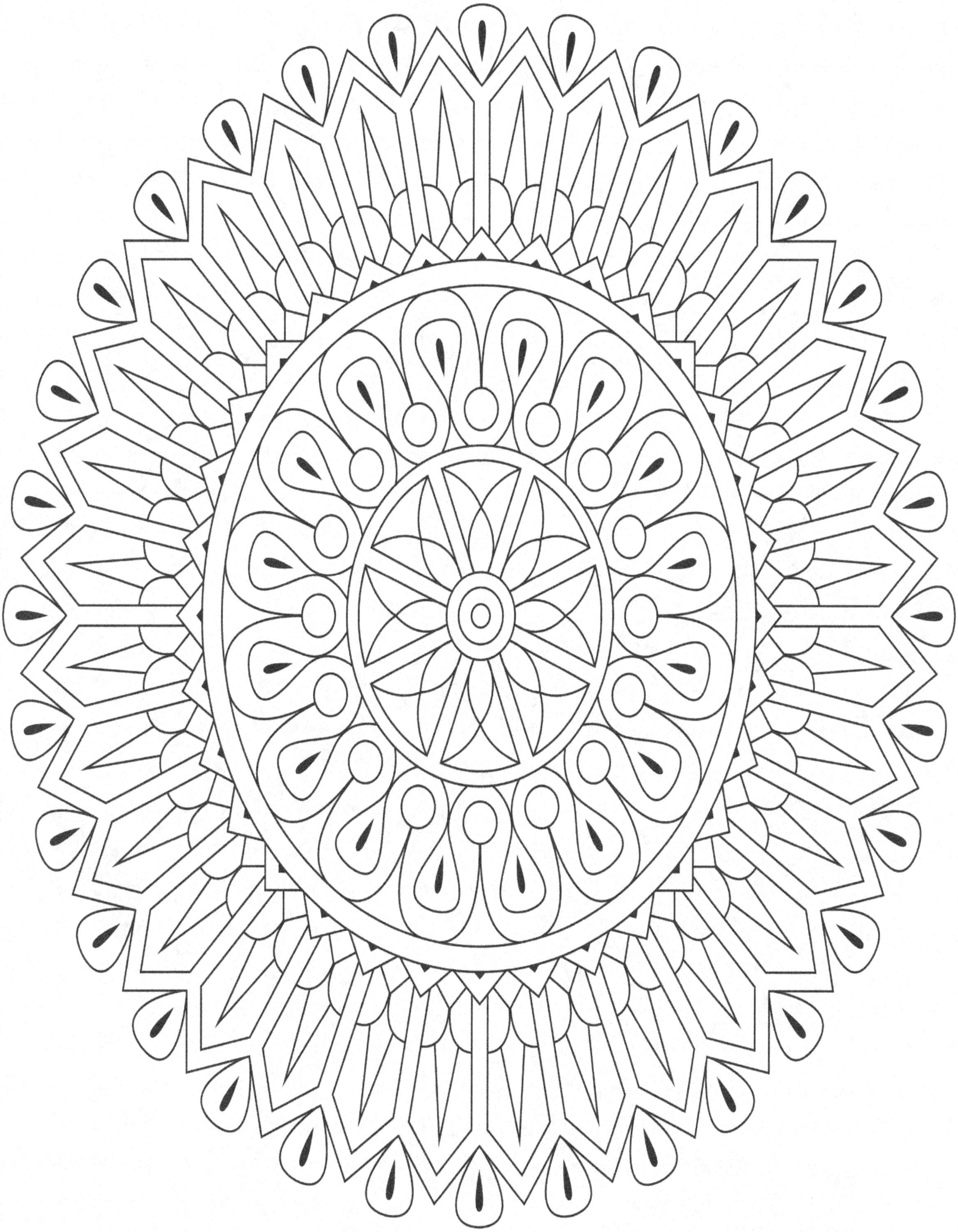

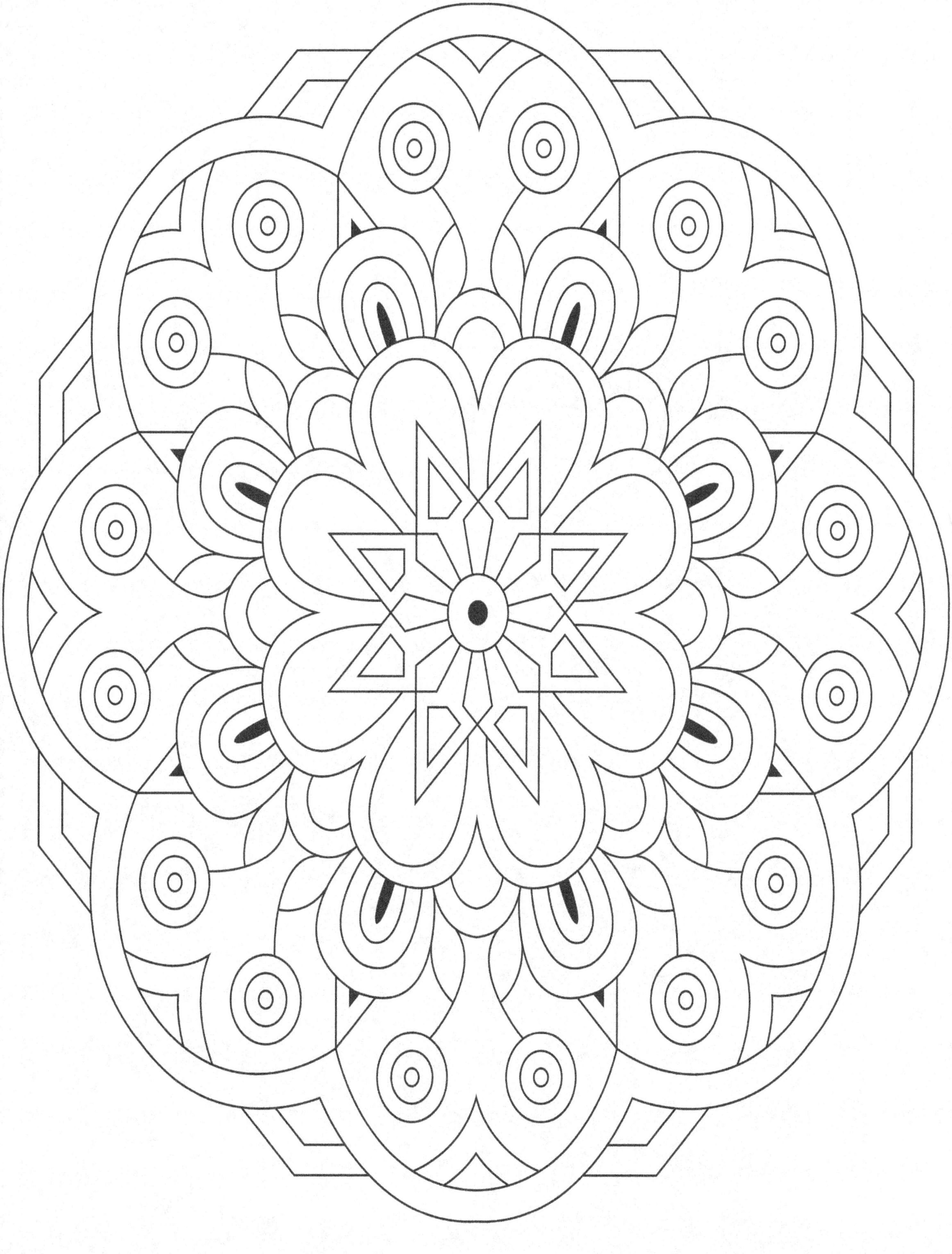

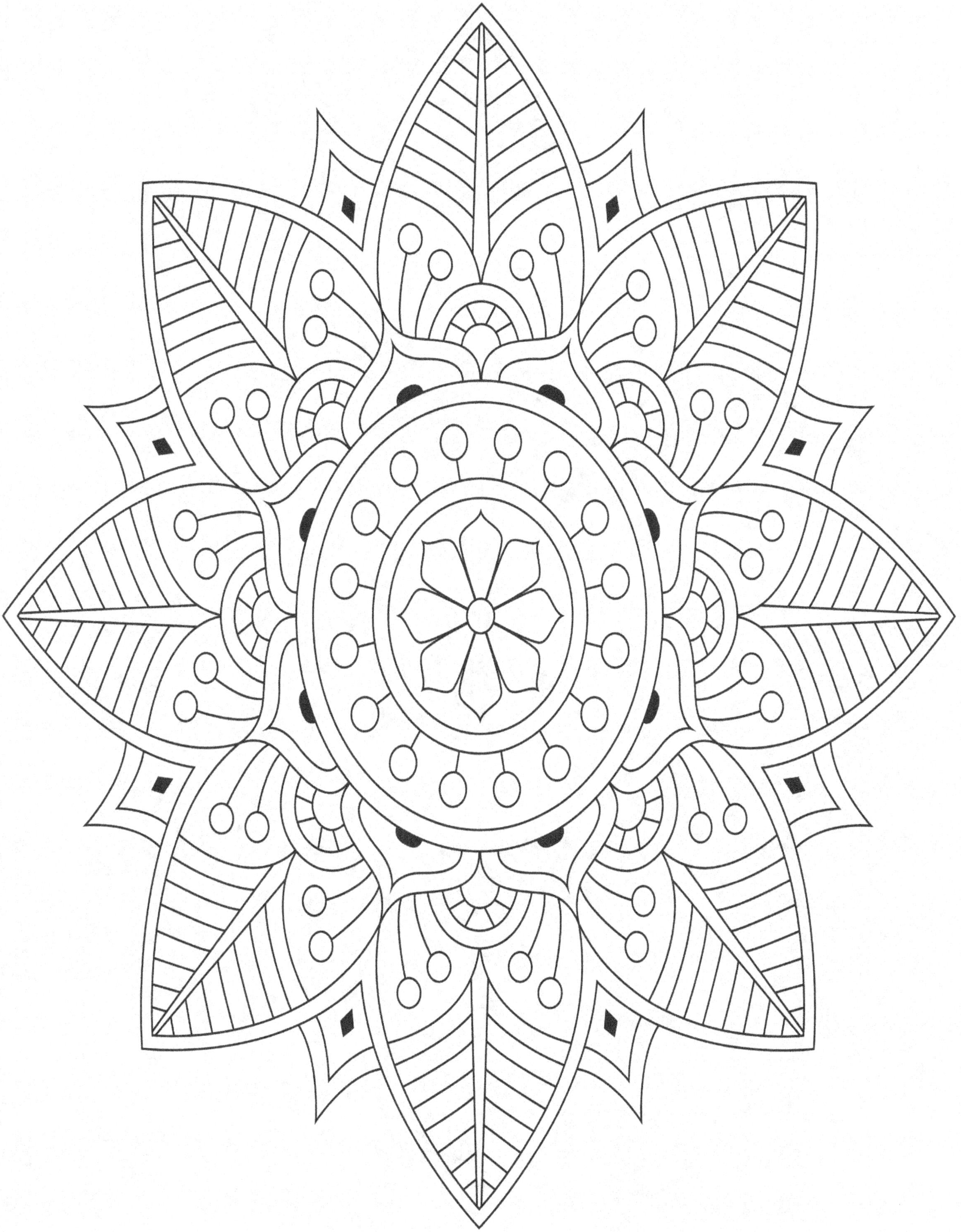

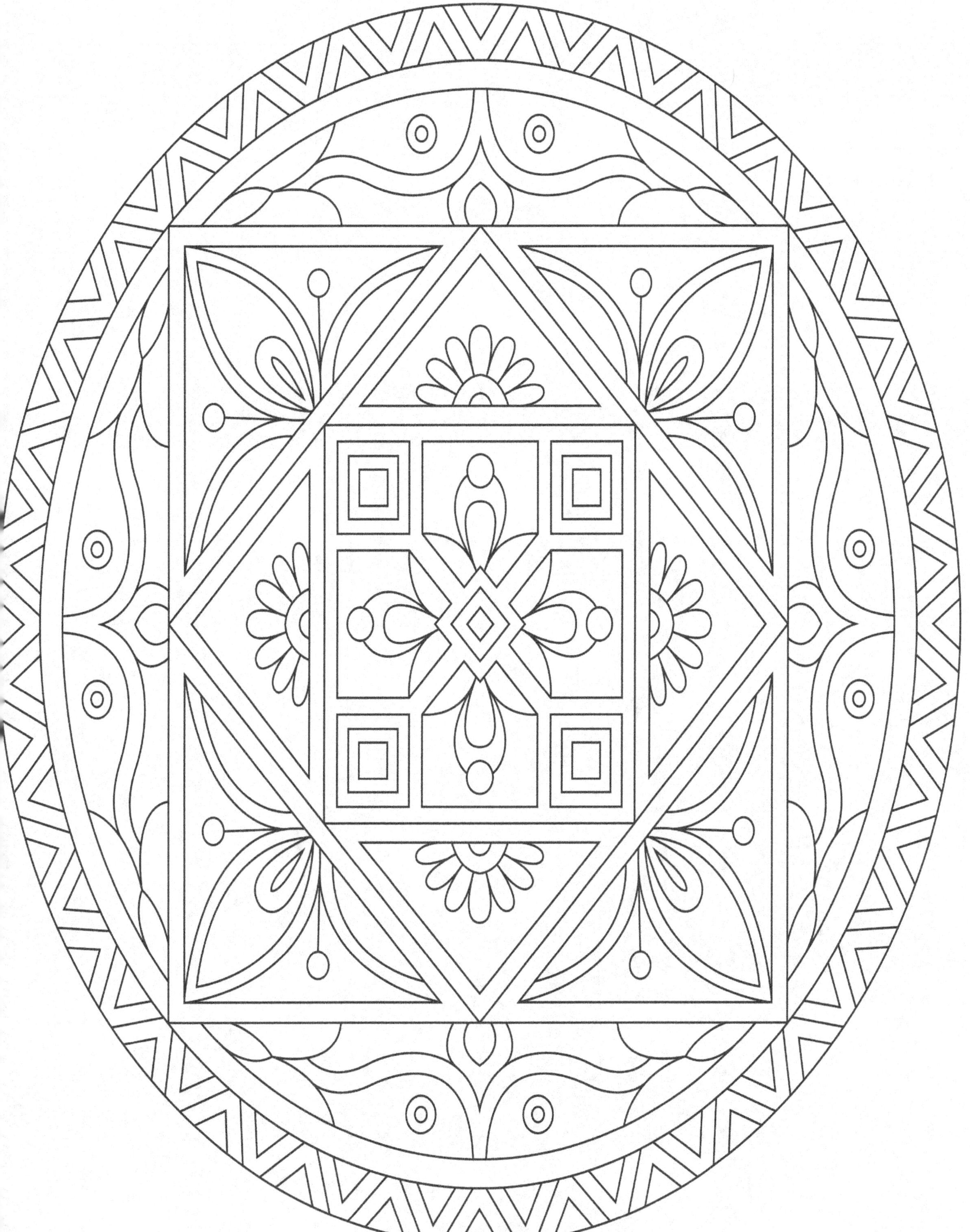

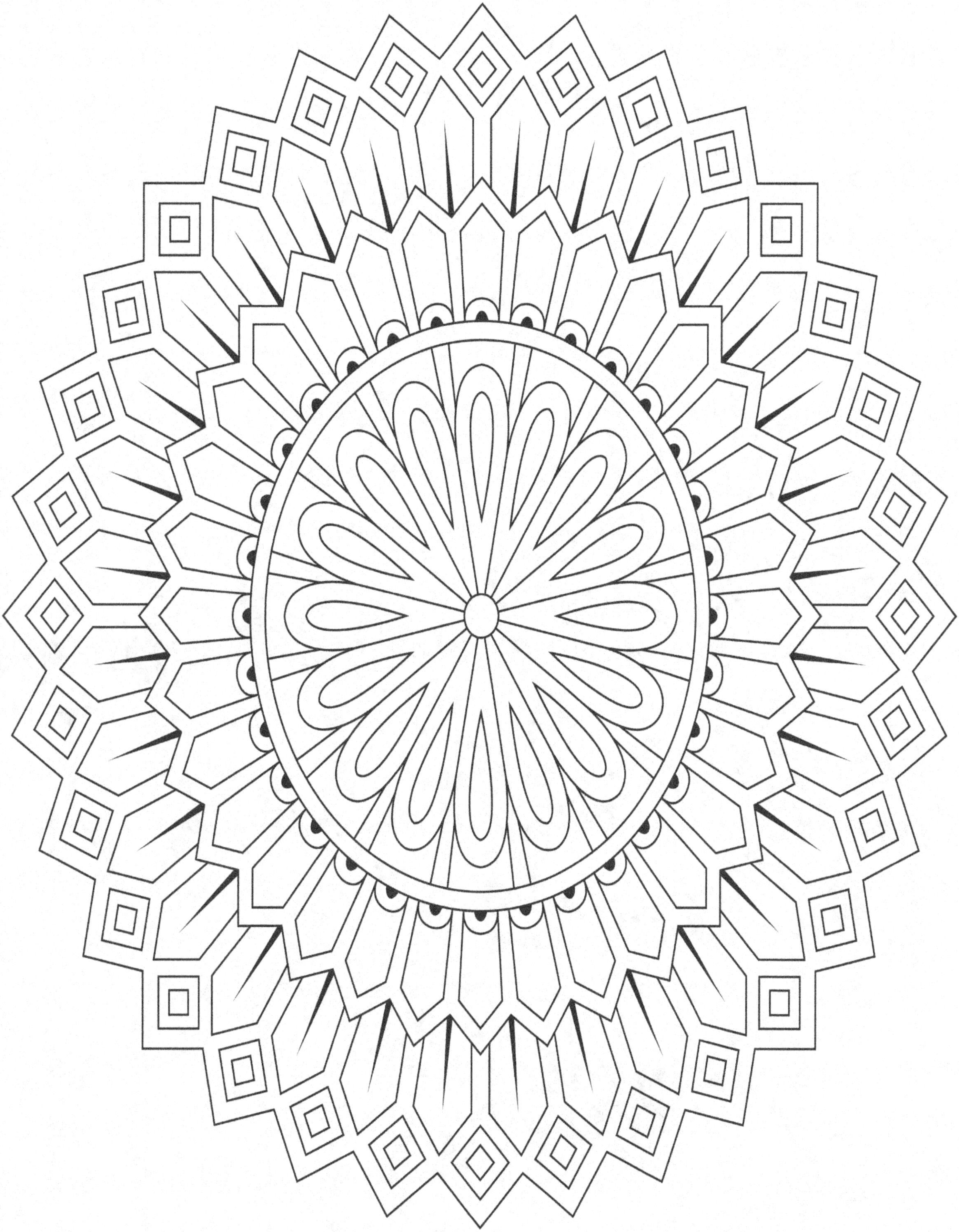

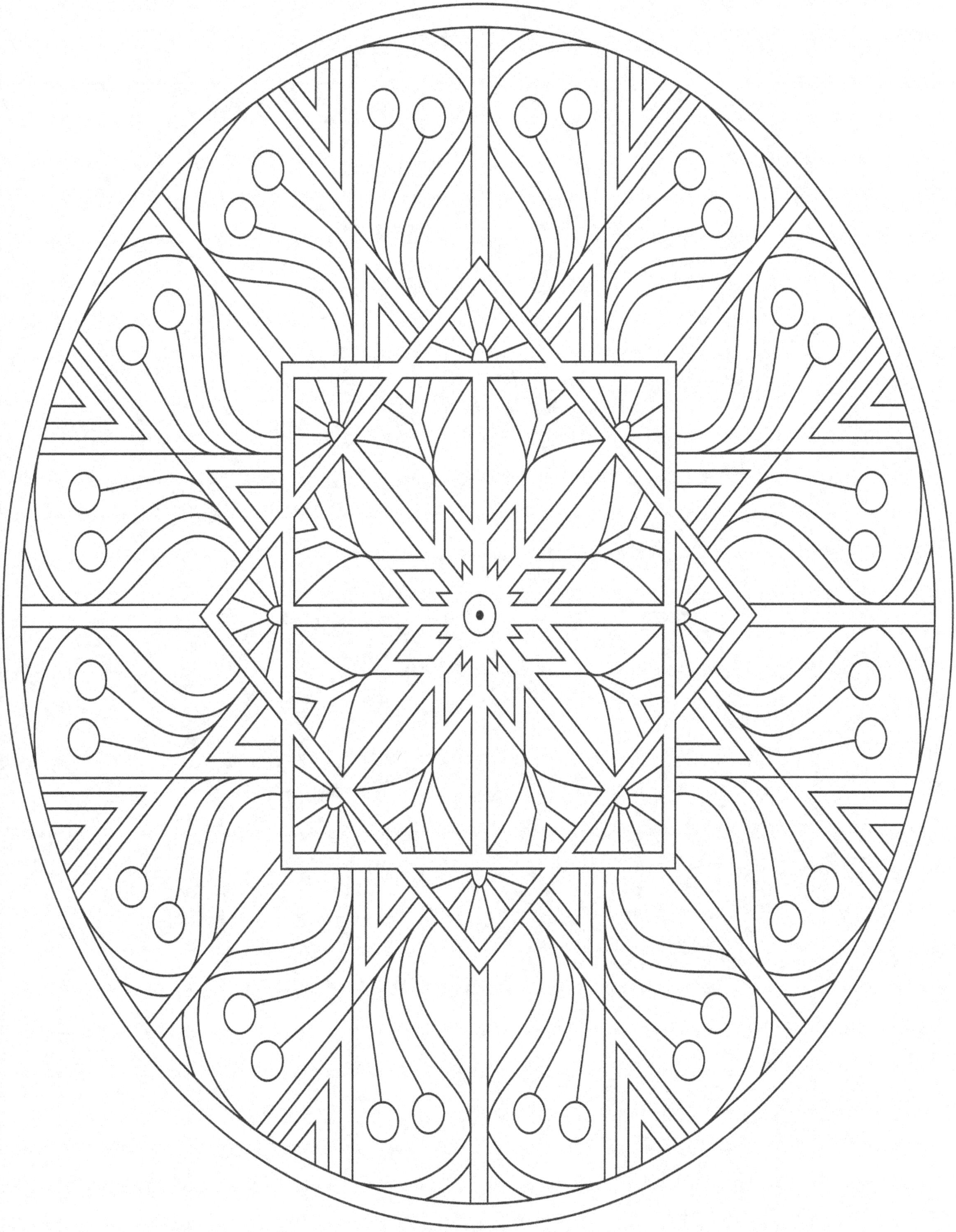

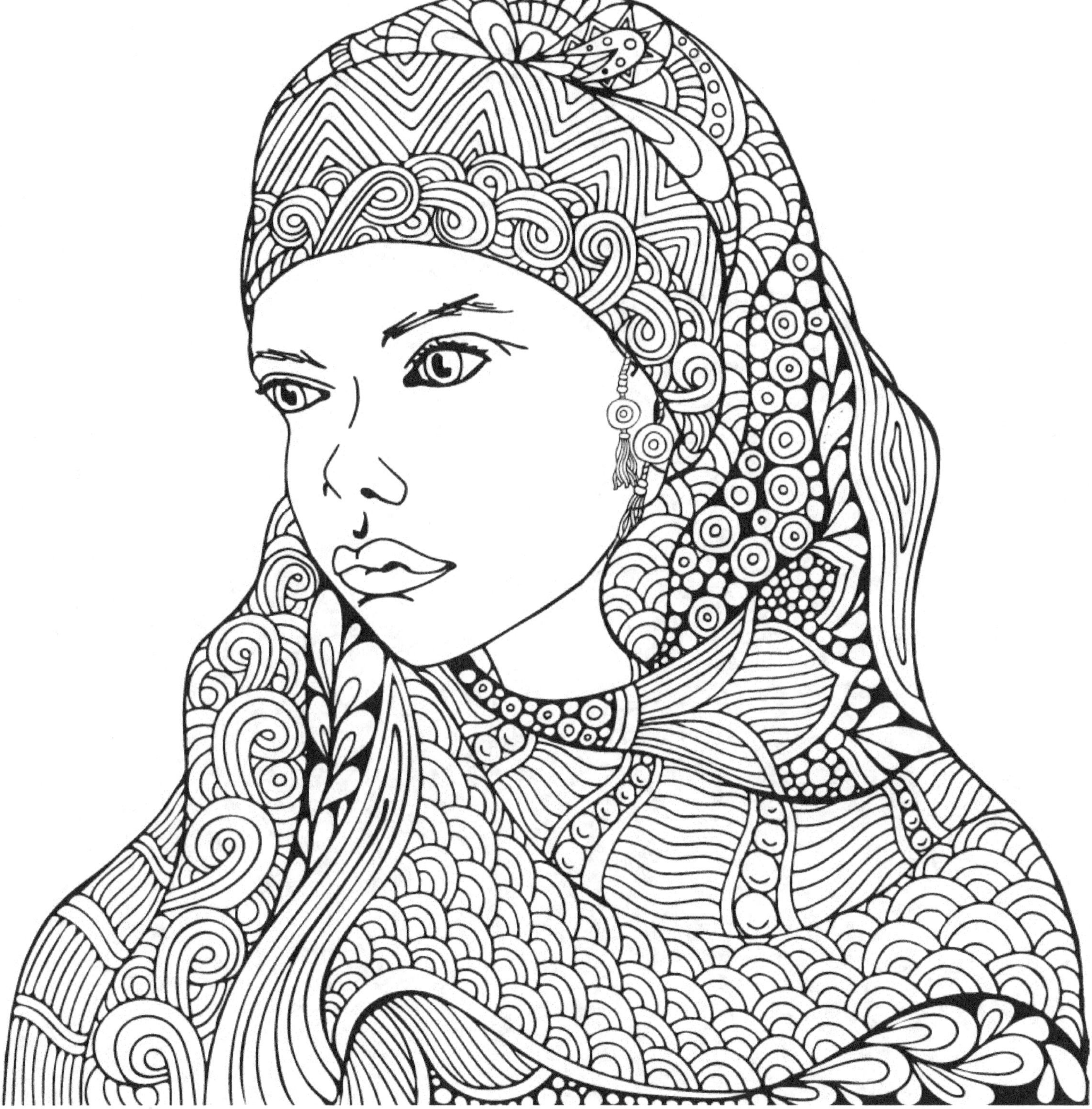

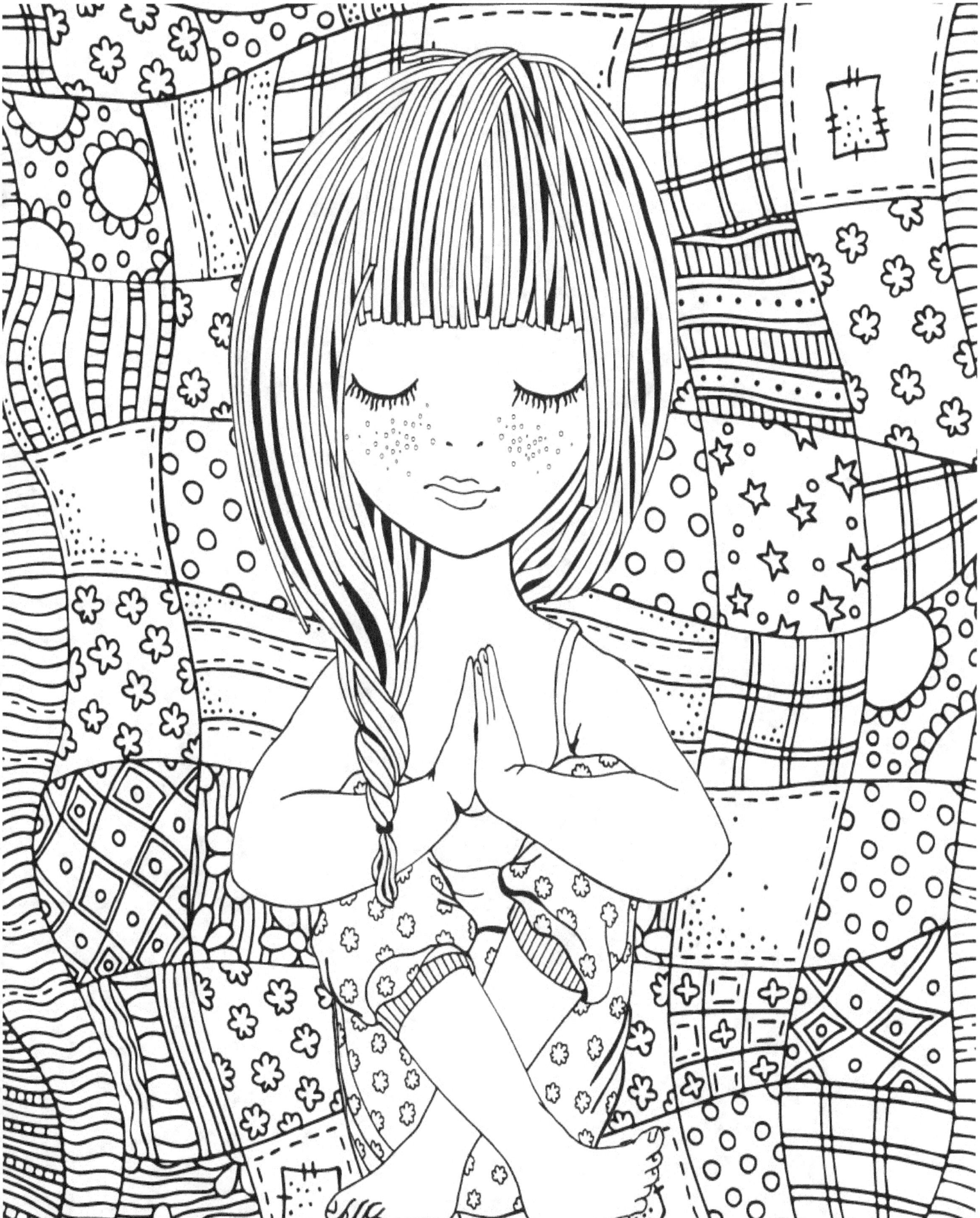

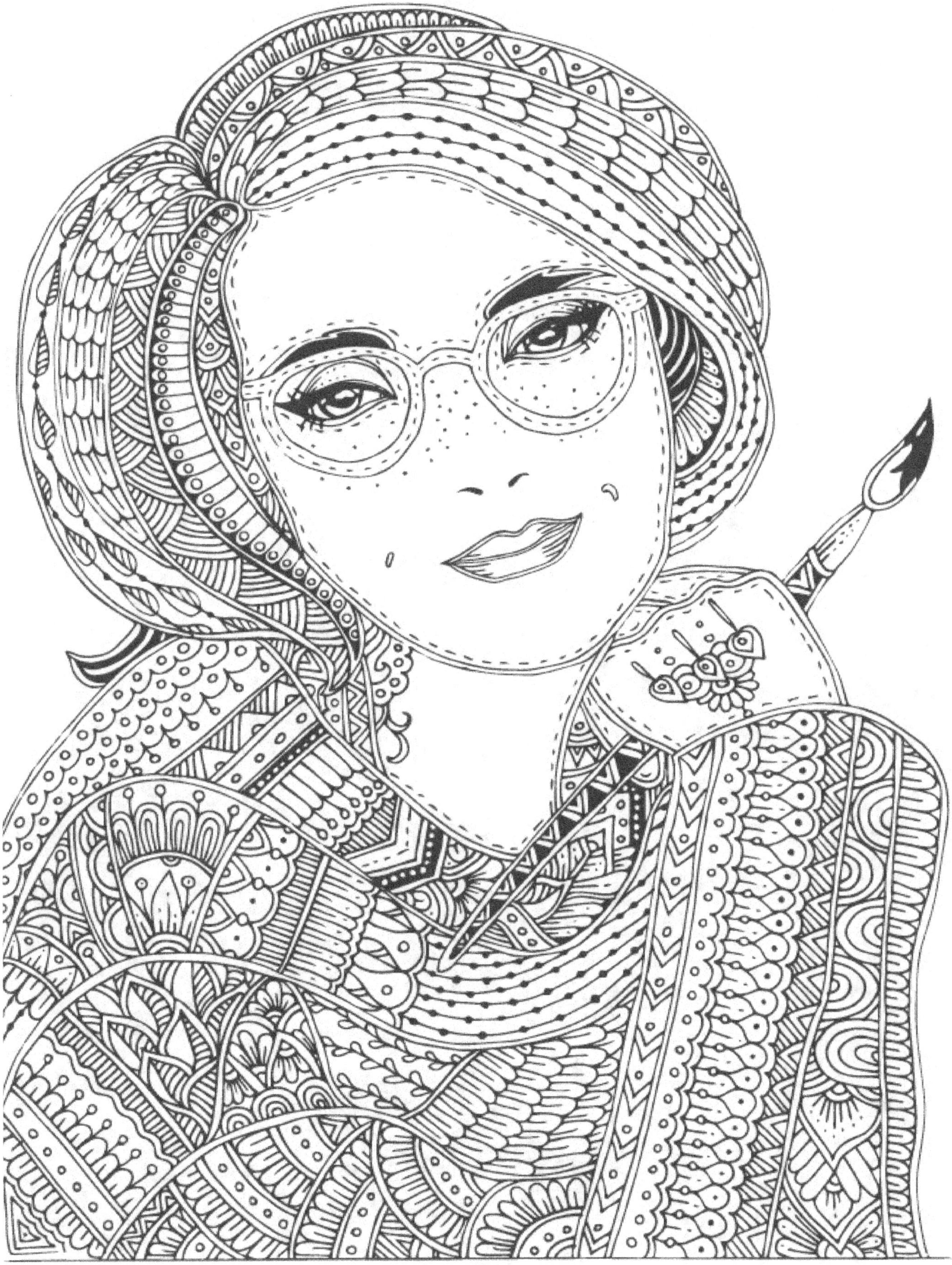

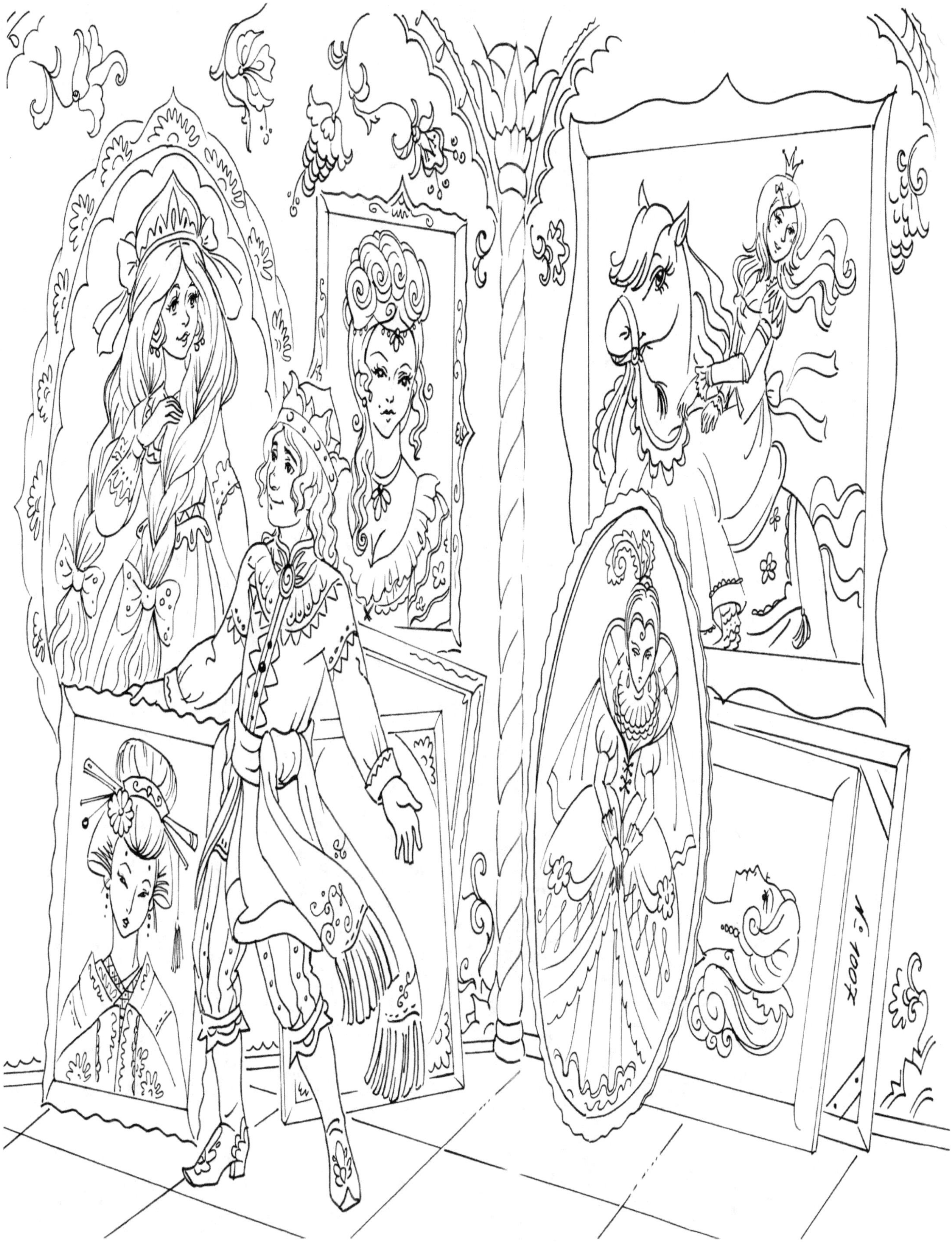
№ 1007

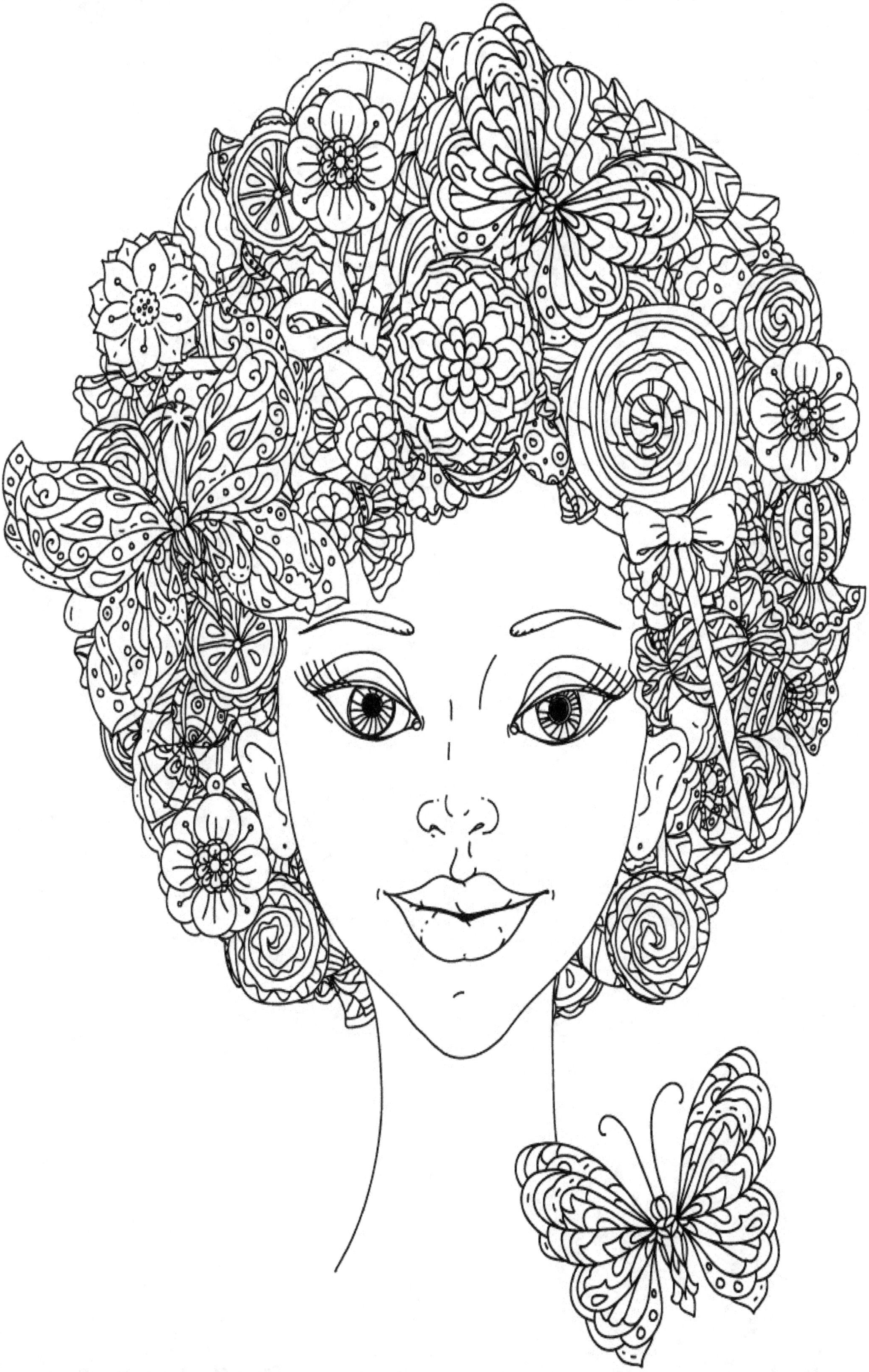

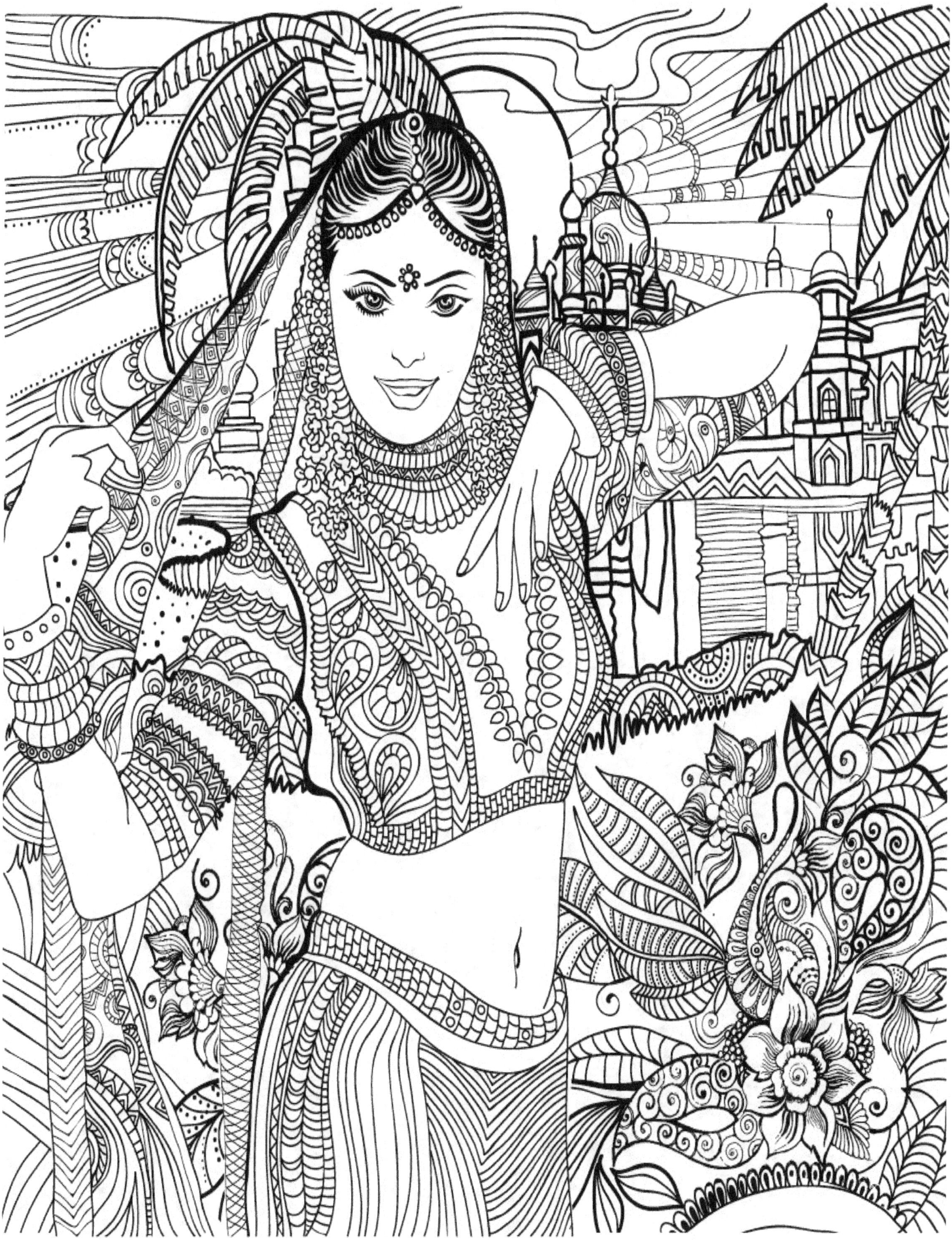

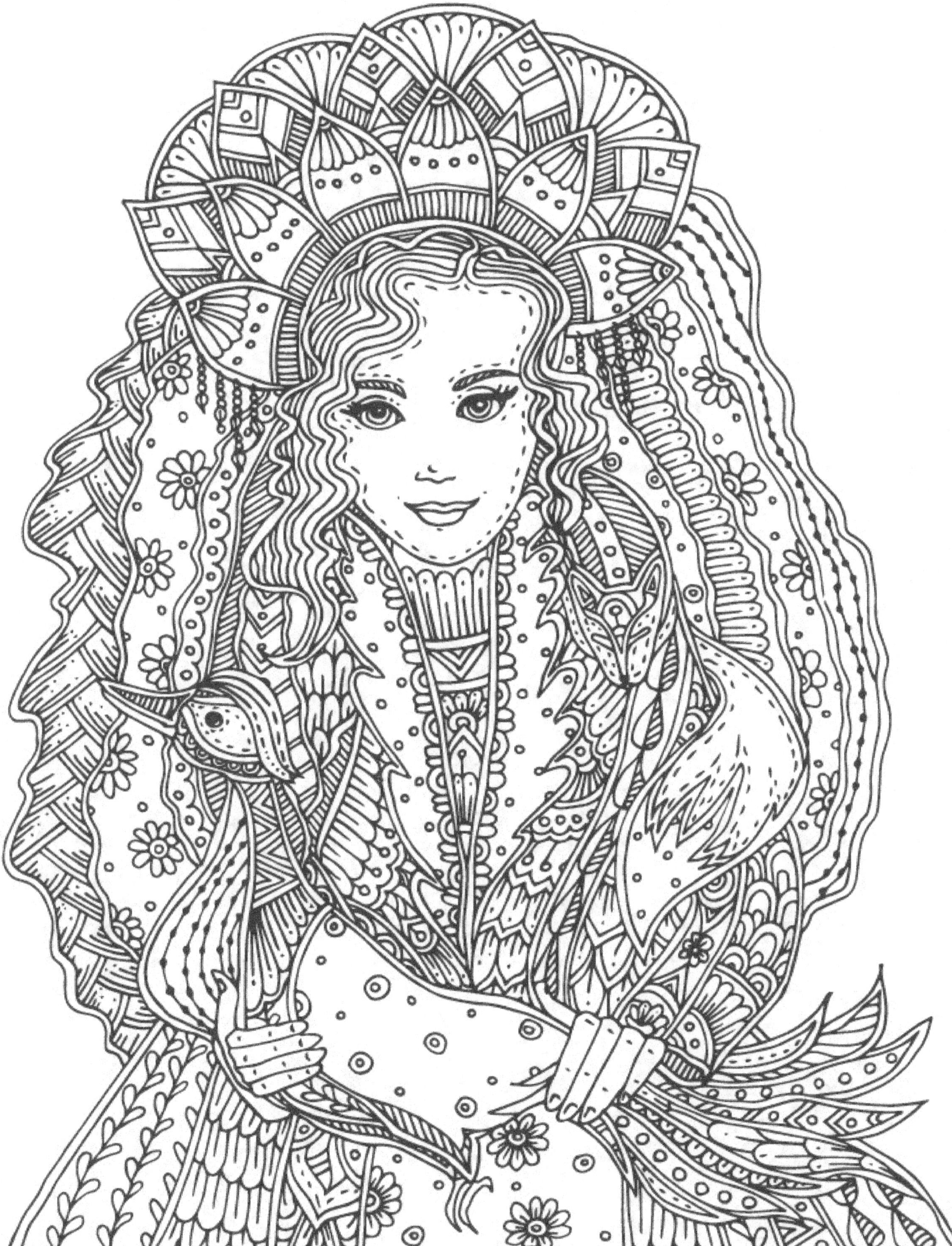

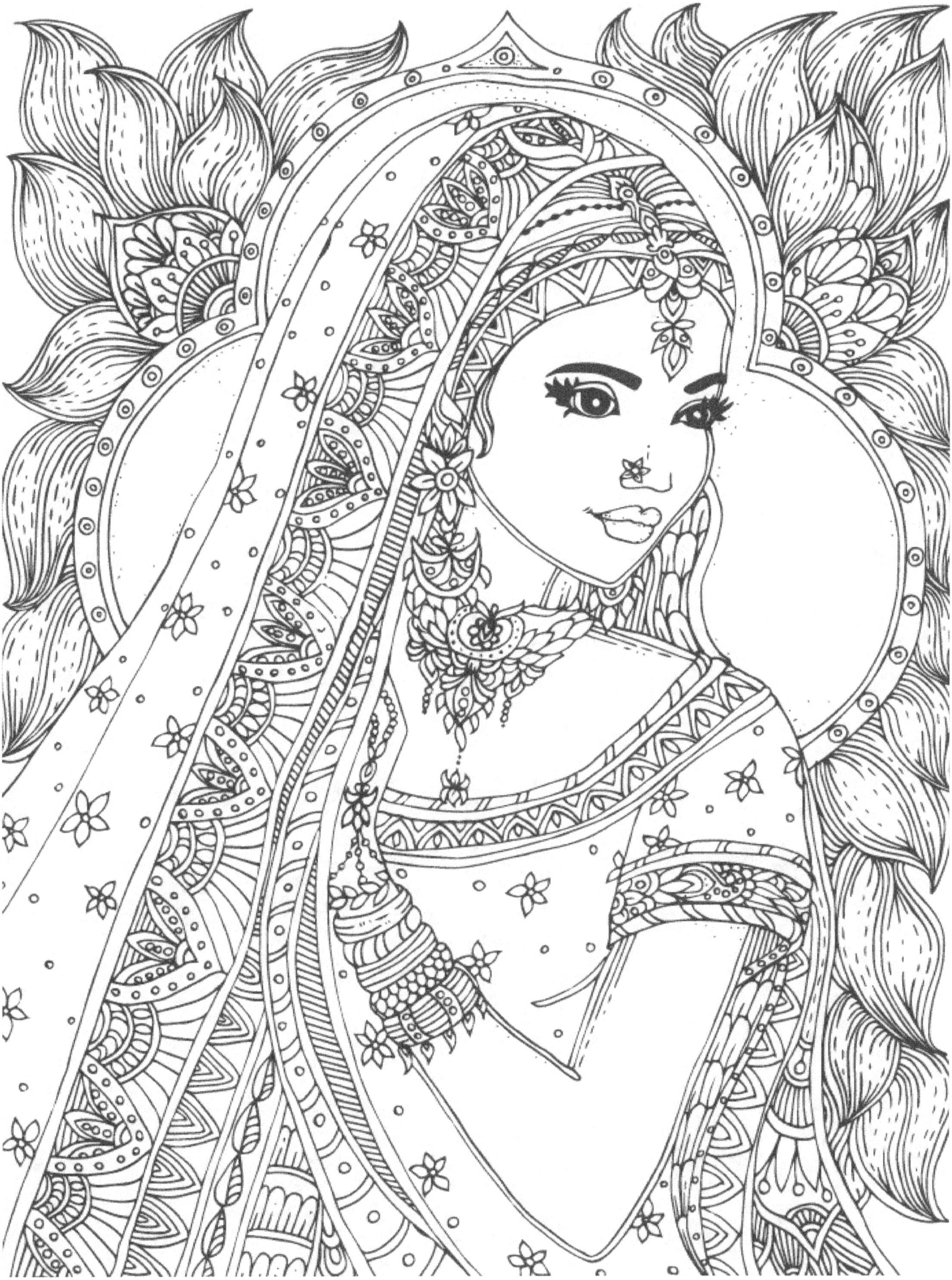

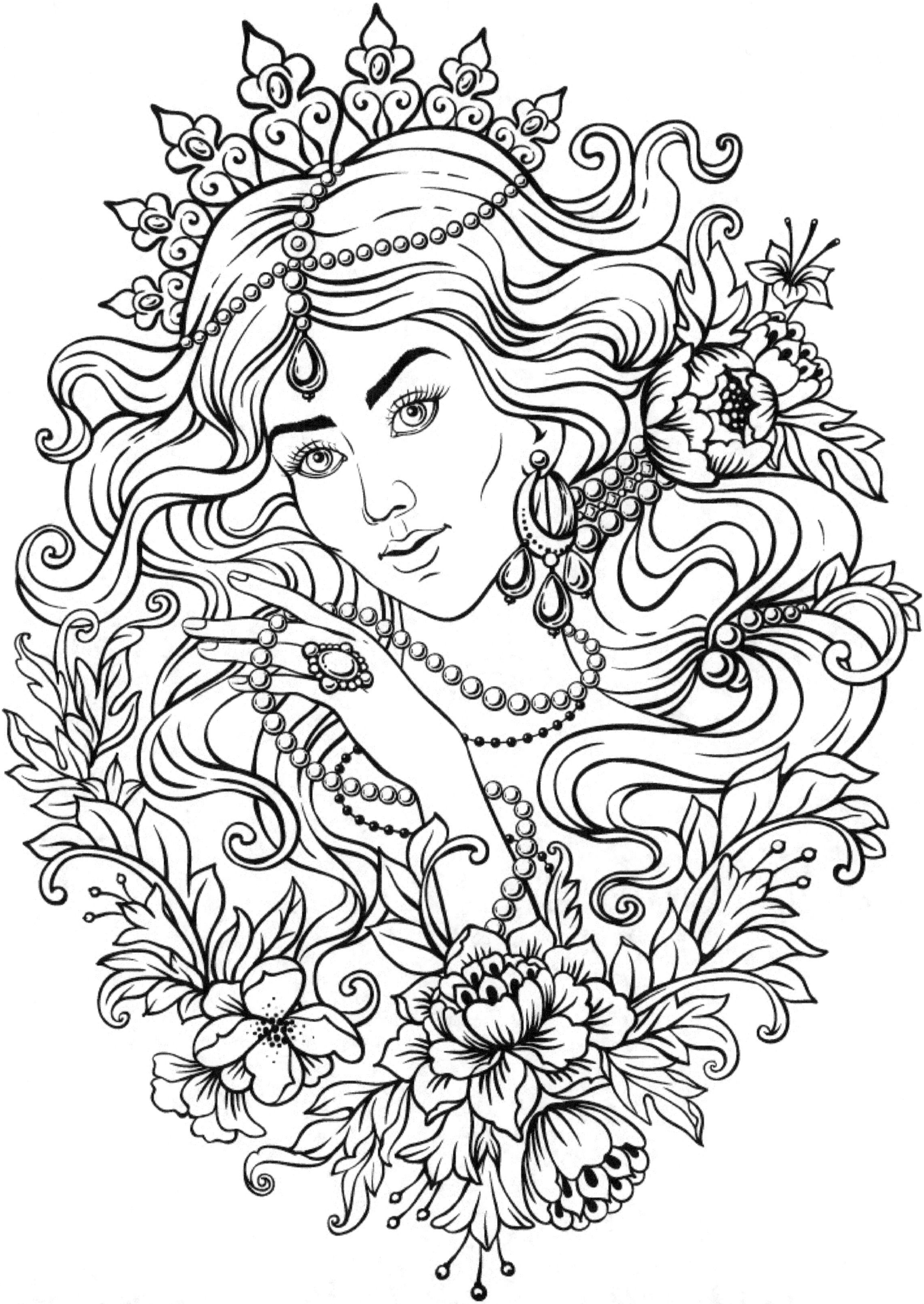

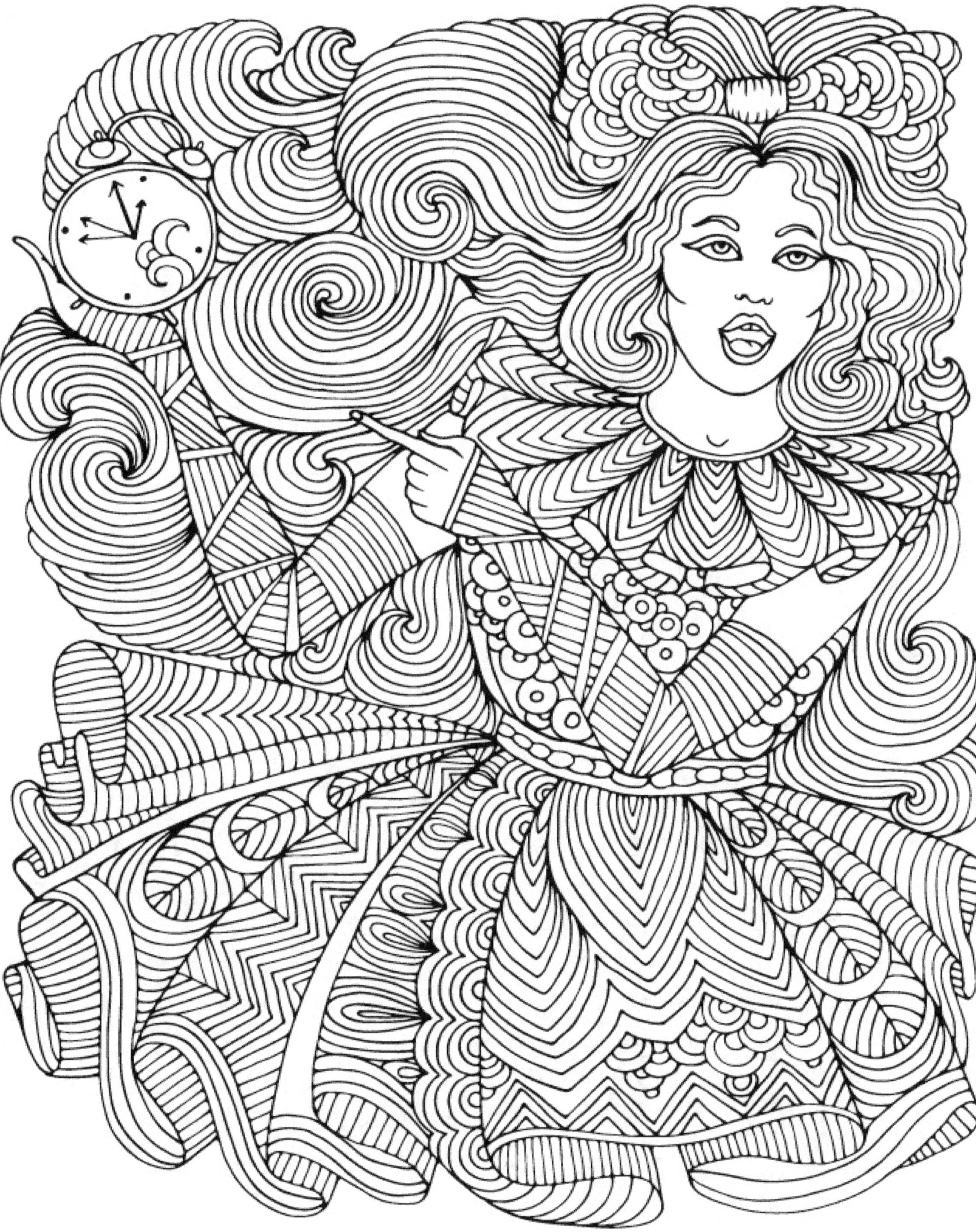

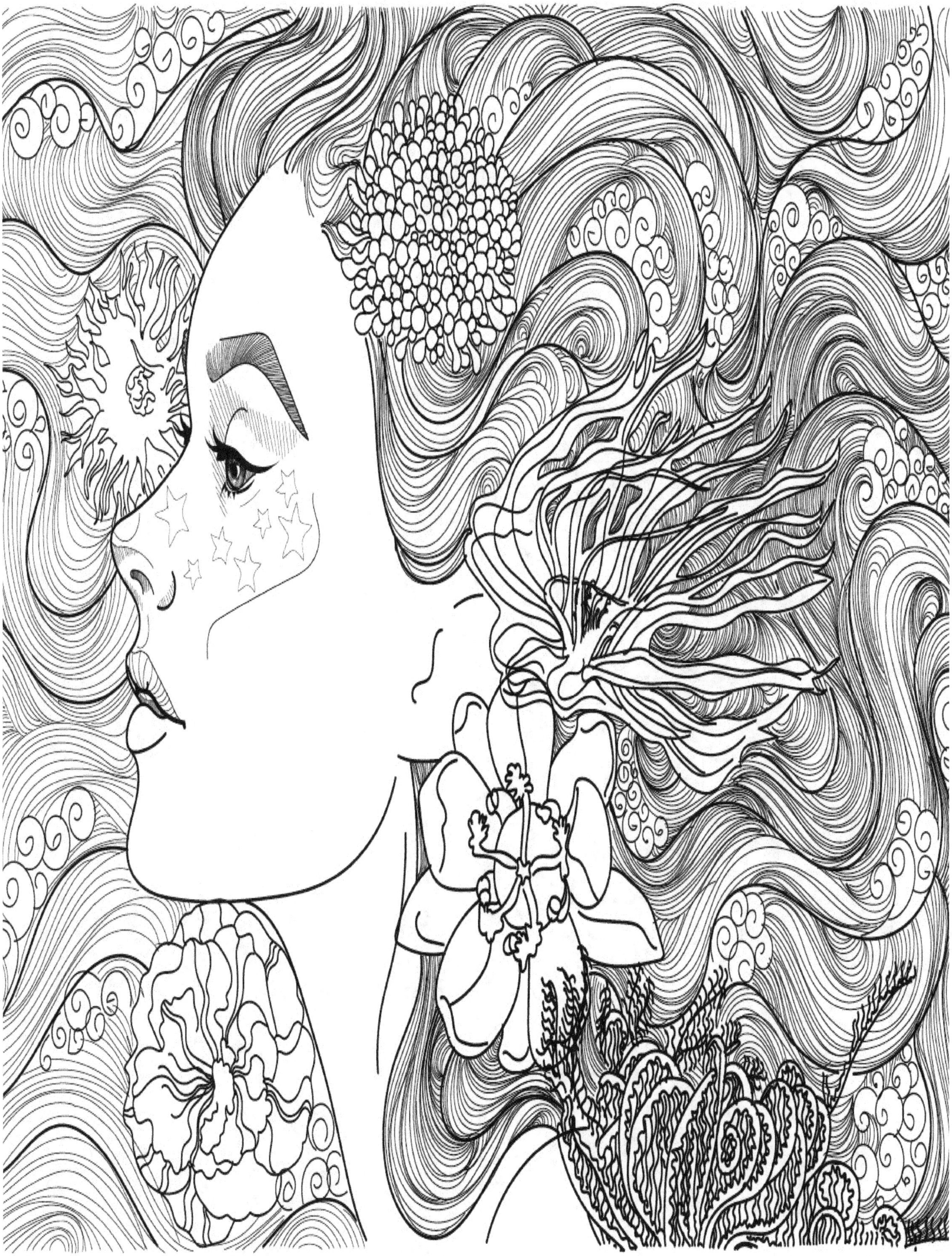

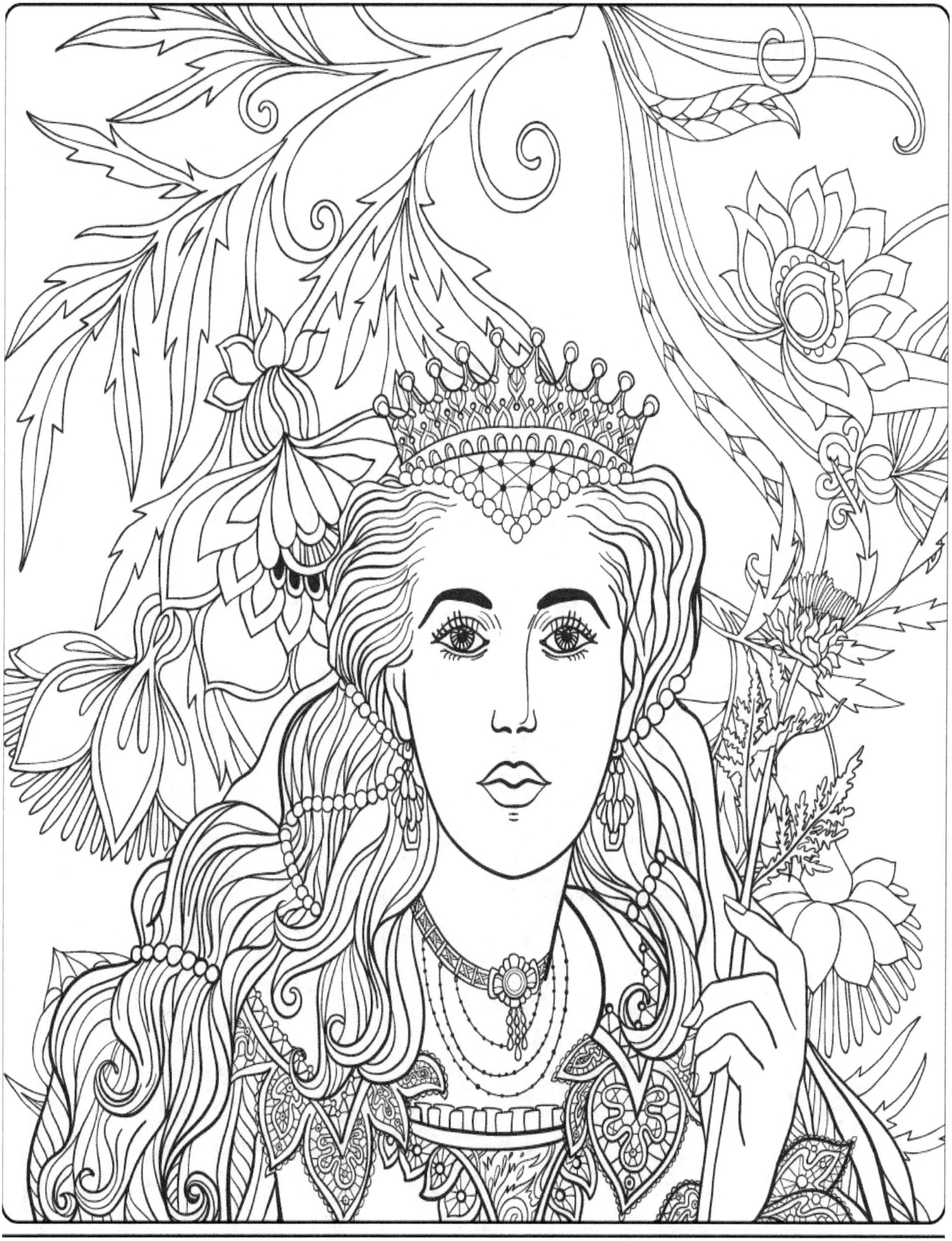

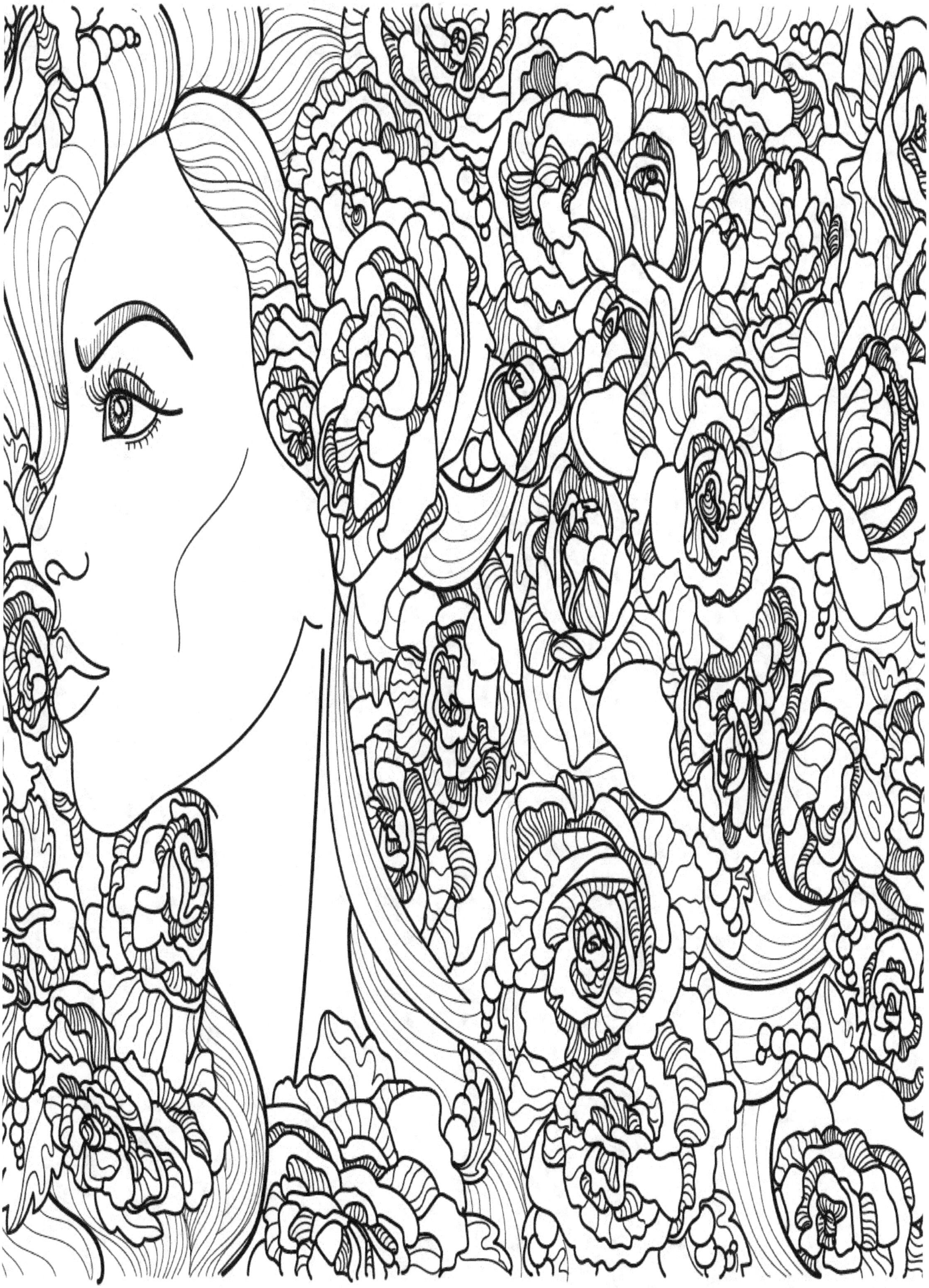

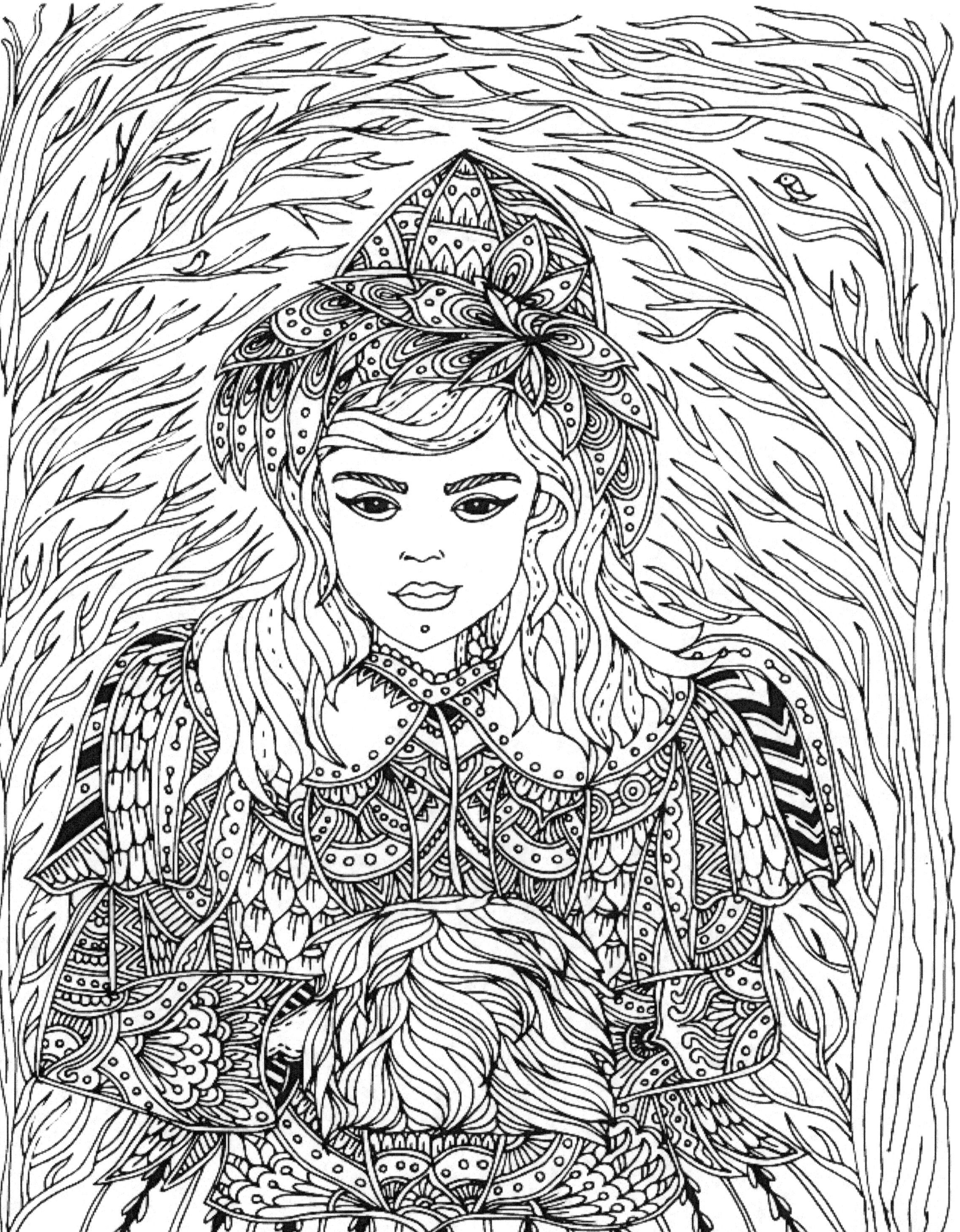

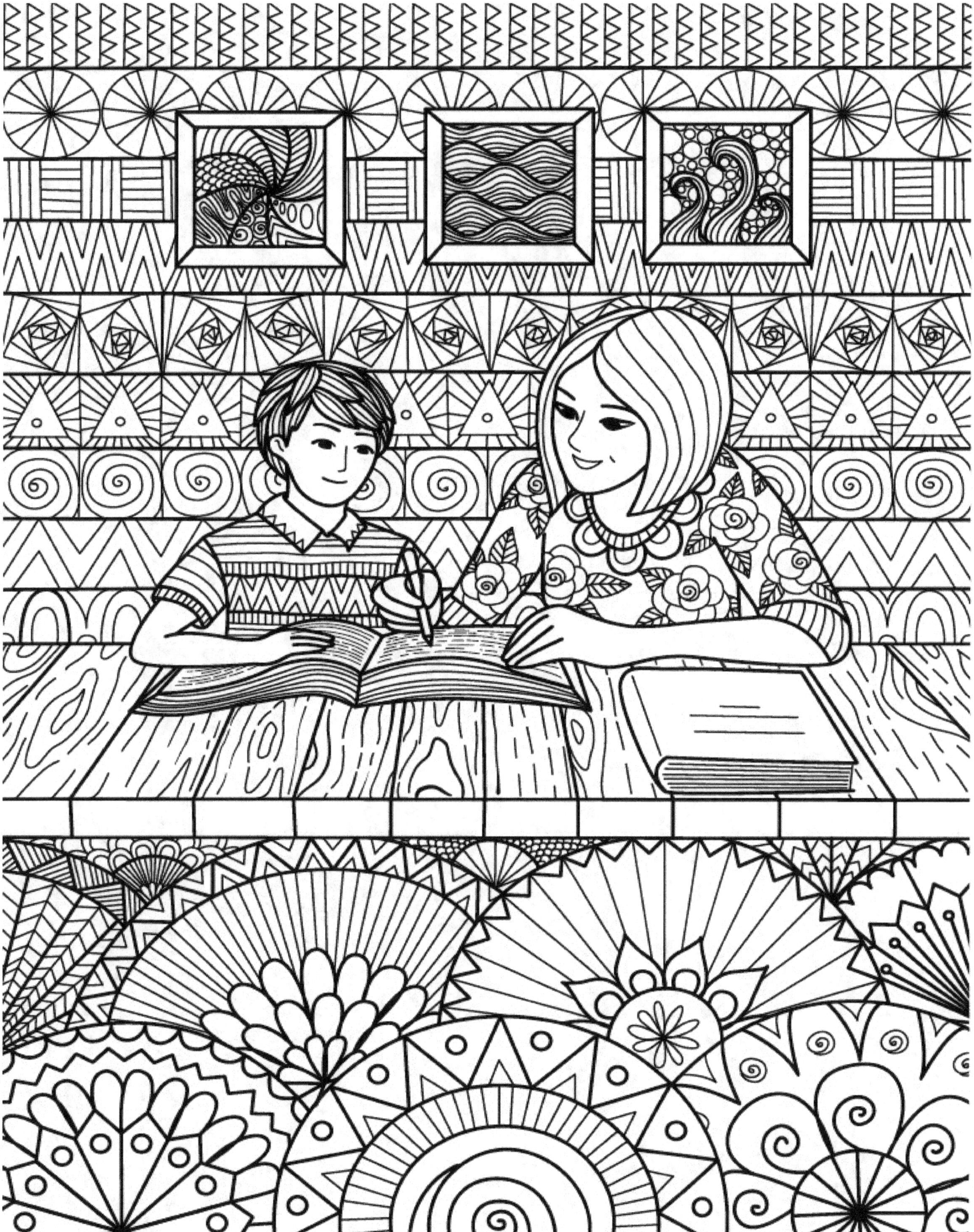

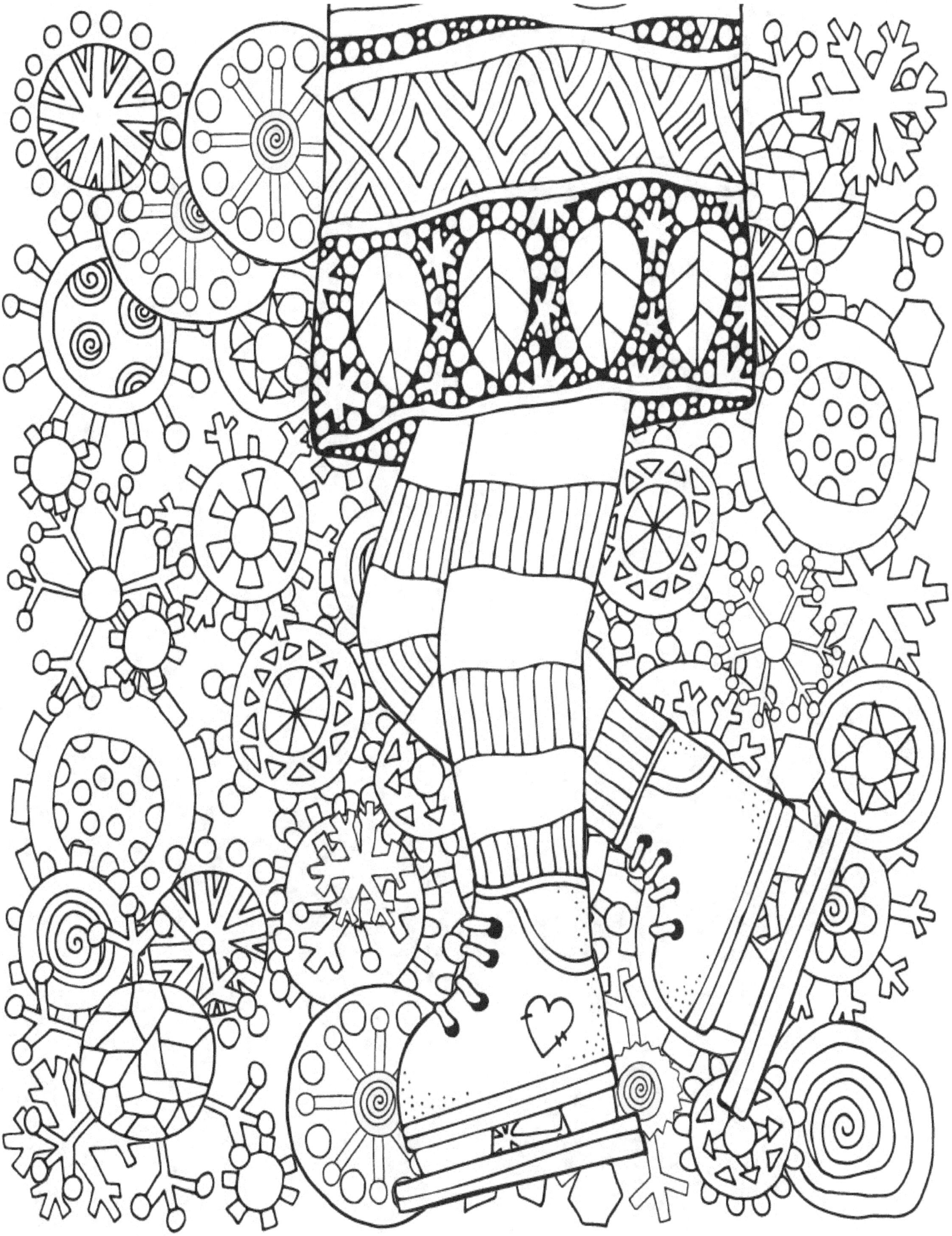

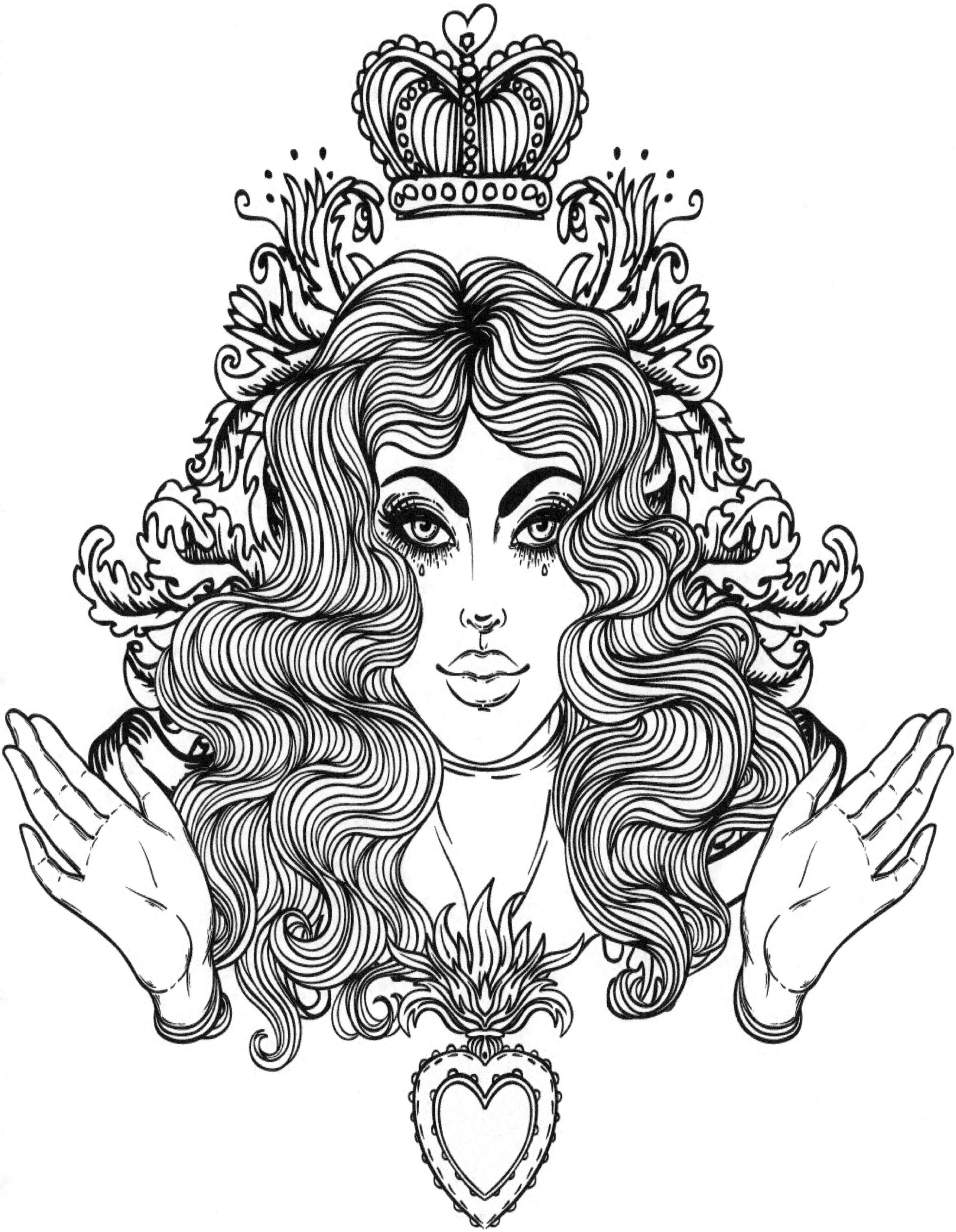

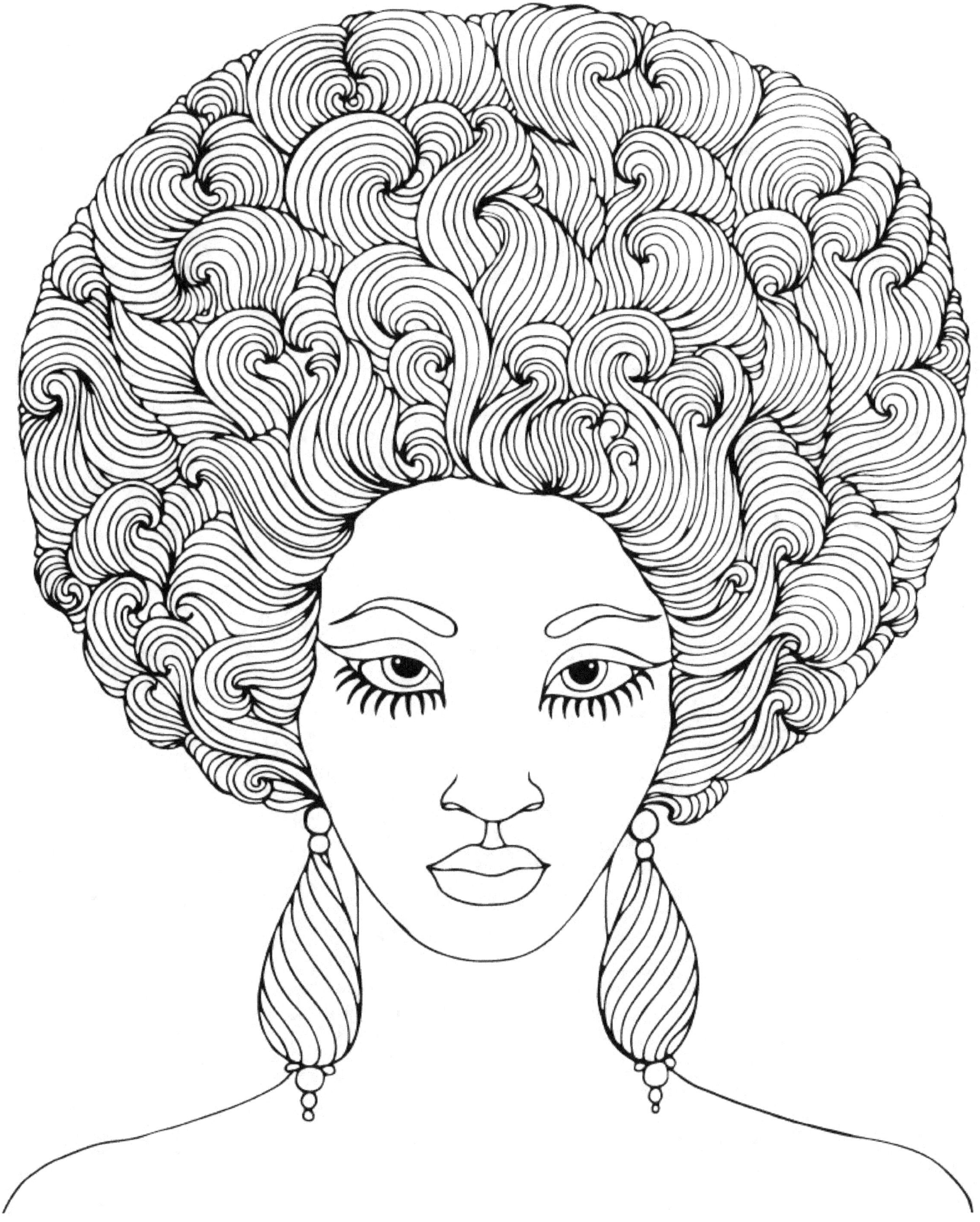

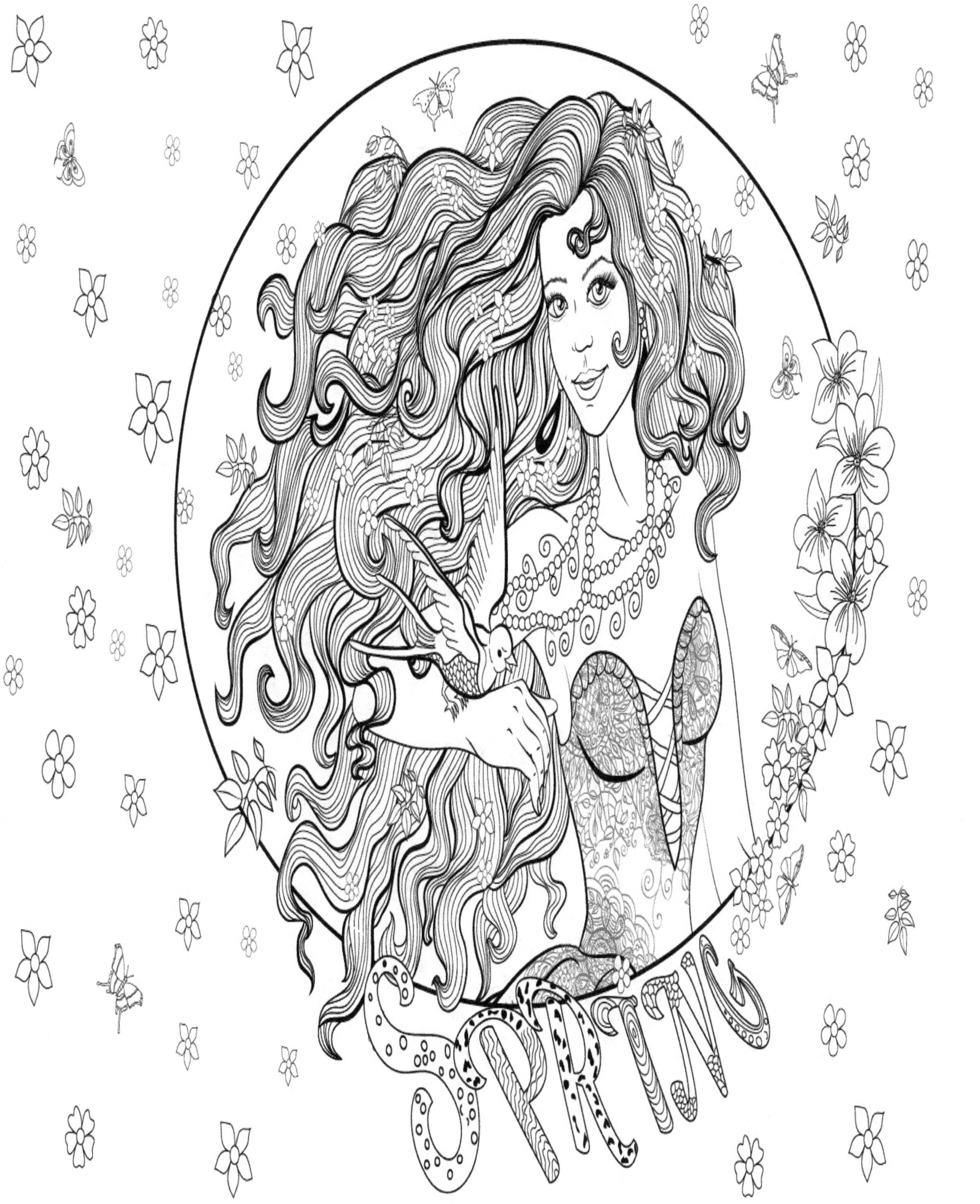
SPRING

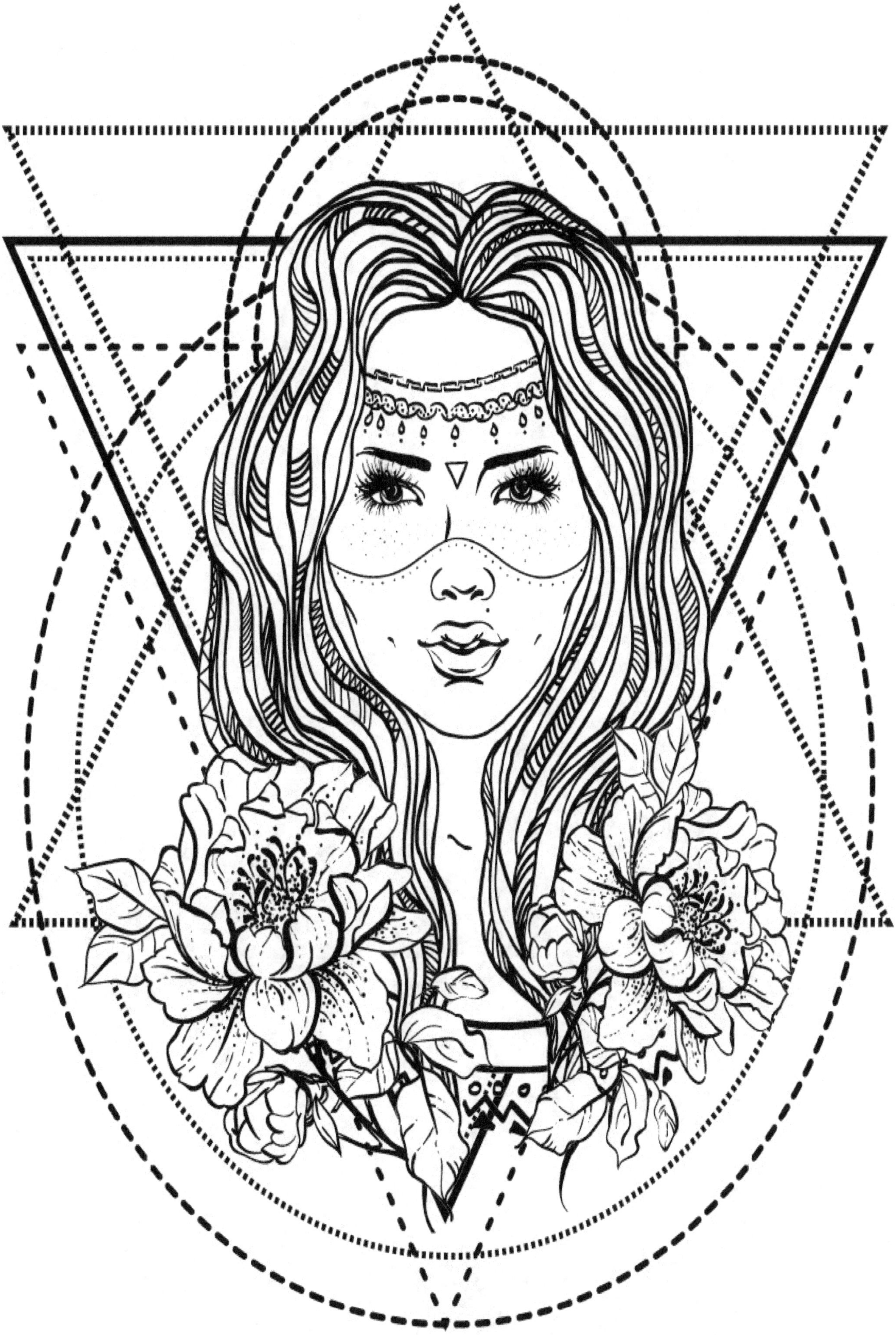

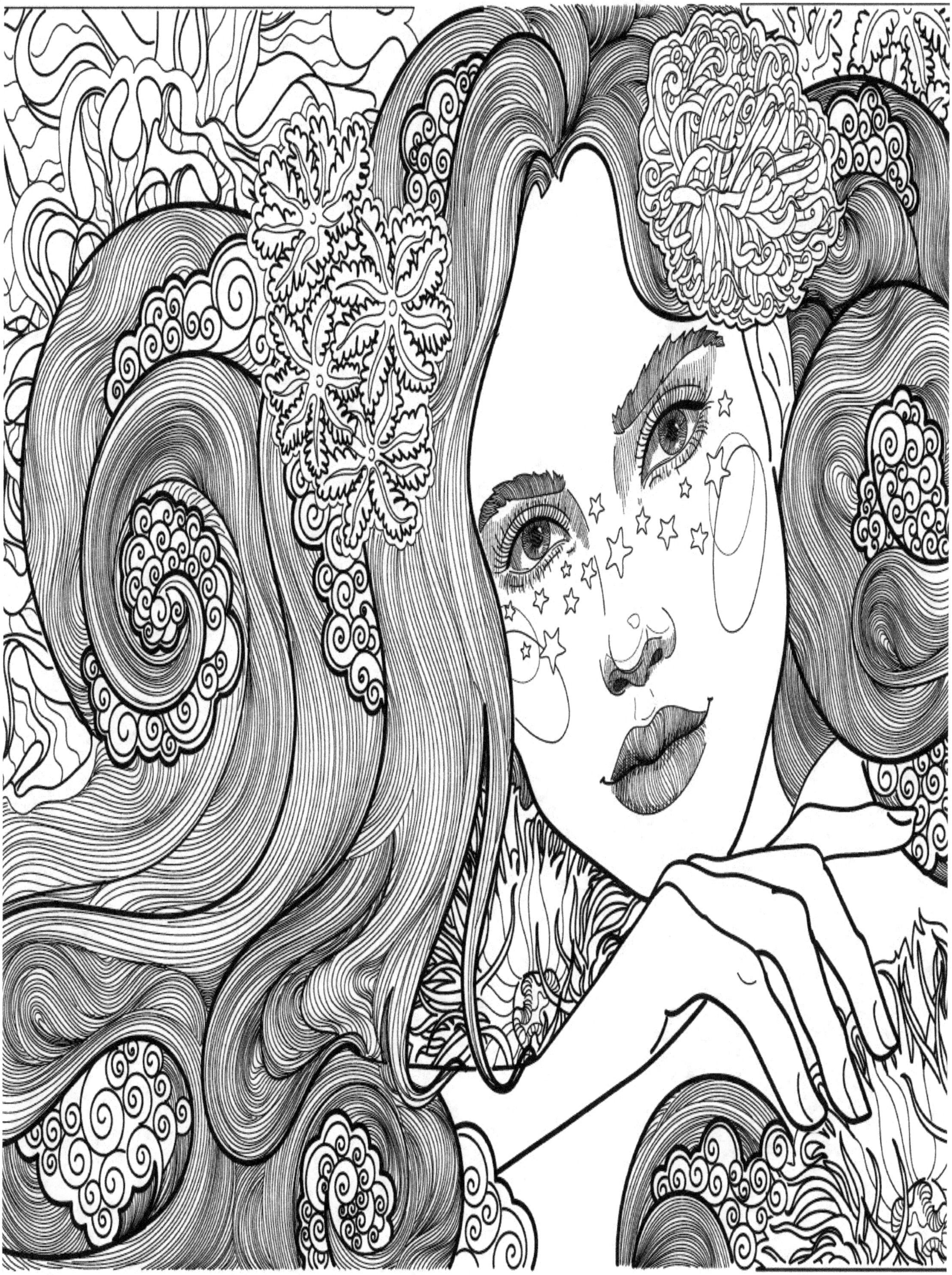

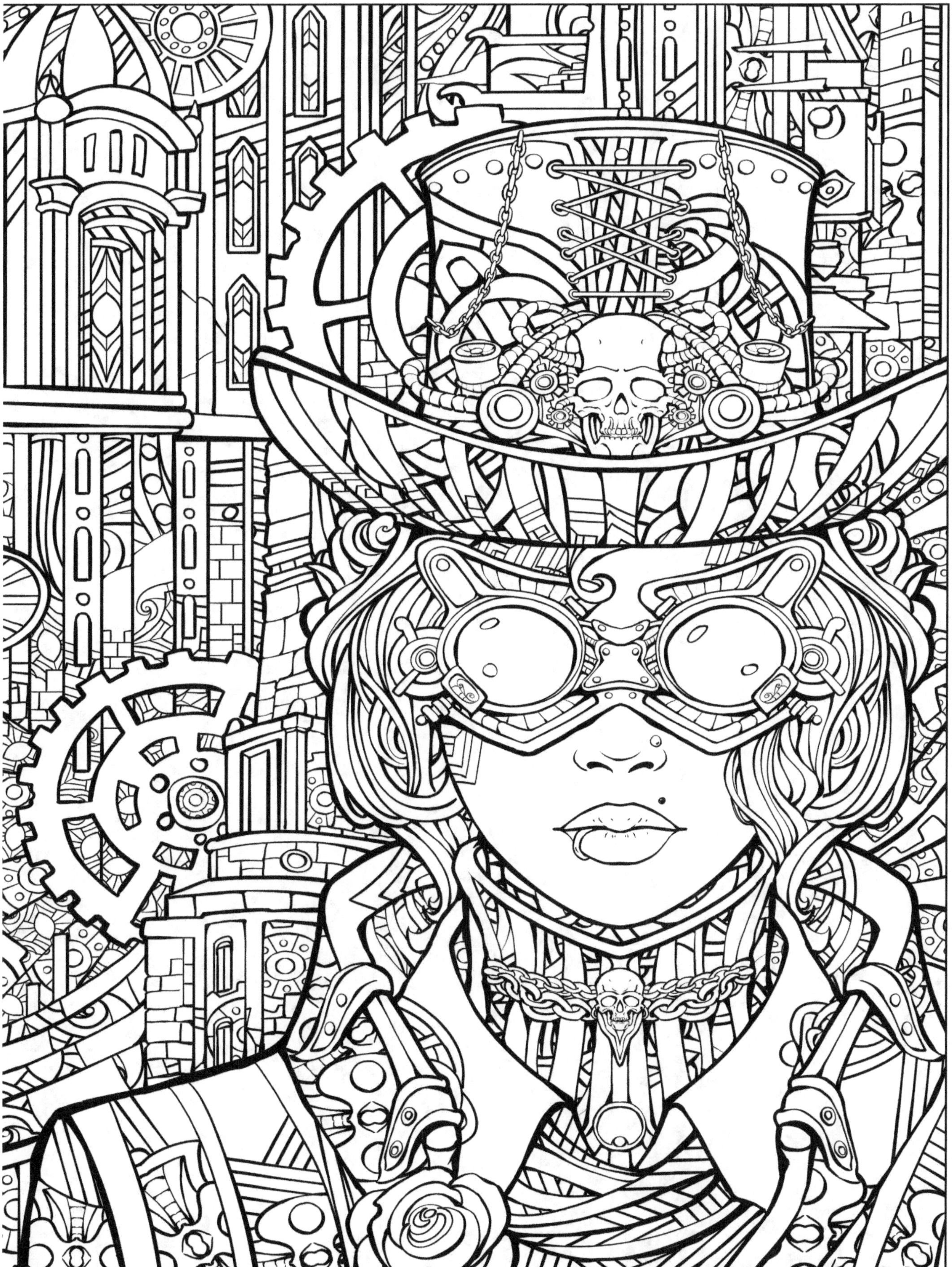

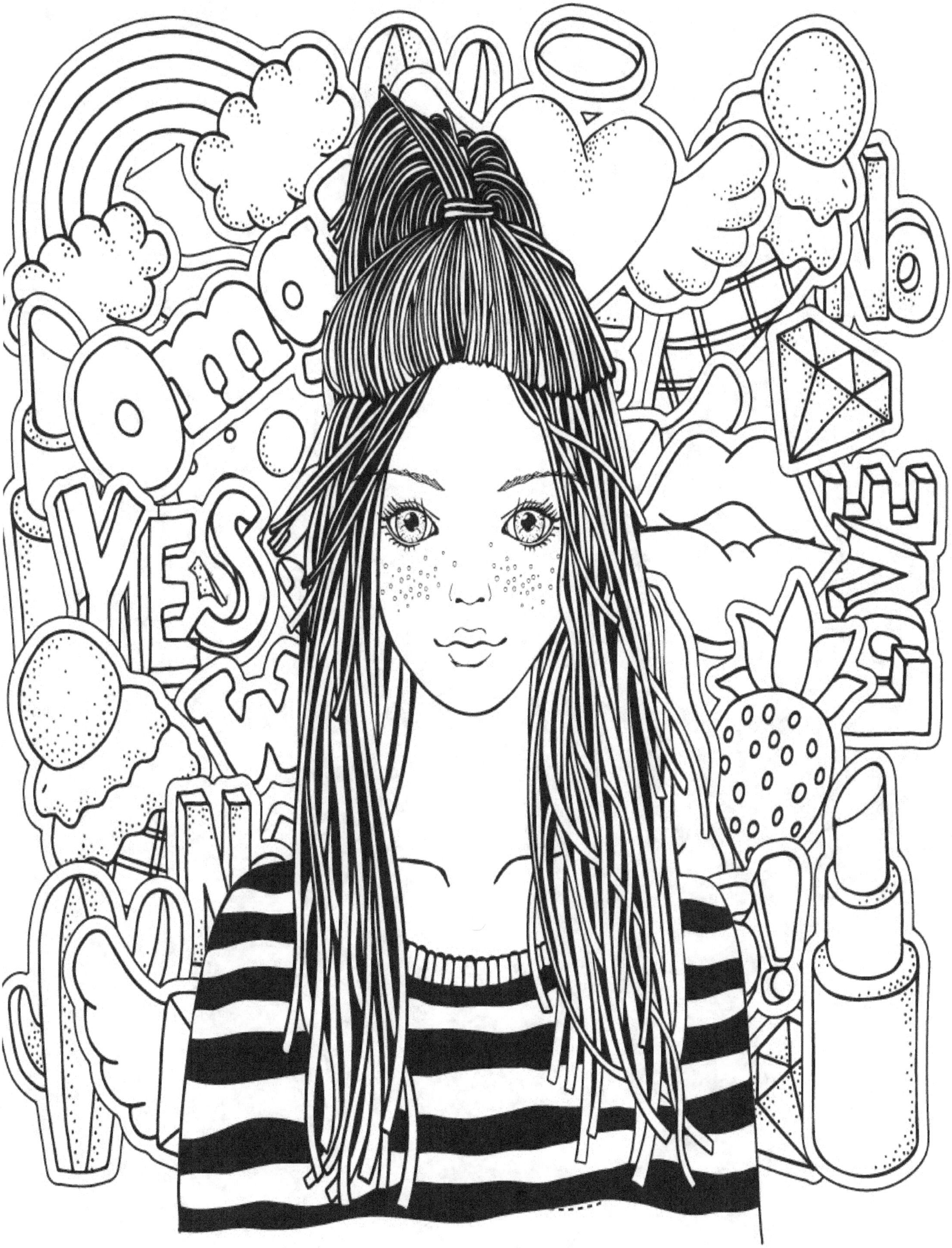
YES
NO

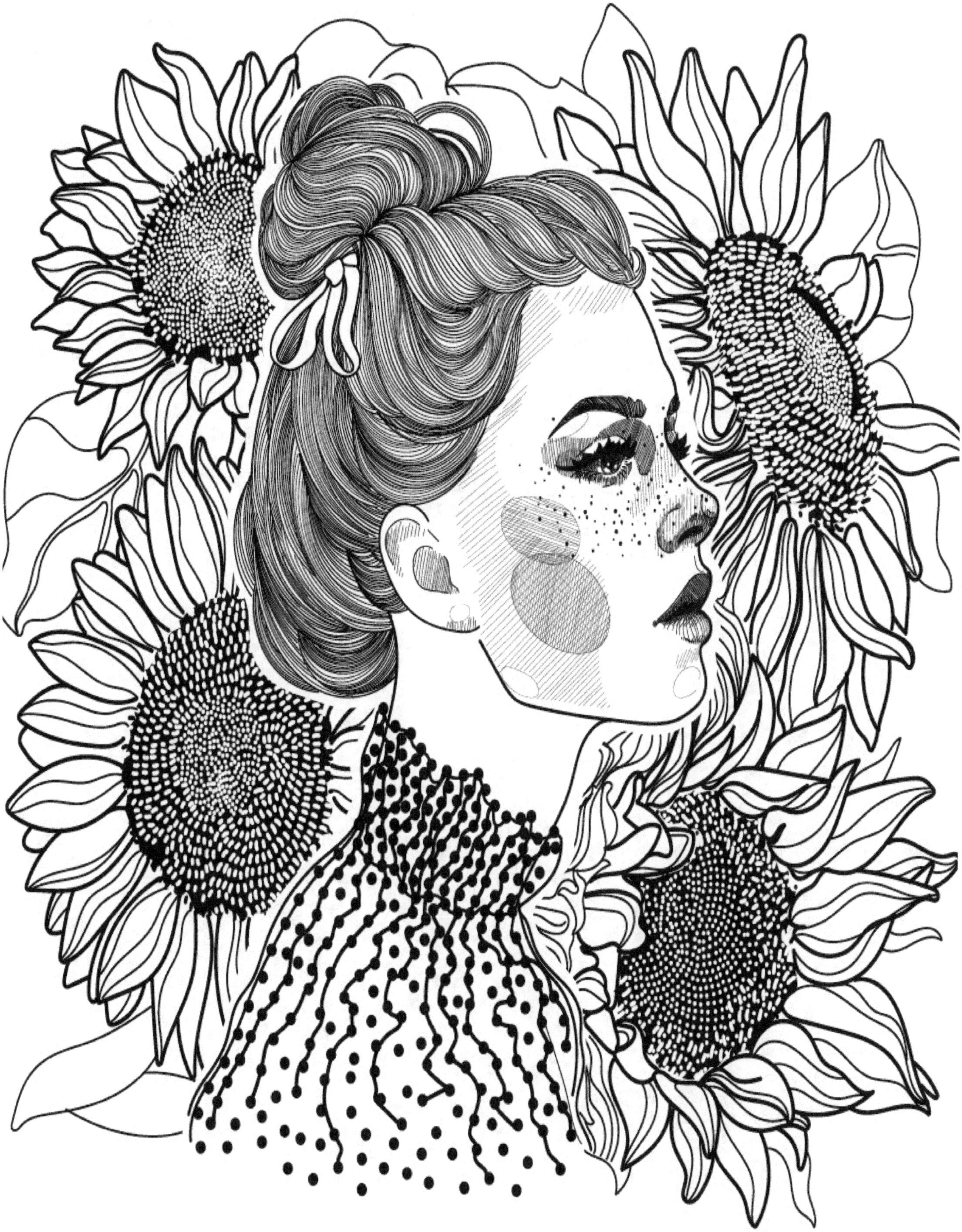

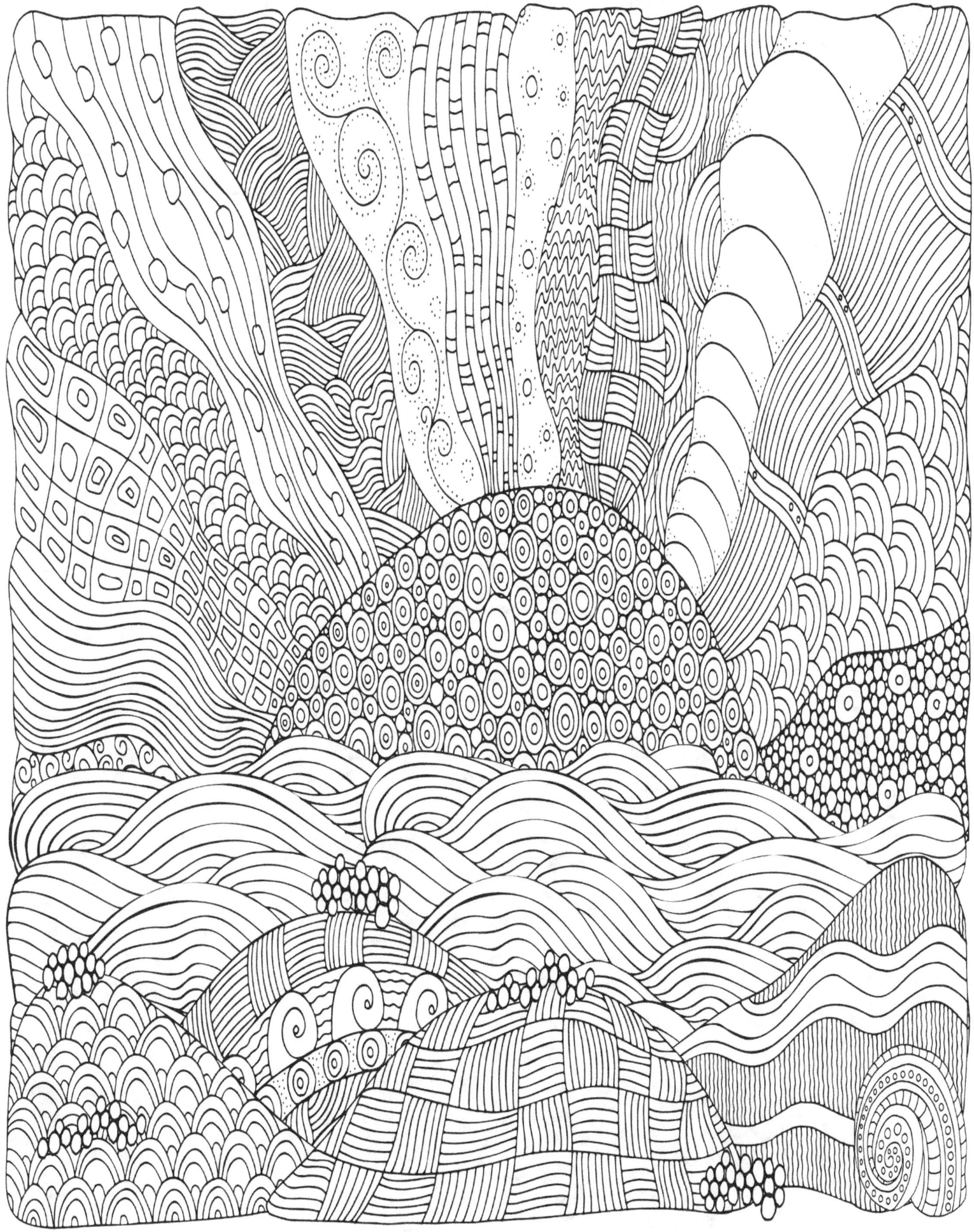

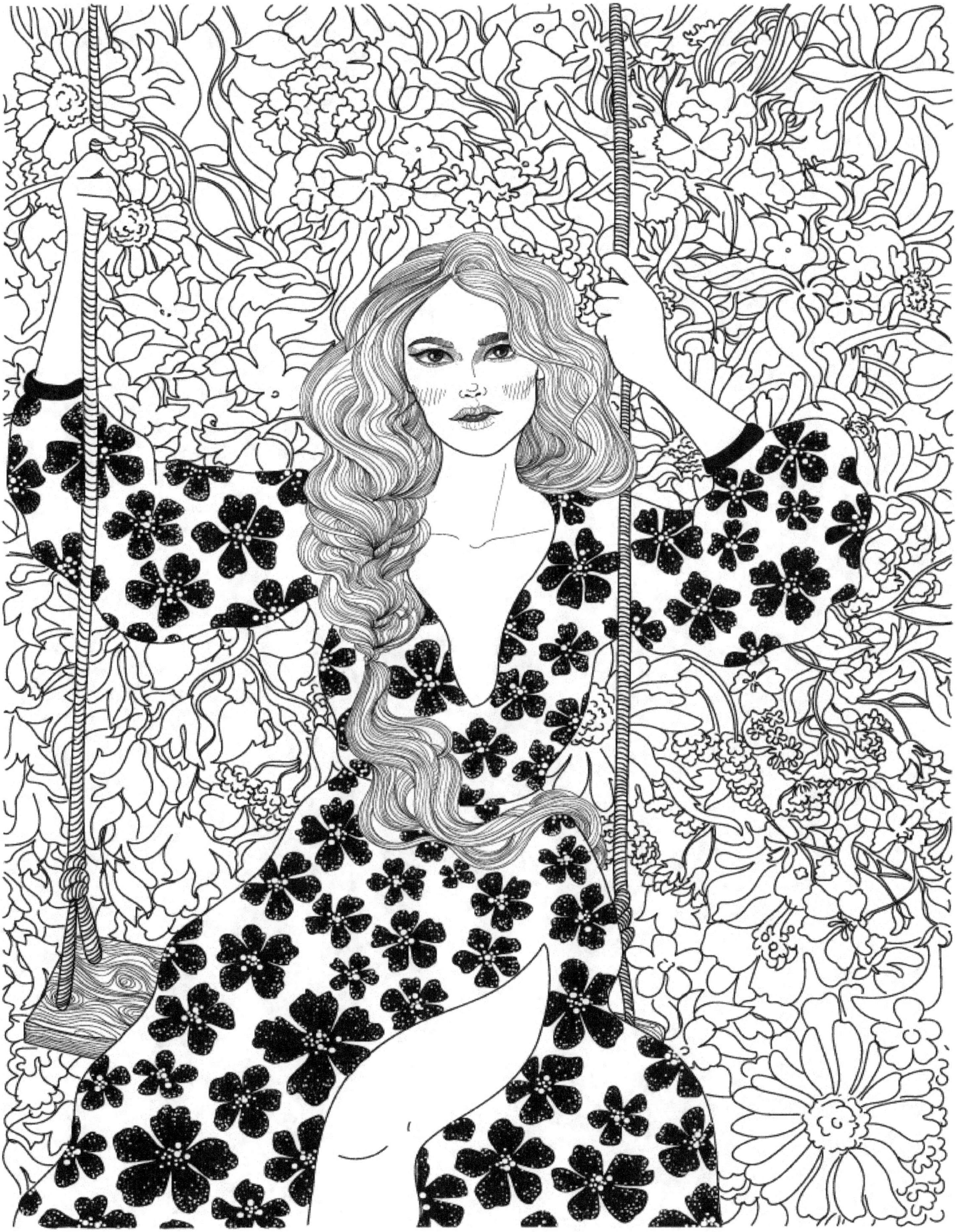

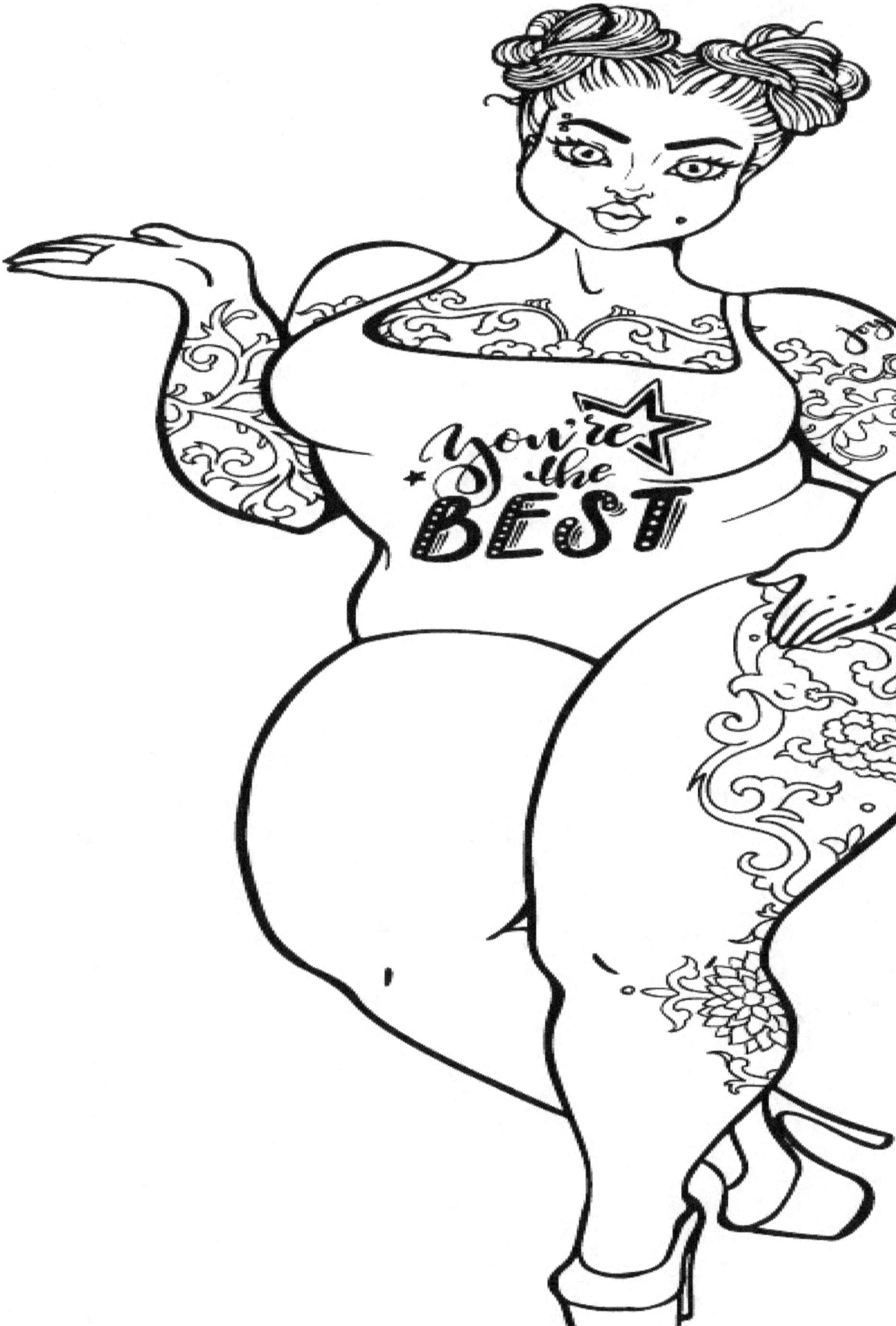

You're the BEST

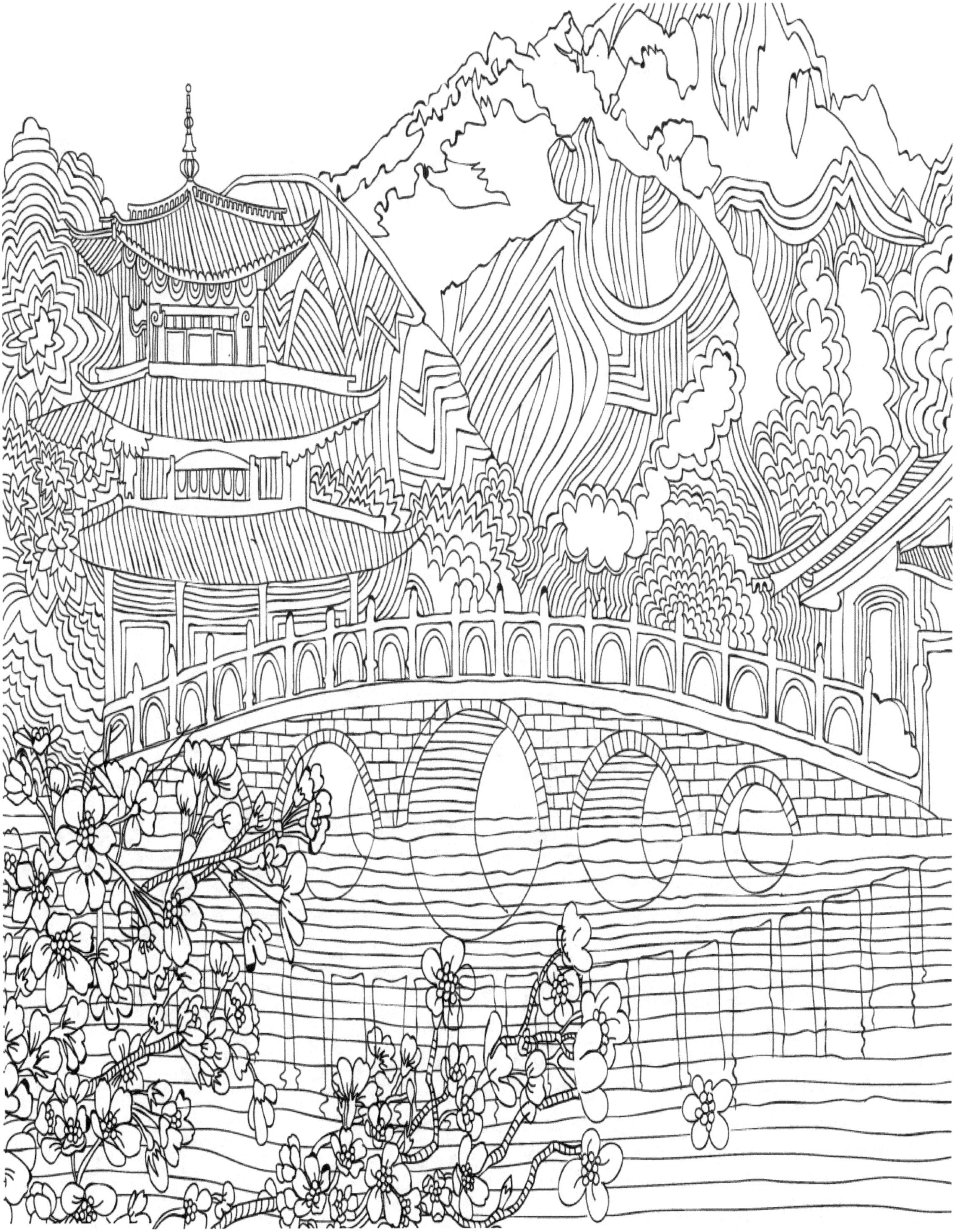

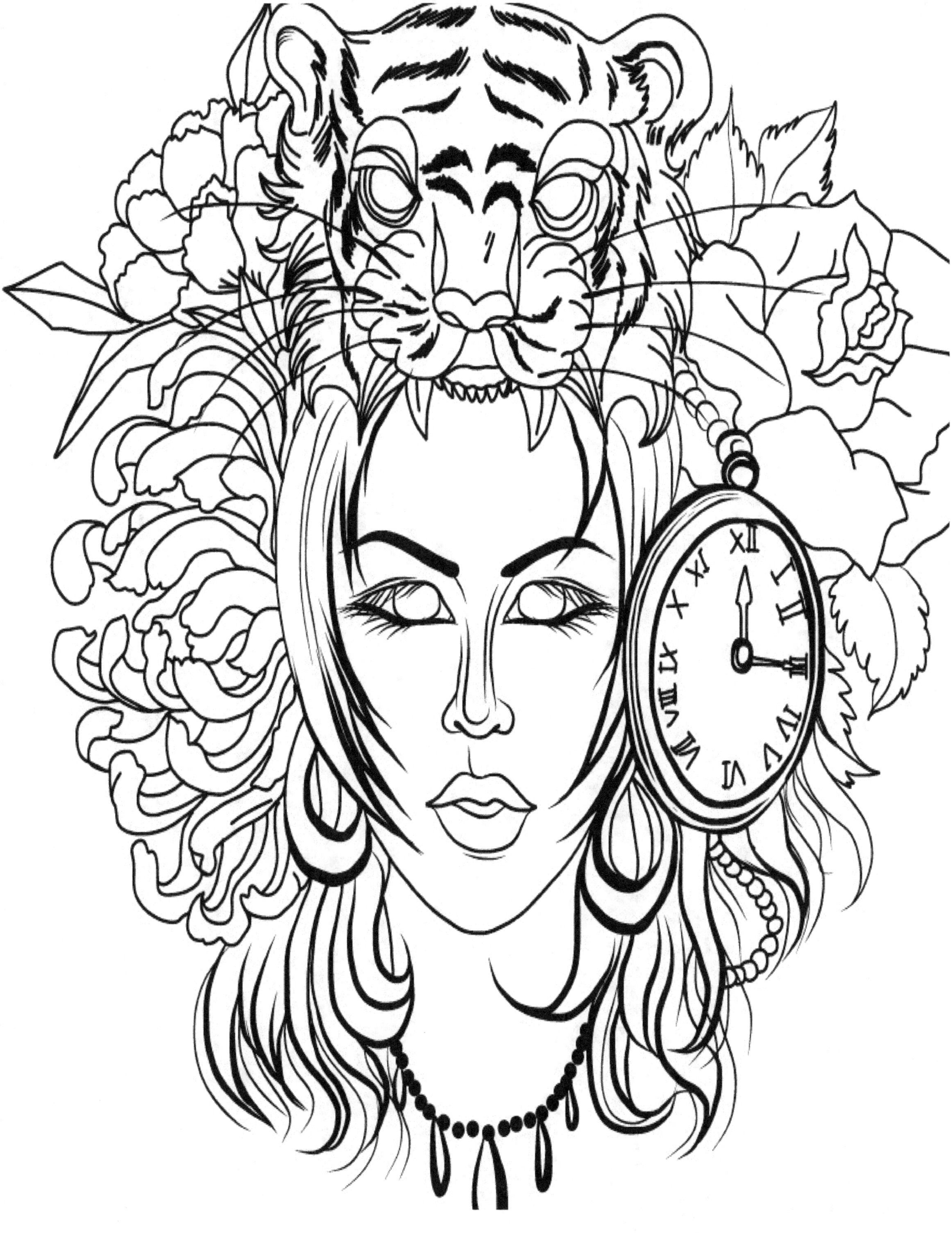

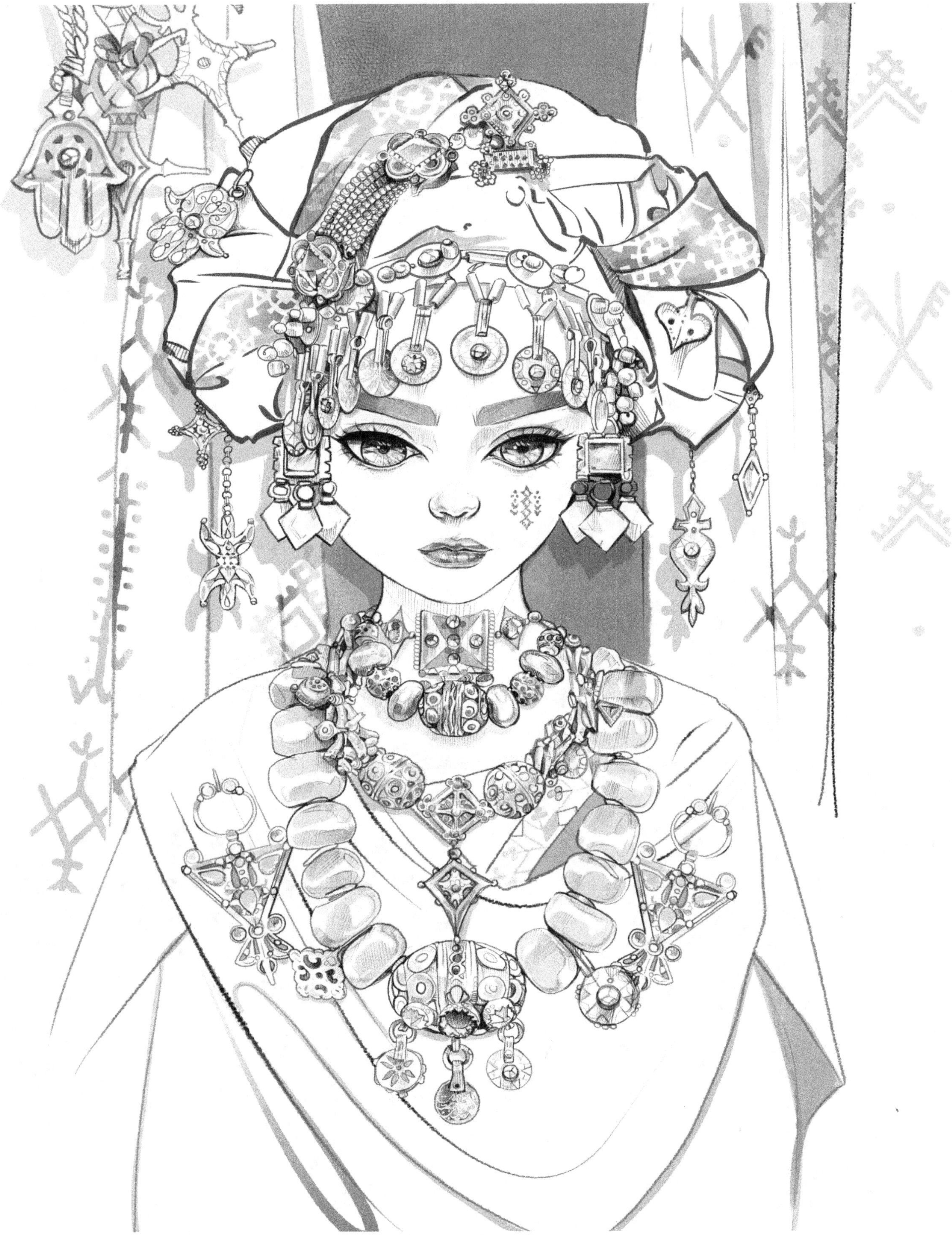

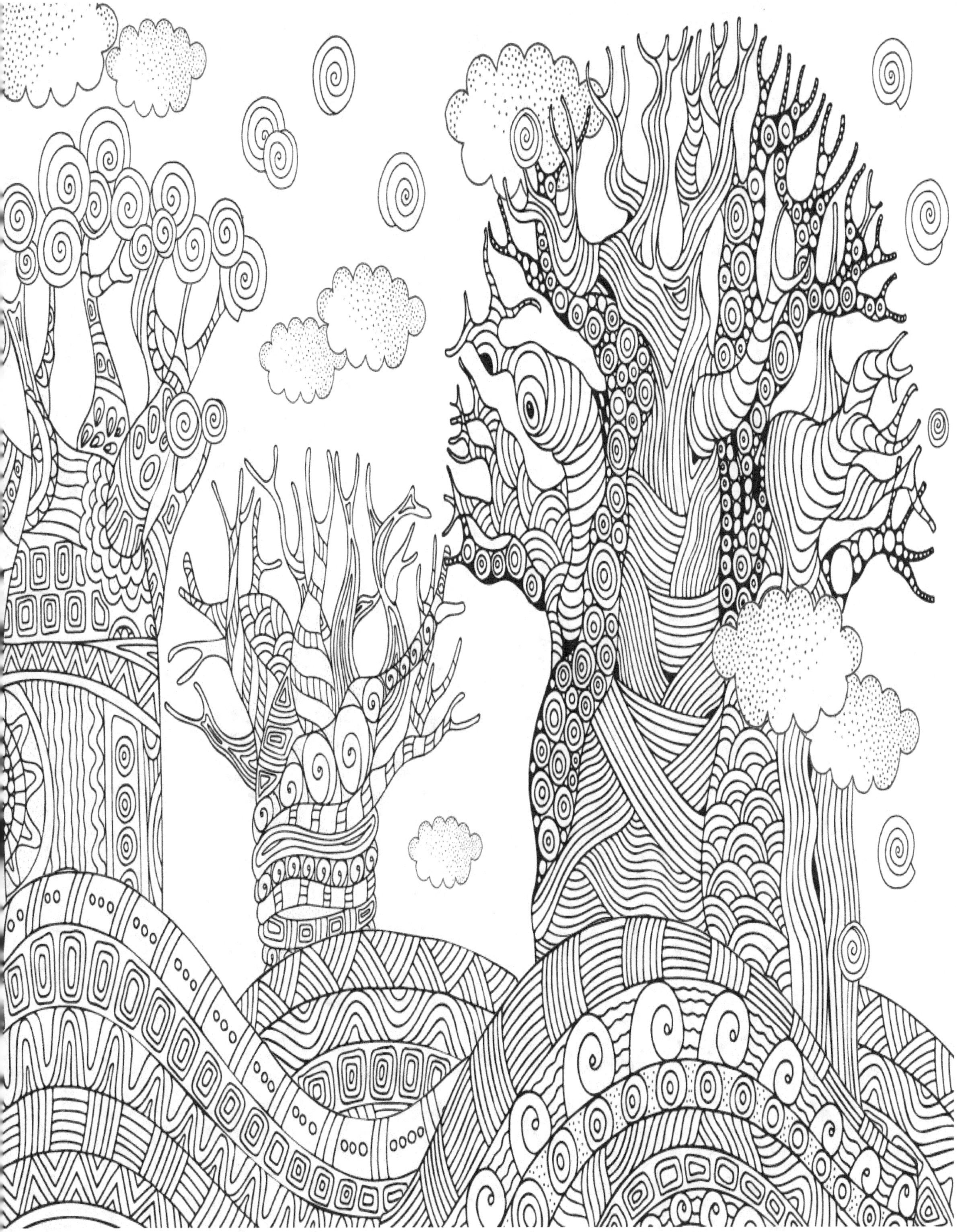

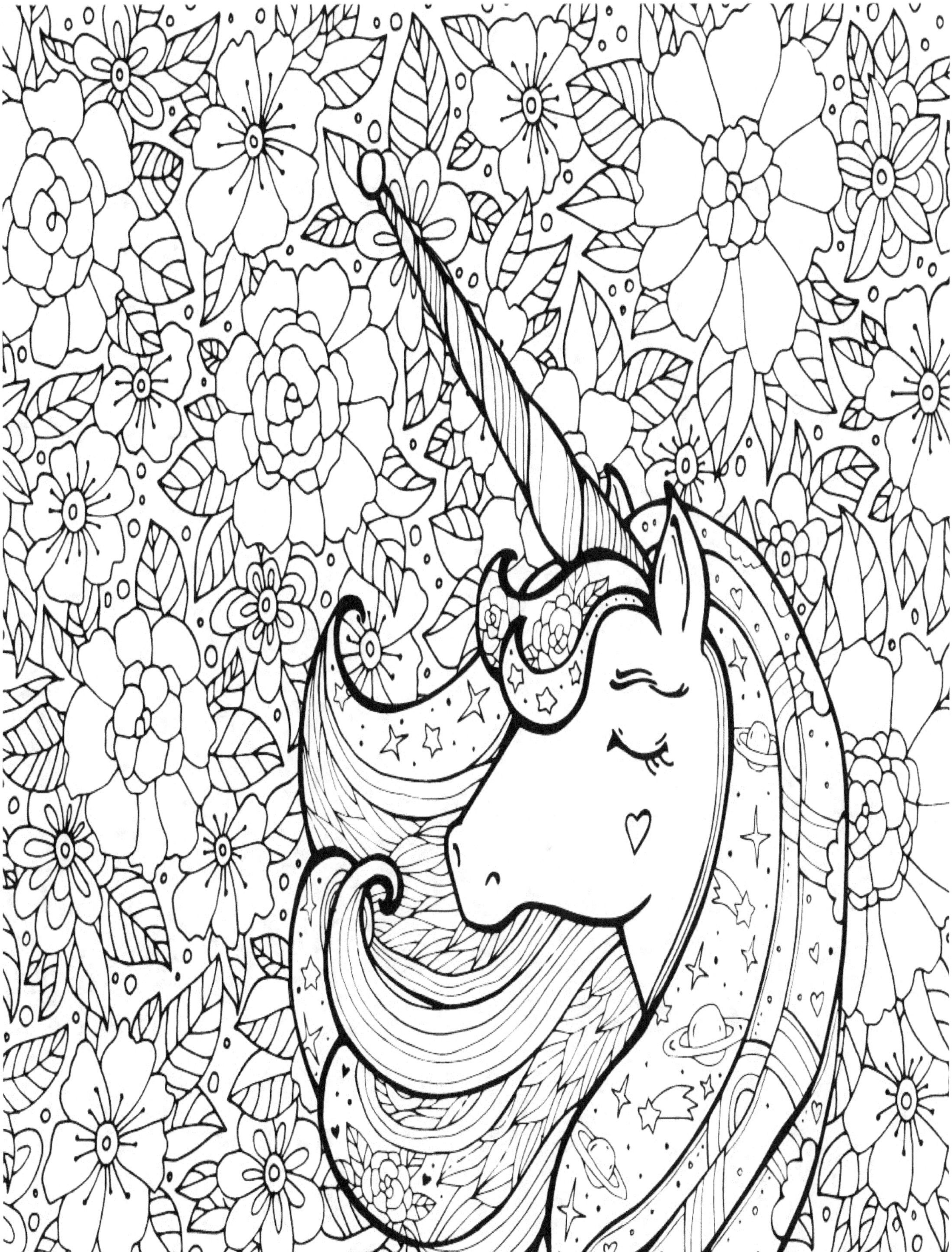

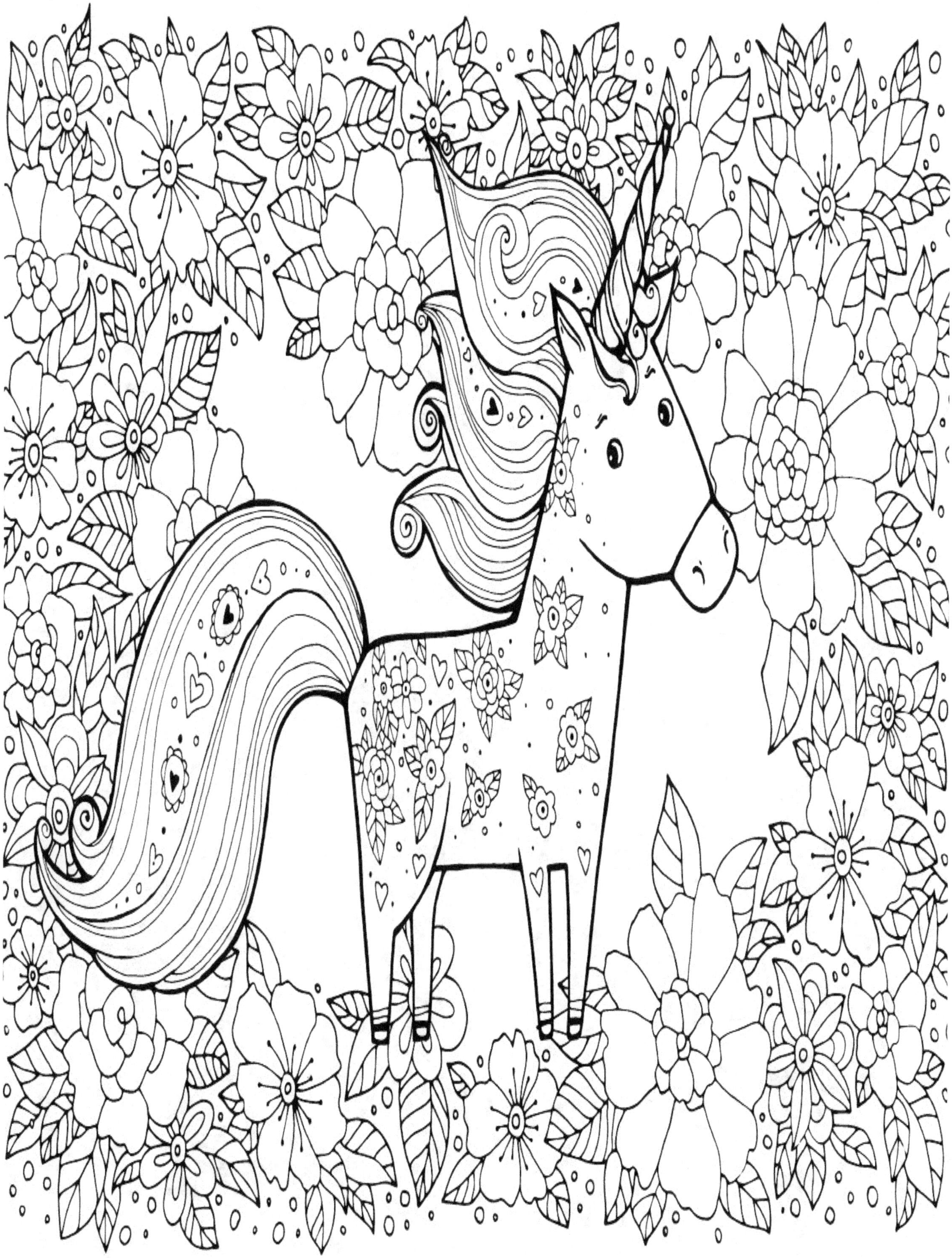

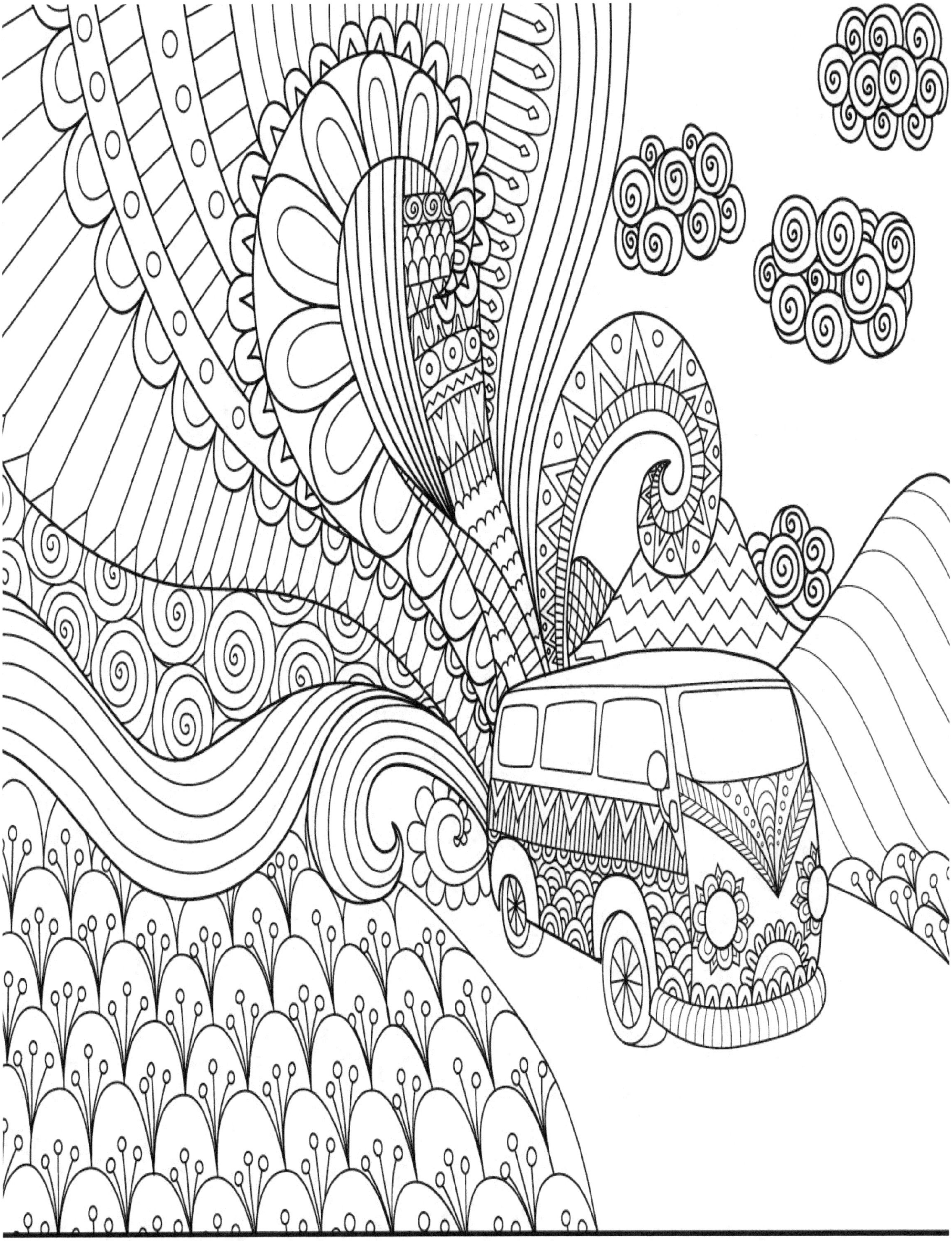

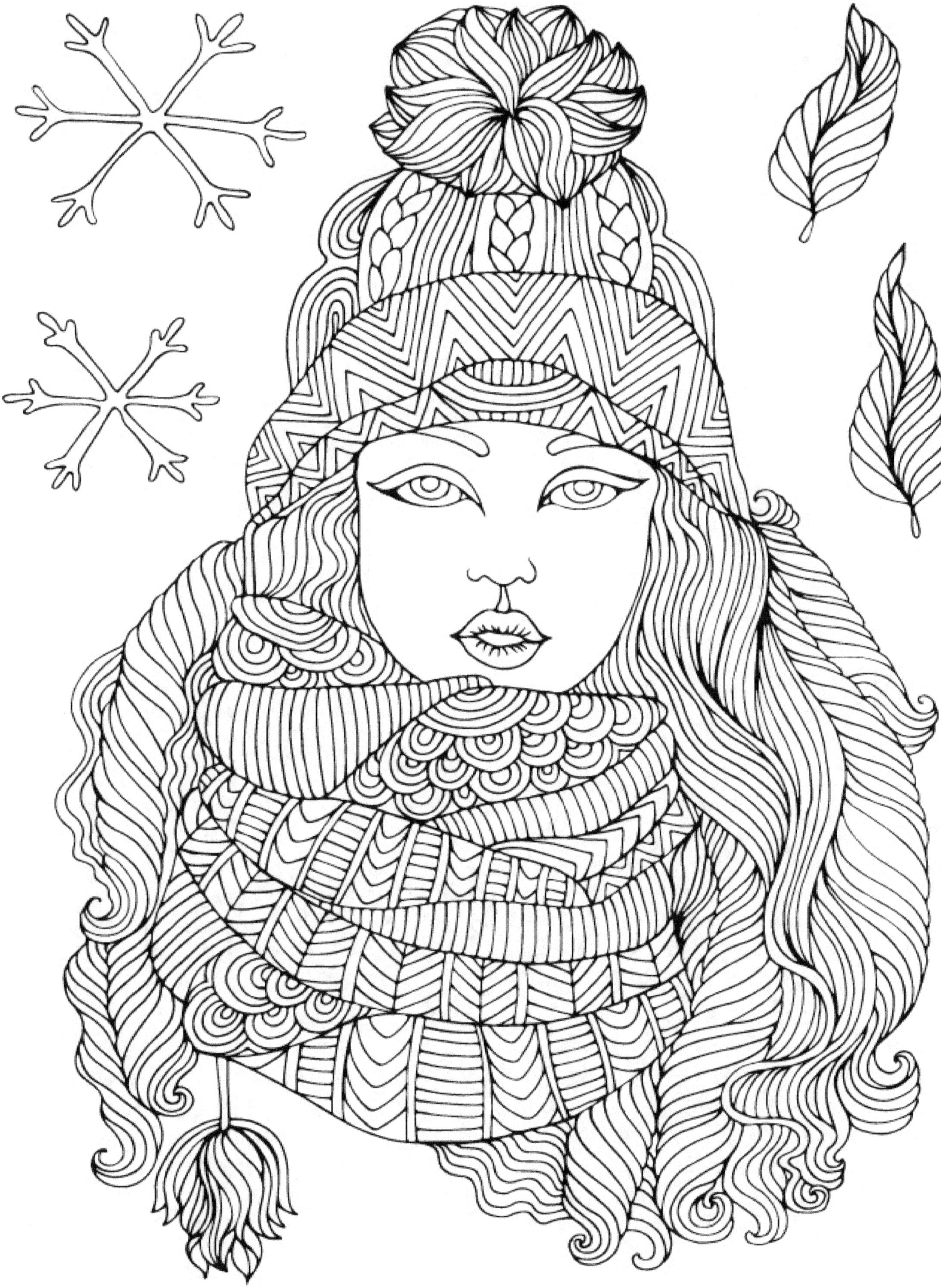

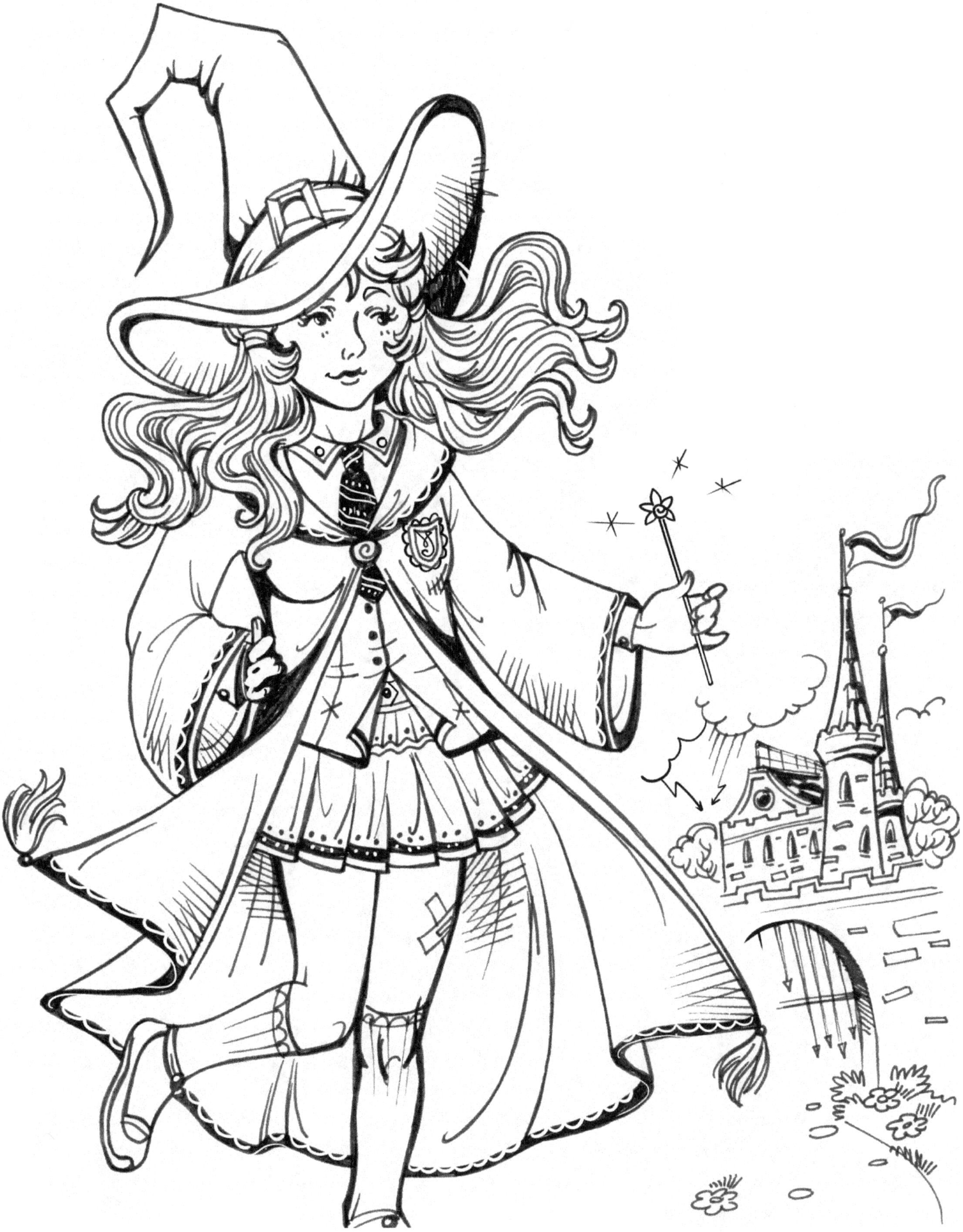

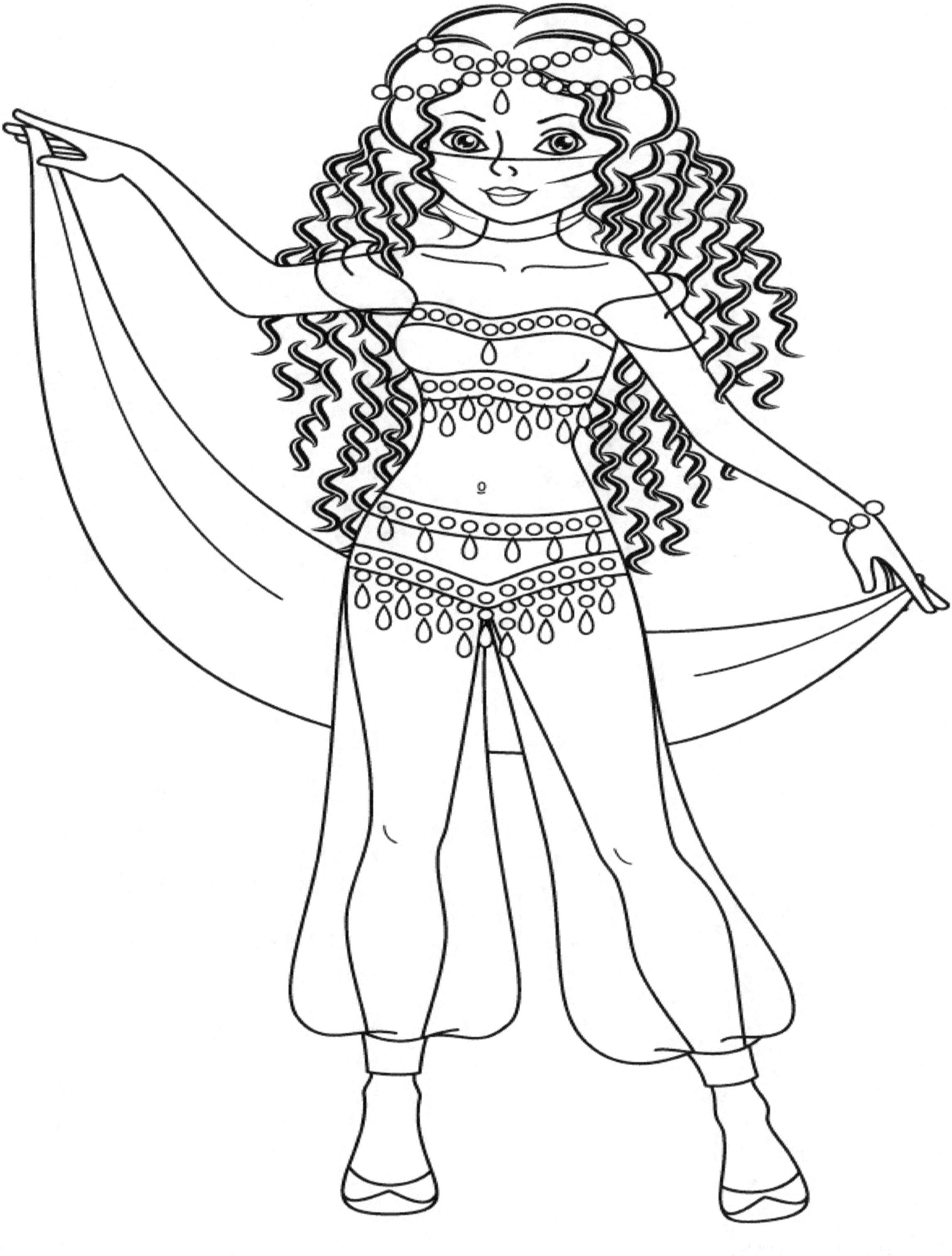

www.ingramcontent.com/pod-product-compliance
Lightning Source LLC
Chambersburg PA
CBHW060412220526
45465CB00008B/2855
* 9 7 9 8 6 5 5 4 6 2 7 0 0 *